DEFENSE MECHANISMS IN THE COUNSELING PROCESS

To my wife, Marybeth,
and my daughters, Heather, Tara, and Kayla,
for their love and support through the years

DEFENSE MECHANISMS IN THE COUNSELING PROCESS

Arthur J. Clark

SAGE Publications
International Educational and Professional Publisher
Thousand Oaks   London   New Delhi

For information:

SAGE Publications, Inc.
2455 Teller Road
Thousand Oaks, California 91320
E-mail: order@sagepub.com

SAGE Publications Ltd.
6 Bonhill Street
London EC2A 4PU
United Kingdom

SAGE Publications India Pvt. Ltd.
M-32 Market
Greater Kailash I
New Delhi 110 048 India

Printed in the United States of America

Library of Congress Cataloging-in-Publication Data

Clark, Arthur J.
    Defense mechanisms in the counseling process / by Arthur J. Clark.
        p.   cm.
    Includes bibliographical references and index.
    ISBN 0-7619-0660-6 (hardcover: alk. paper). — ISBN 0-7619-0661-4 (pbk.: alk. paper)
    1. Counseling.   2. Defense mechanisms (Psychology).   I. Title.
BF637.C6C54   1998
158'.3—dc21   97-45280

98 99 00 01 02 03   10 9 8 7 6 5 4 3 2 1

Acquiring Editor:	Jim Nageotte
Editorial Assistant:	Fiona Lyon
Production Editor:	Diana E. Axelsen
Production Assistant:	Denise Santoyo
Typesetter/Designer:	Janelle LeMaster
Indexer:	Mary Mortensen
Print Buyer:	Anna Chin

CONTENTS

FOREWORD

Psychodynamic constructions of counseling and therapy are alive and well, despite rumors to the contrary. Arthur Clark has presented us with a scholarly summary of defense mechanisms, and his innovative thought brings them alive—and, more important, makes them immediately useful and understandable to the practitioner.

Defenses in clients are often seen by helping professionals as something to overcome. I much prefer to think of defenses as a client's natural way of being, partially learned, partially innate. In effect, I am suggesting that defense mechanisms are a logical result of developmental history of the person in environmental context. When viewed from this light, defense mechanisms become an important way to help us understand and conceptualize the client.

One of Clark's major contributions in this book is the way he helps us understand client developmental history as it relates to various defensive styles. A weakness of much counseling and psychotherapy theory is a lack of client conceptualization. The model of defense mechanisms presented here will be invaluable to both the beginner and the advanced professional through helping them understand where their client "comes from."

Thus, the great strength of this book is in its conceptual richness. I rejoice when I find a scholar such as Arthur Clark who brings to us such a wide understanding of complex constructs but who can also make them clear, significant, and, yes, practical and usable in the daily practice of counseling and therapy.

For example, let us consider Chapter 2—"Denial." Persons use denial to ward off serious external or internal threat—it has a positive function in its origin. But this positive denial has usually outlived its usefulness and, in Gordon Allport's (1961) words, has become *functionally autonomous*. Clark details the several types of denial in a fashion we all can recognize in our clients. This is followed by clear illustrations of how we as counselors or therapists can help clients process the meaning of their defensive structure of denial. We seek to understand, rather than attack, defenses. Through the process of understanding the client's defensive structure—in this case, denial—we then can move to other interventions to help the client reconstruct new meanings from the overly tight defensive position. Then, once this is accomplished, Clark suggests we help the client generate new behaviors, thoughts, and feelings. Here we can integrate psychodynamic thought and much of cognitive-behavioral theory and practice.

I find much to admire in Clark's process model. It is a clear and accurate summary of how we can integrate psychodynamic client and case conception with other theoretical orientations such as humanistic-existential and cognitive-behavioral. Counselors will find the action model of processing defense mechanisms helpful in their own practice: (a) developing relationship with the defensive style and "going with," rather than against, the client; (b) integration in which confrontation, cognitive restructuring, reframing, and interpretation will be helpful; and (c) accomplishment in which the client learns how to catch her- or himself engaging in the defense mechanism and how to substitute newly learned more useful behavior.

Clark also shows an interest in the application of multicultural issues to defense mechanisms. Awareness of race/ethnicity, gender, and other cultural factors is essential for a rich understanding of client defensive structures. Indeed, individuals learn defensive adaptation styles in family and social context.

Clark's discussion of group process from this framework is also helpful. The dynamics of interaction between and among defensive styles become manifest there, particularly in unstructured groups. I appreciate this contribution to generalization of the defensive structure model, and it illustrates Clark's deep understanding of issues that we have not addressed fully in our field.

In short, Arthur Clark is to be commended for his contribution. *Defense Mechanisms in the Counseling Process* will occupy an important place on my bookshelf and in my thinking.

Allen E. Ivey, Ed.D., A.B.P.P.
University of Massachusetts, Amherst

PREFACE

Twenty-five years ago, as a novice school counselor, I first encountered a pattern of behavior in counseling that has intrigued me ever since. Students frequently would tell me that their grades were improving or that episodes of discipline infractions were a thing of the past. We would then continue with our counseling sessions, and I would feel satisfied that my efforts were making a difference. After talking later with the students' teachers, however, I would often learn that their academic performance had deteriorated further or that problems with discipline had actually increased. This pattern repeated itself numerous times as I found clients absolutely convincing when they told me about their improved progress or lack of culpability relating to irresponsible behavior—only to subsequently find out that they were deceiving me. With additional counseling experience, and an increased determination not to be misled by clients, I became more able to detect discrepancies between what individuals report and what they actually do. This awareness, however, created further difficulties for me as a counselor. If I challenged clients about the veracity of their assertions in initial counseling sessions, they would typically become argumentative or withdraw. My untenable choices in counseling were to acquiesce to clients' inaccurate statements or challenge them and undermine the counseling relationship.

Those patterns that I encountered early in my career and have since repeatedly observed in my extensive school and clinical experience are, of course, the manifestation of client defense mechanisms. In recent years, I began to present my thoughts in writing about the defenses in counseling (Clark, 1991, 1992, 1993, 1995c, 1997, 1998a) in a pursuit that culminates in this volume. What I have uncovered in my continuing research is that a substantial body of literature exists on defense mechanisms but that surprisingly little attention has been accorded to identifying and modifying defenses in counseling practice. Various counseling and psychotherapy publications refer to the importance of considering client defenses, particularly as they relate to resistance (George & Cristiani, 1995; Gilliland & James, 1998; Gladding, 1996), but systematic procedures for processing the mechanisms are rarely detailed. Psychoanalytic writings do emphasize the psychotherapeutic management of defenses (Blum, 1985; Gray, 1994; Sandler & Freud, 1985); this material, however, is presented in theoretical formulations and terminology that are difficult to apply directly to more generic counseling orientations. General references that address the various defenses typically focus on conceptual or empirical perspectives that are not immediately relevant to counseling practice (Conte & Plutchik, 1995; Cramer, 1991; Vaillant, 1992).

Although I found the counseling, psychoanalytic, and general resources individually insufficient, in combination the literature offers a knowledge base and potential framework for developing a comprehensive approach for working with clients' defense mechanisms in counseling. Psychoanalytic writings provide a foundation for conceptualizing and treating patient defenses, whereas general references clarify various facets of the mechanisms on the basis of contemporary and wide-ranging research. Counseling and psychotherapy publications that identify and describe selected techniques and processes offer a dynamic structure for effectively managing client defenses. In addition, many current counseling approaches emphasize multicultural considerations (Axelson, 1993; Pedersen & Carey, 1994; Ponterotto, Casas, Suzuki, & Alexander, 1995), and any discussion of defense mechanisms would be incomplete without acknowledging the impact of cultural forces on individuals' development and functioning. In this book, an emphasis will be given to integrating examples from multicultural perspectives when presenting counseling interventions that counselors may use in processing client defenses.

Cultural forces inextricably relate to social influences in the environment of individuals, including the groups with whom a person identifies. Defense mechanisms are primarily a social phenomenon; they are used in response to threatening interpersonal exchanges. Through direct experiences in social-cultural contexts, persons essentially construct and express linguistic and behavioral patterns (Martin, 1994), including the mechanisms of defense. In counseling, clients actively engage the same defenses that they initiate in other interpersonal relationships that evoke psychological disequilibrium. Counselors who conceptualize client behavior through defense mechanisms as theoretical entities also socially construct a reality that is commonly shared by groups of mental health professionals (Hoffman, 1990). Through a collaborative participation with a counselor, clients are encouraged to cocreate new perspectives and meanings that form a basis for more purposeful and adaptive behavior. In this formulation, social interactions become a critical focus for explaining and fostering human change and development (Gergen, 1985; Guterman, 1994).

Both theoretical and practical considerations contribute to the purpose of this book: to present a systematic model for identifying and modifying client defense mechanisms in the counseling process. Three stages of the counseling process provide a framework for detailing specific techniques and strategies for managing individual defenses. Extensive examples from diverse populations of clients emphasize therapeutic change involving 10 defense mechanisms: denial, displacement, identification, isolation, projection, rationalization, reaction formation, regression, repression, and undoing. The examination of each defense will also focus on aspects of the mechanism's theoretical origins, psychopathology, definitions, and, where delineated, types. Because this book stresses the work of the counselor in individual treatment with clients, a separate chapter focuses on defense mechanisms in the counseling process in groups. An integrative case example will illustrate a client's multiple defense change through the counseling stages.

Chapter 1 includes perspectives on the importance of defenses in counseling, definitions and properties of the mechanisms, and developmental and assessment considerations. Ten classic defenses are then introduced, in addition to a brief overview of the three-stage model of the counseling process. Chapter 2 focuses on denial as the first of the defenses to be reviewed regarding theoretical and practice implications. Denial serves as a lead chapter both for the significance of a prominent defense and for clarifying the counseling process and techniques that are also represented in the subsequent nine chapters on individual defenses. With each chapter on separate defenses organized in a standard format, the reader may study for comparative purposes specific counselor interventions in the counseling process. I have based my selection of the defense mechanisms examined primarily from those defenses most frequently referred to in the literature and my judgment of the mechanisms more commonly encountered in counseling practice. The group and case study chapters conclude the book.

In this volume, counseling is viewed as a therapeutic process involving client development during three stages. Throughout the counseling experience, essential interventions focus on clarifying individuals' functioning and establishing more adaptive behavior. Although the defense mechanisms originated in the psychoanalytic modality, the use of the constructs has broad and sustained application to practitioners in the helping professions with diverse orientations. With this in mind, I have written this book for counselors, psychologists, social workers, and other direct service professionals. Although the term *counselor* is used almost exclusively, this designation applies to the complementary roles of therapist and psychotherapist. The book is pertinent as a text in graduate courses that focus on techniques of counseling, theories of counseling and psychotherapy, or the counseling practicum.

ACKNOWLEDGMENTS

I wish to express my gratitude to William P. Brown, whom I first met in his position as director of Pupil Personnel Services in the Sharon Public Schools in Massachusetts. Bill has been a mentor and friend for many years, and he made a significant contribution to the completion of the book through his perceptive critiques. Allen Ivey, distinguished university professor, University of Massachusetts—Amherst, deserves special credit for his encouragement during the development of the manuscript. I am also grateful to Barry Jackson, chief psychologist, Durham Board of Education, Whitby, Ontario, for his discerning comments in reading each chapter. I also wish to acknowledge Jim Nageotte, sponsoring editor from Sage Publications, for providing supportive direction in shaping my manuscript. For their review of my book, I appreciate the assistance of the following: Denise Twohey, Susan Neufeldt, Merith Cosden, and Linda Berg-Cross. Thanks to my graduate assistants at St. Lawrence University—Angelita M. Dobson, Stephanie de Vera, Lorraine Lyndaker, and Judy Gibson—who were helpful in numerous ways. Finally, I appreciate the efforts of the university's senior secretaries, Bonnie Enslow and Faye Martin, for their typing and logistical support.

1

INTRODUCTION

The greatest of faults, I should say, is to be conscious of none.

—Thomas Carlyle, 1841/1993, p. 41

Perhaps one of the clearest examples of defense mechanisms in counseling occurs with persons who deny or rationalize their chemical dependency despite obvious and urgent conflicts. In counseling, a client may state, "I don't have any problems controlling my drinking" but is in treatment for multiple infractions for driving while intoxicated. Another individual who states that he has been free of substances during the week appears to be high from smoking marijuana on meeting with a counselor. Yet another client, recognizing that she has problems with controlling her use of alcohol, employs rationalization as a defense to justify her habit: "Hey, anybody with all my troubles needs a drink from time to time." Although defense mechanisms are prevalent in treatment with individuals with alcohol and substance abuse issues, defenses also frequently occur with individuals in counseling from diverse backgrounds with a variety of presenting problems. Defenses protect persons from

1

perceived threat, and for many clients, aspects of the counseling experience are destabilizing and threatening. Counselors need to be prepared to respond effectively to the inevitable emergence and persistence of client defenses that constitute both a challenge and an opportunity for therapeutic progress.

In addition to an awareness of the impact and significance of defense mechanisms in counseling, other aspects of the defenses contribute to a comprehensive understanding of their function and characteristics. A surprisingly large number of defenses and definitions of defense mechanisms have been proposed in the literature since Sigmund Freud's earliest formulation of the construct, late in the 19th century. An examination of the specific properties of the defenses assists in clarifying a reasonable working number for counseling purposes. Attempts to assess defense mechanisms also have a lengthy history, although many psychometric instruments and procedures are not directly relevant to counseling. Any review of defense mechanisms must make a determination as to the selection of defenses to be included; specified here are 10 classic mechanisms that clients frequently employ in counseling. An understanding of the nature of defenses assists the counselor when processing client mechanisms in counseling through a coherent and systematic therapeutic model.

SIGNIFICANCE OF DEFENSE
MECHANISMS IN COUNSELING

Client use of defense mechanisms frequently restricts the development of open communication and trust in the counseling relationship. If a counselor indiscriminately challenges individuals' defenses, the counseling alliance may be jeopardized, and those mechanisms become further entrenched. Yet if a counselor is reluctant to explore dynamics of client defenses, affect and conflicts relating to the mechanisms may remain fragmented and therapeutically inaccessible. Failure to adequately process defenses also precludes the opportunity to clarify clients' subjective distortions inherent in the mechanisms. Individuals who rely on defenses to avoid or escape uncomfortable situations often encounter interpersonal difficulties, and social context is a key dynamic in the operation of the mechanisms. Counselors may understandably be hesitant about challenging clients' defenses because of uncertainties about how to proceed once defenses are observed, as multiple defenses may be operating at the same time. It is possible, however, to identify and describe a comprehensive approach in working with client defenses that is both supportive and challenging.

Client Resistance

Persons using patterns of defense attempt to control disclosure to reduce threat and potential reproach. If a counselor challenges individuals by expanding discussion into threatening areas, clients typically become more adamant about the veracity of their assertions or emotionally withdraw. On the other hand, if the counselor acquiesces and supports clients' distorted contentions, the focus of counseling becomes limited to the frames of reference of particular persons, regardless of their accuracy. As an example, a student employing the defense of rationalization asserts that his academic failure is due to an inadequate teacher, an outdated textbook, and a boring subject. When the counselor suggests that other possibilities, including effort and level of concentration, may contribute to the client's scholastic failure, the individual refuses to consider these alternative perspectives. The other option of the counselor, to acknowledge client perceptions and avoid arousing threat, does not permit consideration of broader motivational forces. The counselor's task is to develop trust and rapport within the counseling relationship for clients to become less resistant to exploring topics and issues that are threatening but also potentially growth enhancing.

Indiscriminate Counselor Processing

A counselor may undermine the counseling relationship through intrusive or premature interventions. Excessive threat occurs when a counselor attacks or "strips" clients' defenses. A counselor may intentionally decide to forcefully challenge client defenses in an effort to disrupt what is perceived as a dysfunctional pattern. In other instances, a therapist may become impatient with individuals who persist in relying on their defenses and may imprudently begin to apply pressure to induce behavior change. In either case, through strategic choice or intolerant responses, a counselor can overwhelm and discourage clients through an outright assault on their defenses. A counselor's ill-advised actions may produce client duress and disequilibrium to the point of emotional decompensation. A counselor may also assume a role by de- fault and avoid addressing maladaptive patterns of client defense mechanisms. Attacking or avoiding individuals' defenses is untherapeutic and may represent the presence of unresolved personal issues for a therapist. A counselor is also susceptible to engaging defense mechanisms to the detriment of clients. Supervision, self-reflection, and, when abusive or avoidance behaviors persist, personal counseling can be effective in limiting indiscriminate processing in the counseling experience.

Avoidance of Conflict Examination

In counseling, the counselor frequently presents a threat when at- tempting to identify or clarify individuals' conflicted and contradictory behavior. Employing various defense mechanisms, clients may divert direct examination of potentially therapeutic issues, including central assumptions and convictions. Critical client dynamics avoided through the use of client defenses may remain obscure and unaddressed as sources of psychological and physiological dysfunction. Shedler, Mayman, and Manis (1993) provide research support indicating that psychological defense involving the process of inhibiting thoughts and feelings is a cumulative stressor and increases susceptibility through time to a variety of illnesses. A client, for example, experiences distress relating to expression of feelings and, using the defense of isolation, controls and inhibits affect. At the same time, however, conflict relating to expression of feelings remains unassessed and unchanged, and the person experi- ences high blood pressure. Further, some individuals maintain a sus- tained pattern of defense even after the resolution of those conflicts that initially prompted the employment of the mechanisms (Freud, 1965). It is also a possibility that what initiates an individual's behavior is re- inforced or perpetuated by other motivational forces. Gordon Allport (1961) referred to this process as *functional autonomy,* and the concept may be applicable to persons who do not reverse their defense use despite diminution of circumstantial threat. Therapeutically, the counselor must attempt to develop a relationship that enables clients to clarify conflicts and contradictions inherent in the use of their defenses.

Client Subjective Distortions

Defense mechanisms operate largely outside individuals' awareness and mitigate intolerable affect and conflict. Defense responses are an automatic reaction to threat, rather than more considered attempts to cope with sources of difficulty more directly. A function of the mechanisms is that persons construct safeguards that are immediately responsive to their subjective perspectives. Defenses are distorting to the degree that they are contradictory and inconsistent in relation to client behavior or in relation to various environmental conditions. For example, a client using the defense of projection attributes unacceptable behavior to others that is actually characteristic of the individual. Other persons may, in fact, possess none of the specific qualities attributed by the client, and a contradiction exists between the two realities that is accounted for by the individual's distorted perceptions. The objective in counseling is to clarify client distortions and inconsistencies and to encourage persons to construct more coherent and adaptive perceptions.

Interpersonal Dysfunction

An individual's defense use can evoke adverse interpersonal consequences that result in troubled relationships. In a continuation of the previous example, a client employing projection attributes hostility to another individual who in actuality is not angry. The client responds to the targeted person presumed to be hostile in an aggressive manner, and an argument results. In other instances, individuals may resent a client's using deceptive maneuvers that are perceived as self-serving, rather than dealing more directly with situations. As an example, a client uses the defense of rationalization and justifies arriving late for organizational meetings, voicing a variety of somewhat plausible statements. The client's pattern of self-justifications, however, is perceived as "excuse making" by her irritated coworkers, resulting in disputes and disagreements. The counselor's task is to collaborate with clients in recognizing the adverse effects that defenses typically evoke in interpersonal relationships and subsequently in developing alternative and more purposeful actions.

Use of the Counseling Process

Without a coherent framework for processing client defense mechanisms in counseling, the counselor's interventions may prove to be ineffective, and essential strategic questions and issues can remain unresolved. An initial concern emerges about how the counselor determines the functional quality of client defenses. Once specific mechanisms are detected, a major counseling issue then becomes whether maladaptive defenses should be relinquished, worked around, or in some way replaced with more effective strategies (Vaillant, 1997). Another matter relates to how the counselor may involve clients in modifying their defenses while respecting the idiosyncratic functioning of individuals. A further concern is the sequence of client defense change and what specific techniques and strategies promote therapeutic progress. These significant counseling issues may begin to be addressed by conceptualizing the counseling process into sequential stages (Sampson, Weiss, Mlodnosky, & Hause, 1972). Within each of the three major stages of counseling, counseling interventions may be intentionally employed to identify and modify client defenses in adaptive directions.

CONCEPTUALIZATIONS AND PROPERTIES OF DEFENSE MECHANISMS

Classic Conceptualizations of Defense Mechanisms

Sigmund Freud's understanding of the nature and significance of defense mechanisms changed through many years of scattered commentary on the constructs. At various times, he made reference to as many as 17 relatively distinct defenses (Vaillant, 1992). In "The Neuro-Psychoses of Defence" (1894/1962b) and "Further Remarks on the Neuro-Psychoses of Defence" (1896/1962a), Freud described conversion, displacement, isolation, projection, repression, and retreat or withdrawal from reality as separate defenses. He theorized that varied symptoms "arose through the psychical mechanism of (unconscious) defence—that is, in an attempt to repress an incompatible idea which had come into distressing opposition to the patient's ego" (p. 162). Subsequent to 1896, however, nearly all the defense mechanisms introduced by Freud were used interchangeably with repression, as repression became synonymous with defense (Mahl, 1969). After 30 years, Freud (1926/1959) made a major change in his conceptualization of defenses when he reintroduced the term:

> It will be an undoubted advantage, I think, to revert to the old concept of "defence," provided we employ it explicitly as a general designation for all the techniques which the ego makes use of in conflicts which may lead to a neurosis, while we retain the word "repression" for the special method of defence. (p. 163)

Sigmund Freud was already in his late 60s when he reformulated the defense mechanisms in his 1926 publication. To that point, Freud had not written a definitive analysis of the defenses, and it was left to his daughter, Anna Freud (1936/1966), to fulfill this task in *The Ego and the Mechanisms of Defense*. She lists the following defense mechanisms in this volume: regression, repression, introjection, reaction formation, isolation, undoing, projection, turning against self, reversal, and sublimation. Freud does not, however, clearly differentiate reversal from reaction formation or isolation from intellectualization (Suppes & Warren, 1975). The status of sublimation as a defense is questionable because of its unique function of pursuing creative activity in response to threat, presenting more of a coping, rather than a defensive, process.

Further Conceptualizations of Defense Mechanisms

A multitude of defense mechanisms have been proposed during the past hundred years, and there is little consensus on identifying the defenses because researchers and practitioners have held different perspectives on the number and nature of the constructs. Since Sigmund and Anna Freud's accountings of the defense mechanisms, the number of identified defenses from various enumerations has escalated to more than 50 (Cramer, 1991; Laughlin, 1979). Proposals for specific sets of defense mechanisms generate a variety of selections with a number of rather obscure defenses sometimes suggested. Bond, Gardner, Christian, and Sigal (1983) list 24 defense mechanisms, including inhibition, pseudoaltruism, and as-if clinging behavior. In a comprehensive text on ego defense mechanisms, Laughlin (1979) identifies 22 major ego defenses that are more clearly delineated and professionally accepted and 26 minor ego defenses. The *Diagnostic and Statistical Manual of Mental Disorders (DSM-IV;* American Psychiatric Association, 1994a) contains a glossary of 27 defense mechanisms and coping styles divided into seven levels on a defensive functioning scale. Certain defenses, such as denial, projection, and repression, appear on virtually every published list. A defense mechanism that was not identified by either of the Freuds but that has gained wide acceptance in the literature is rationalization, first conceptualized by Ernest Jones (1908).

Defining Properties of Defense Mechanisms

In addition to lack of consensus on a universally accepted list of defenses, there is also disagreement on even a more basic consideration: What are the criteria for a mechanism of defense? No definitive definition of a defense mechanism prevails in the literature, and various sources provide diverse and sometimes conflicting meanings (American Psychiatric Association, 1994a, 1994b; English & English, 1958; Rycroft, 1995). In attempting to clarify this central question from a counseling perspective and to arrive at yet another definition of a defense mechanism, it is helpful to consider what constitutes the defining properties or characteristics of the mechanisms of defense. It is generally accepted in counseling that defenses are relatively discrete mental constructs that may be inferred from behavioral observations of clients (Sampson et al., 1972) or from collateral information, such as observations of a parent or spouse, available to the counselor. Identifying additional properties of defense mechanisms beyond this level generally is subject to the varying views of researchers and counselors. From my perspective, after an extensive review of the literature, the properties of a defense mechanism include the following defining characteristics: unconscious processing, subjective distortion, intolerable affect and conflict, and automatic and undifferentiated responses. Each of these properties will be discussed in the following sections, concluding with a definition of a defense mechanism.

Unconscious Processing. When persons react to threat when employing defense mechanisms, the conflicted source of the response is largely outside their conscious awareness. Sigmund Freud emphasized the significance of the unconscious as a repository for data that had never been conscious or that had been conscious briefly but had been subsequently repressed (American Psychiatric Association, 1994b). Alfred Adler (1931/1958) contended that what is considered the unconscious is simply parts of human consciousness that are not fully understood. A crucial aspect of the unconscious process of an individual relates to the core convictions that a person maintains in relationship to the self, the world, and life (Adler, 1931/1958; Kelly, 1955; Liotti, 1987). At this core level, a person lacks understanding or awareness of influential convictions or assumptions that are fundamental to the individual's functioning. In conjunction with the core level of mental activity is an intermediate level or a "protective-belt" relating to the explicit verbal descriptions that a person expresses (Liotti, 1987). Defense mechanisms function at this intermediate level, as individuals express statements directly influenced by assumptions outside their awareness. In counseling, for instance, a client maintains core convictions that he is an inadequate person in a noncaring world and that life is futile and bleak. Repeatedly, when challenges occur in the individual's life, he employs the defense of rationalization to justify his lack of participation in experiences that predictably end in failure. When the client refuses to examine motives beyond those expressed through rationalization, his prevailing core assumptions and psychological equilibrium are maintained.

Subjective Distortion. Inherent in defense mechanisms is a phenomenal distortion that becomes evident in individuals' conflicted and contradictory behavior. For example, a client employing the defense mechanism of projection attributes hostile feelings to a counselor, when in actuality, the counselor responds benignly toward the person. Until clients become aware of the contradictions in their behavior, however, they may not perceive that their functioning involves subjective distortions. As persons use a repetitive pattern of a defense or defenses, the breadth or scope of distortions may be widened, with direct implications for questions of normal and abnormal behavior. It is necessary, however, to employ some type of criteria or standards to evaluate individuals' idiosyncratic psychological functioning. Anna Freud's (1965) framework for differentiating functional outcomes of defense mechanisms on the basis of age adequateness, balance, intensity, and reversibility will be used in this text. Freud tended not to stress environmental forces when assessing the psychopathology of the defenses, and the addition of context represents an extension of her conceptualization. Age adequateness implies that the relative age of a person is significant when considering the appropriateness of defense mechanism use. Balance relates to the degree of flexibility in defense use; a single mechanism employed in a stereotyped way suggests a limited repertoire in response to threat. Intensity or frequency of defense engagement manifests a compelled quality to an individual's functioning and frequently disrupts interpersonal relationships. Reversibility indicates the ability of a person to reduce defense employment when perceived threat diminishes or no longer exists. Context involves the cultural and social forces that influence an individual's use of particular defense mechanisms.

Intolerable Affect and Conflict. Sigmund Freud observed that defense mechanisms ward off unpleasurable anxiety as a result of intrapsychic conflict of drives occurring between the id and the ego or the ego and the superego (English & English, 1958). A contemporary view of defenses expands the range of affect mitigated by the mechanisms to include anxiety, embarrassment, grief, humiliation, remorse, shame, and other painful emotions (Dorpat, 1987). Although Freud's emphasis on drives is more limited to adherents with a psychoanalytic orientation, intrapsychic conflict between incompatible internal forces of an individual's personality is a widely accepted contemporary perspective. Anna Freud (1936/1966) was instrumental in beginning to expand the focus of conflict to include external as well as internal forces. Extrapsychic or external conflict occurs between an individual and some demand or requirement of the environment (American Psychiatric Association, 1994b). Although defenses are more apparent when clients experience extrapsychic conflict, they are also influenced by intrapsychic conflict between incompatible demands within clients' personalities. For example, a client maintains an internal conflict between dependency and autonomy and employs the defense mechanism of rationalization to justify both needs in social interactions. Defenses may restore persons' psychic equilibrium, but the escape-avoidance quality of the mechanisms does little to address either internal or external conflicts.

Conflict may also occur between here-and-now situational demands or between the pressure of demands and referents to developmental experiences. In an immediate conflict, an individual may employ a defense mechanism to ameliorate opposing demands in a specific context. A client, for instance, using the defense of isolation discusses societal implications of adolescent substance abuse to avoid becoming emotionally involved in a discussion of his son's recent arrest for dealing drugs. The client encounters an immediate conflict over expressing intimate feelings in the counseling context, and isolation as a defense reduces his duress. Individuals may also incur conflict relating to developmental experiences that prompt the use of defense mechanisms. In the example cited, the client employing isolation may have a long-standing conflict over expressing affect relating to a parental injunction that family members do not show their emotions. Conflicts of a developmental type may relate to a person's unquestionable assumptions about self and reality, involving schemas constructed during childhood (Liotti, 1987).

Automatic and Undifferentiated Responses. Although individuals' use of defenses is an escape-avoidance reaction, the mechanisms are enacted without a deliberate attempt to be evasive. The automatic responses of defenses are rigid and stimulus bound (Haan, 1977), lacking a reflective or discriminating quality. Persons tend to immediately employ the mechanisms in generalized contexts of perceived threat, instead of assessing specific situations that may elicit more versatile and purposeful reactions. Defenses frequently become habitual or compelled because they have reduced conflicted affect and thus are not modulated depending on changing circumstances or conditions. This is the case in counseling in which potential for growth is encouraged, but the nature or expectation of the therapeutic experience that presupposes client self-disclosure is inherently threatening to many individuals. Instead of being open to new directions and development, clients react to the perceived threat of the counselor and focus on maintaining self-structures that are unchallenged and unchanged and seemingly safe (Rycroft, 1995). Further, clients' feelings of threat may not simply be linked to immediate circumstances or discussion topics in counseling but relate in an automatic, tacit way to their core assumptions. As an example, a client maintains a conviction that men cannot be trusted and are hurtful, and a male counselor's best attempts to be sensitive and supportive are immediately perceived as rejecting by an individual using the defense of projection. It may be evident that this example also suggests the phenomenon of transference, and clarification is required. Although both core convictions and transference relate to schemas developed in early life, the former refers to assumptions an individual maintains about people in general, and the latter represents attitudes and feelings associated with important persons in particular, such as parents and siblings (American Psychiatric Association, 1994b).

The selected properties of the mechanisms of defense contribute to an eclectic definition of a defense mechanism: an unconscious subjective distortion that reduces intolerable affect and conflict through automatic and undifferentiated responses.

DEVELOPMENTAL ASPECTS OF DEFENSE MECHANISMS

A question that has been of interest to researchers and practitioners since Sigmund Freud's initial formulation of a defense mechanism focuses on developmental factors or influences that predispose an individual to assume a particular defense or defenses. Freud suggested that a person's choice of possible defense mechanisms is a function of an inherent constitutional factor that determines developmental tendencies and reactions (Hartman, 1939/1958). Anna Freud (1936/1966) was less conclusive about formative influences relating to an individual's employment of particular defenses: "The considerations which determine the ego's choice of mechanism remain uncertain" (p. 50). In recent years, research has focused on various developmental factors contributing to the use of particular defenses, such as age and gender (Safyer & Hauser, 1995). The formation of defense mechanisms also relates to cultural and family influences that individuals experience in their development (Ivey, Ivey, & Simek-Morgan, 1997). Culture and family environments affect the construction of persons' core assumptions used in conjunction with the mechanisms of defense. Defense mechanisms have also been categorized along developmental hierarchies, such as defensive and coping processes and levels of maturity (Cramer, 1991).

Developmental Factors of Defense Mechanisms

Chronological Age. Studies pertaining to the differential age use of defenses relate several mechanisms to developmental stages. Denial appears most prominently during early childhood and declines with age; projection is more characteristic during late childhood and preadolescence; identification increases during middle childhood and once again during middle adolescence (Cramer, 1991). Intellectualization, as a type of isolation, is prominent during adolescence (Mahl, 1969). One view suggests that the emergence of particular defenses depends on their relative degree of cognitive complexity and an individual's developmental ability to process and conceptualize (Safyer & Hauser, 1995). Anna Freud (1965) emphasized an adequateness dimension relating to chronological age when she stated that defenses "are more apt to have pathological results if they come into use before the appropriate age or are kept too long after it" (p. 177).

Gender. Investigating the possibility that gender relates to particular defenses assists in clarifying a central developmental variable. Studies conducted using the Defense Mechanism Inventory (Cramer & Carter, 1978; Ihilevich & Gleser, 1995) with college-age students indicated that in comparison with women, men consistently score higher on item preferences for projection and turning against object; in comparison with men, women score higher on items relating to turning against self and reversal. Turning against object includes defenses of identification with the aggressor and displacement, and reversal includes denial and reaction formation (Ihilevich & Gleser, 1995). As they relate to the defenses on an external-internal dimension, male defenses are more outer directed, and female defenses are more inner directed (Safyer & Hauser, 1995). Defense mechanism preference may also be related to sex role orientation (Brems, 1990; Evans, 1982; Levit, 1991). In a study conducted with college students, men who consistently employed outer-directed defenses tended toward a strong masculine gender identity, and women who used inner-directed defenses were characterized by a strong feminine gender identity (Evans, 1982).

Culture and Family. Broad and varying forces inherent in culture and family influences affect a person's development (Grieger & Ponterotto, 1995), including the construction of the mechanisms of defense. Developmentally, an individual begins to use escape-avoidance responses when interacting with others in threatening situations, and defenses that are relatively "successful" tend to persist, as with other socially learned behavior. For example, a child living in a harsh and insecure urban environment employs the defense of denial to protect herself emotionally from fearful interactions with others. From a social learning perspective, a longitudinal study recognized the influence of parent modeling of particular behaviors as an important determinant for children's development of defense mechanisms (Weinstock, 1967). An earlier study found parental communication and discipline patterns related to the use of defense mechanisms among early male adolescents (Miller & Swanson, 1960). The importance of understanding defenses of individuals that may developmentally relate to unmet dependency needs and neglect and abuse within their family of origin has also been cited (Ivey et al., 1997). In counseling, for example, a client subjected to parental abuse as a child employs the defense mechanism of displacement when shifting his anger from the original target of a parent to the vulnerable substitute of a spouse.

Developmental Hierarchies

In addition to investigations that consider developmental factors pertaining to defense mechanisms, another type of research arranges defenses along developmentally related hierarchies (Safyer & Hauser, 1995). Considerations of coping and defensive processes (Haan, 1977) and maturity levels of defenses (Vaillant, 1977) offer comprehensive models for clarifying developmental aspects of the mechanisms of defense.

Defense and Coping Processes. Identifying 10 classic defenses, Norma Haan (1977) provides a model of ego processes that differentiates defensive from coping functions on a qualitative basis. Haan conceptualized a taxonomy composed of 10 generic processes, with each process having modal functions in a hierarchy of fragmentation, defense, and coping. The fragmentation mode presents common clinical labels describing disorganized, pathological behavior. Characteristics of defenses as modal processes include rigidity, distortion of present reality, pressure from the past, undifferentiated thinking, magical thinking, and gratification of subterfuge. The coping processes, in contrast to defenses, are flexible, open to choice, oriented to present reality as well as the future, and focused on realistic compromises between wishes and affects. Defense and coping processes were rated by clinicians after reviewing tape-recorded interviews with adult participants in a longitudinal study. Theoretically, according to Haan, most people have a preferred generic process and move up or down the hierarchy of modal functions in dealing with life challenges. If individuals do possess a preferred generic process and express themselves within modal functions, the implications for counseling would be obvious. Clients could be assessed for their generic processes, and strategies could be effected to promote their respective coping processes. As an example, a client who possesses a generic process of sensitively reacting to others' thoughts and feelings may progress from expressing delusion and ideas of reference (fragmentary mode) to projection (defensive mode) to empathy (coping mode). Empirical research, however, does not provide statistical support for Haan's model. With the exception of people with high ratings on the coping process of intellectuality and equally high ratings on the defense process of intellectualization, there are no significant tendencies for specific coping processes to be related to counterpart defenses (Swanson, 1988).

Defense Maturity. Conceptualizing the maturity of defense mechanisms as a developmental dimension, George Vaillant (1977) identified 18 defenses on a hierarchy from immature to mature. Longitudinal studies involving questionnaires and interviews initiated with college students resulted in differential levels of the defenses presented in clinical and developmental categories. *Narcissistic* or psychotic defenses include denial, distortions, and delusional projection. *Immature* defenses are acting out, schizoid fantasy, hypochondriasis, projection, and turning against the self. *Neurotic* defenses include displacement, dissociation, intellectualization, reaction formation, and repression. *Mature* defenses are altruism, anticipation, humor, sublimation, and suppression. A central assumption of the defense hierarchy is that individuals employing mature defenses are happier and enjoy more optimal mental health than people using less mature defenses. The use of mature defenses increases with age, and emotional health in childhood is related to higher levels of mature defense use in adulthood (Safyer & Hauser, 1995). It is disputable whether the defenses that Vaillant labels mature are not more appropriately conceptualized as coping processes because of their more flexible, conscious, and often creative qualities for purposefully managing conflict and emotions (Plutchik, 1995). Another semantic point of contention with the hierarchy is that an "immature" defense used by an adult is qualitatively the same defense that may be age-appropriate when used by a child (Cramer, 1991).

ASSESSMENT OF DEFENSE MECHANISMS

The wide variations in assumptions concerning the essential nature and number of defense mechanisms among theoreticians and practitioners make it difficult to establish sound methods for evaluating the constructs. Numerous attempts have been made to measure defenses; 58 empirical procedures for assessing the mechanisms have been identified (Cramer, 1991). Variations also occur in the methodologies and databases that researchers use to evaluate defenses, although in recent years, distinct systematic approaches have evolved for assessing the constructs (Conte & Plutchik, 1995; Cramer, 1991; Vaillant, 1992). Research methods for measuring defenses relate to three basic approaches: clinical observer ratings, self-report instruments, and projective techniques.

Clinical Observer Ratings

Despite the obvious difficulties inherent in the assessment of defenses, numerous researchers have made significant attempts to conceptualize and measure the mechanisms. Vaillant's (1977) longitudinal studies, accomplished through interviews conducted during 30 years and his subsequent ratings on the maturity of defenses, are outlined in *Adaptation to Life.* Haan (1977), also employing extensive clinical interviews, provided a detailed analysis of her approach to rating defenses from a constructivist perspective in *Coping and Defending.* Other researchers have employed clinical judgments and ratings for assessing defense mechanisms with various participants including women during pregnancy and early mother-child relationships (Bibring, Dwyer, Huntington, & Valenstein, 1961); adolescent diabetic and psychiatric patients (Jacobson et al., 1992); and persons diagnosed with schizophrenia (Semrad, Grinspoon, & Feinberg, 1973). Psychodynamically oriented clinical interviews and life vignette data, emphasizing personality and affect disorders, were used in the development of the Defense Mechanism Rating Scale (DMRS; Perry & Kardos, 1995). The DMRS conceptually organizes 27 defenses in a hierarchy of seven levels of maturity or adaptiveness. Although interview-based rating systems allow for the inferential assessment of unconscious processes, the procedures are complex and subject to observer bias and are not directly applicable with individual clients for use in the counseling process.

Self-Report Instruments

In contrast to clinical observer rating approaches that require extensive interviews, self-report procedures use questionnaires to derive participant responses to conflict situations that identify the presence or absence of defensive functioning (Hentschel, Ehlers, & Peter, 1993). A critical assumption of the various self-report instruments is that a limited number of standardized statements consciously evaluated by participants support inferences relating to unconscious defense mechanism processing (Jacobson et al., 1992). Self-report instruments are also susceptible to distortion and faking (Safyer & Hauser, 1995). The Defense Style Questionnaire (Bond, 1995) is an 88-statement questionnaire measuring the self-report of four defense styles: maladaptive, image-distorting, self-sacrificing, and adaptive. The Life Style Index (Conte & Apter, 1995) assesses the conscious derivatives of eight defense mechanisms through ego defense scales in a self-report format of 97 items.

The most widely recognized and researched self-report instrument for evaluating defenses is the Defense Mechanism Inventory (DMI; Ihilevich & Gleser, 1995). The DMI organizes 15 defense mechanisms into five clusters that yield participant preferences for each category. For example, principalization is a cluster that includes the defenses of isolation, intellectualization, and rationalization. Although the classification of clusters of defenses on the DMI expands the scope of behavior for research purposes, the instrument may be relatively insensitive to the effects of individual defenses and should be used cautiously (Vickers & Hervig, 1981). From a counseling perspective, because of the discrete nature of defenses demonstrated by clients, a focus on individual defenses may be more relevant to practice than clusters or defense styles.

Projective Techniques

A fundamental assumption of projective techniques is that individuals express or "project" their personality characteristics through relatively unstructured and ambiguous tasks that permit a virtually unlimited variety of responses (Anastasi & Urbina, 1997). Several prominent instruments have entailed the assessment of defense mechanisms, including the Rorschach, the Thematic Apperception Test, sentence completion tasks, and human figure drawings. The most well known of the projective techniques, the Rorschach, has produced only equivocal or uncertain findings for assessing defense mechanisms (Ritzler, 1995). The Thematic Apperception Test has been used to provide definitions of defenses with examples for detecting eight mechanisms in stories expressed by individuals (Bellak & Abrams, 1997). The test has also been used in discussing a detailed procedure for assessing the defenses of denial, projection, and identification in projective stories (Cramer, 1991). Human figure drawings have been related to various defenses (Hammer, 1958), and the operation of 13 defense mechanisms in drawings and the graphic productions of disturbed children and young adults has been illustrated (Levick, 1983). The open-ended format of sentence completion tasks assists in ascertaining defense mechanisms in the counseling process (Clark, 1995d), and the Defense Mechanism Profile (Johnson & Gold, 1995) provides 40 sentence stems and a manual with definitions of nine defenses and specific scoring criteria.

Although the assessment of defense mechanisms continues as a research pursuit, projectives have not proved to be sound measurement devices for the constructs because of a variety of methodological and psychometric weaknesses (Heath, 1958; Johnson & Gold, 1995). Projective techniques in general are known more for cautions and prohibitions among theoreticians and practitioners than for potential resources in counseling (Clark, 1995d). Reservations about the therapeutic use of projectives include marginal validity and reliability levels, the proliferation of various types of these measures, and the considerable training required for many instruments. These considerations, although legitimate, are of less concern if projective techniques are viewed as informal, hypotheses-generating tools that are integral to the counseling process (Clark, 1994a, 1995d). Within these parameters, their use can assist in developing inferences that may later be confirmed or invalidated. Data on defense mechanisms derived from projective techniques may also be corroborated through observations of client behavior and collateral sources available to the counselor.

DEFENSE MECHANISMS
IN THE COUNSELING PROCESS

Given the vast number of defenses proposed in the literature and variations in the properties of the mechanisms, identifying defense mechanisms that are pertinent to the counseling process requires specific criteria to guide the selection process. Arriving at a definition of a defense assists in identifying qualities that will apply to some mechanisms while excluding others. Once counselors become familiar with a working number of defenses, it is possible for them to process the mechanisms in counseling through a three-stage model.

Selection of Defense Mechanisms

My selection of defense mechanisms discussed in subsequent chapters of this book is based on the following criteria: identifiable defining properties, personal observations in counseling with a diverse range of clients in schools and clinics, and individual mechanisms commonly referenced in the literature. Defining properties of defenses emphasized in this book—unconscious processing, subjective distortion, intolerable affect and conflict, and automatic and undifferentiated responses—is inclusive of a number of defenses. Other defenses proposed in the literature, such as humor, compensation, and sublimation, are outside circumscribed limits of the defining properties. Although the choice of defense mechanisms has been clearly influenced by the psychoanalytic model, other counseling orientations extend the conceptualization of the mechanisms from a broader perspective. For a hundred years, certain defense mechanisms have been consistently referenced in the literature, whereas others have been proposed but have not been widely accepted as constructs among communities of researchers and practitioners. Counseling and psychotherapy texts that list individual defenses (e.g., Gladding, 1996; Hansen, Rossberg, & Cramer, 1994; Ivey et al., 1997) are of course another contemporary resource for recognizing individual defenses. On the basis of the criteria suggested, the following 10 defense mechanisms are included as a focus of this book: denial, displacement, identification, isolation, projection, rationalization, reaction formation, regression, repression, and undoing. Table 1.1 provides definitions of the defense mechanisms with examples of client statements reflecting substance abuse issues.

The Counseling Process

A generic three-stage model of the counseling process has been detailed (Patterson & Welfel, 1994) that is compatible with the structure of the present text. In my own writings on counseling practices (see references), I also use a three-stage framework for working with a diverse range of clients. Within each sequential stage, multiple theories of counseling and psychotherapy contribute to a coherent and compre-

TABLE 1.1   Defense Mechanism Definitions With Examples of
Client Statements Reflecting Substance Abuse Issues

Definitions	*Examples*
Denial	
Negating the meaning or existence of perceptions	"People say things about me taking drugs for no reason."
Displacement	
Redirecting feelings to a vulnerable substitute	"After I have a few joints, I forget about how much I hate school."
Identification	
Assuming desired attributes of another person through fantasized associations	"I really admire his cool, and drugs are just a part of what he does."
Isolation	
Severing verbalized cognitions from associated affect	"Perhaps I have a propensity to mind-altering substances."
Projection	
Attributing intolerable behavior to others that is characteristic of oneself	"Stop staring at me. I think you have a problem with drugs."
Rationalization	
Justifying objectionable behavior through the use of plausible statements	"Everybody around here is into using dope."
Reaction formation	
Demonstrating exaggerated moralistic actions that are directly contrary to cognitive and affective functioning	"Anybody who is into drugs is mentally deranged."
Regression	
Reverting to developmentally immature behavior	"What's really wrong with getting high?"
Repression	
Excluding from awareness intolerable cognitions and affect	"I can't recall having any problems with chemical abuse."
Undoing	
Nullifying a perceived transgression through a reverse action	"I like getting high, but I never do it."

hensive conceptualization of therapeutic change. In the initial or relationship stage, person-centered (Raskin & Rogers, 1995), Adlerian or Individual Psychology (Adler, 1931/1958; Dinkmeyer, Dinkmeyer, & Sperry, 1987), and psychodynamic (Freud, 1936/1966; Gray, 1994) orientations are prominent in establishing a supportive and trust-inducing climate for assessing client defense mechanisms. The middle or integration period emphasizes Gestalt (Clarkson, 1989) and cognitive behavior (Beck & Weishaar, 1995; Ellis, 1995; Meichenbaum, 1977) and continues with the psychodynamic approach. An in-depth exploration challenges individuals to clarify contradictory and conflicted behavior inherent in defenses. In the final or accomplishment stage, strategies from Individual Psychology and cognitive-behavioral formulations encourage clients to control defense use and consolidate purposeful actions. Although defense mechanisms represent only one dimension of individuals' functioning, the constructs are integral to broad forces in human development and psychopathology and are essential considerations in the counseling process. The next chapter on denial specifically describes the three-stage framework and therapeutic interventions that will be used in subsequent chapters on identifying and modifying defenses in counseling.

2

DENIAL

Nature never deceives us; we deceive ourselves.

—Jean Jacques Rousseau, 1764/1911, p. 166

Counselors must continually be alert to challenges presented by clients' use of denial and related mechanisms of defense. Individuals employ denial by distorting perceptions in response to threat, and numerous examples of the defense in counseling may be cited. In one instance, a client insists that she is not using drugs when the counselor is aware of the person's continuing chemical abuse. Another client denies the urgency of making up incomplete assignments, while reporting that his academic performance is improving. Yet another person is noncompliant with her medication for a life-threatening condition and states, "I'm doing much better, and I really don't need the treatment anymore." The counselor may be placed in the untenable position of either appearing to agree with or contesting a client's use of denial. If the counselor chooses not to dispute statements manifesting clients' denial, individuals may feel affirmed in their employment of the defense. On the other hand, if the counselor questions the veracity of persons' assertions, the counseling relationship may be jeopardized because clients feel threatened or even attacked by the counselor. Defining denial as a defense mechanism emphasizes negating the meaning or existence of perceptions.

THEORETICAL ASPECTS OF DENIAL

Prior to considering how a counselor may process a client's use of denial in counseling, it is instructive to examine conceptual issues that help identify various qualities of this defense mechanism. Although Sigmund Freud first described denial as a construct late in the 19th century, its conceptual base has expanded so that the defense is pertinent to the practice of contemporary practitioners with a range of orientations clearly beyond the psychoanalytic modality. Anna Freud was instrumental in categorizing defenses and differentiating between functional outcomes of the mechanisms. Evaluating such elements as the intensity, context, and reversibility of denial assists in determining the adaptive or maladaptive nature of a client's defenses. Although denial may be considered a discrete defense, it is possible to distinguish specific types of denial that become manifest in counseling.

Emergence of Denial

More than a century ago, Freud (1894/1962b) first made reference to denial in one of his early writings when he described a case of a woman who falsely believed that a man who came to her home to visit another woman was in love with her. After his relationship ended with the other woman, the man stopped coming to the house. The woman hallucinated that the man came to stay with her as she denied the torment of her situation through a distortion of reality. In a later work, Freud (1923/1961b) theorized that young boys believed that they saw a penis on a female because they could not accept its anatomical absence. In these references, and in other scattered commentary, Freud alludes to denial or disavowal, but beyond this he does not expound on the role or place of denial in defense.

It was left for Anna Freud (1936/1966) to delineate denial in her classic work *The Ego and the Mechanisms of Defense*. Denial, however, was deemed by Freud to be involved only in the preliminary stages of defense. She did not regard denial as meeting the criteria for defense mechanisms to protect against internal "instinctual demands" but tended to view the response only as a means to avoid pain or danger due to external or more objective conditions in the life of a person. Only in subsequent psychoanalytic writings does denial emerge as a widely recognized defense mechanism with a capacity to ward off both internal and external threat.

Psychopathology and Denial

In one of her more contemporary writings, Anna Freud (1965) outlined a framework for differentiating the functional outcomes of defense mechanisms on the basis of age adequateness, balance, intensity, and reversibility. It is possible to use Freud's framework to determine differential client functioning in adaptiveness relating to the various dimensions of denial and related defenses. Context is added to Freud's framework to account for environmental considerations affecting defense use.

Age Adequateness. Anna Freud (1936/1966) considered denial to be a normal process for young children, although she made it clear that reliance on the response should decline as a child enters latency; the relative age of a person contributes to determining the appropriateness of denial. For example, in a counseling session, a 6-year-old girl denies that her parents have separated, even after her father has moved out of the child's home. In this instance, the counselor may view the child's denial as age-appropriate, albeit requiring supportive intervention and parental consultation. If, however, a high school student employs denial in a similar situation, the counselor may recognize pathological implications of the defense. The age of individuals is also significant in attempting to assess the normalcy of their fantasies and daydreams. Freud considered that fantasies become abnormal the moment that "fantasy activity ceases to be a game and becomes an automatism or an obsession" (p. 86). An individual engaging in extensive fantasy or daydreaming beyond childhood may be self-absorbed to the degree that the person is using the activity as a substitute means to meet life tasks. Denial is also integral to delusions, hallucinations, manic conditions, and other psychotic phenomena, and the counselor must consider a client's age, in addition to other factors, when discerning psychopathology.

Balance. Anna Freud (1965) noted that the healthiest defense organization occurs when an individual uses several defenses instead of being restricted to a single mechanism employed in a stereotyped way. A client's predominant pattern of denial suggests that the person has a reduced range of methods to deal with threat and instead relies on a repetitive and inflexible response. Rigidity in the employment of denial to the exclusion of all other defenses implies an entrenched quality, as is the case when an individual singularly and repeatedly uses the mechanism to stave off threat. For example, a client, in treatment for substance abuse, refuses to acknowledge the extent of his drug problems despite abundant evidence in the form of job and relationship losses.

Intensity. Freud (1965) observed that when defenses are used to excess, they frequently lead to symptom formation and produce disturbed interpersonal relationships. When a client engages in automatic and habitual denial responses, the person fails to address conflicts or issues inherent in the threat or develop constructive alternative behaviors (Dorpat, 1985). A hostile female adolescent client, for example, repeatedly denies feelings of anger, although her behavior has resulted in numerous altercations with peers and authority figures. As long as the young person persists in denying her hostile affect, the exploration of the source of her feelings remains largely unexamined in counseling. In addition to the frequency of a client's denial pattern, intensity may also imply the relative degree of distortion of denial. Some client expressions of denial involve minor and circumscribed distortions of reality; in other instances, clients manifest massive distortions of a psychotic type that pervasively affect persons' functioning.

Reversibility. Defense mechanisms that may have been useful in individuals' past to ward off threat, according to Freud (1965), should be subject to reversibility and not employed when perceived dangers subside or become nonexistent. An aspect of mental health is flexibility in adapting to changing conditions, but for clients who maintain an irreversible and out-of-date quality to their defenses, adaptation rarely occurs. Clients may use denial by refusing to acknowledge conditions, when in reality, situations have changed, but they fail to recognize new circumstances. For example, a client instigates a pattern of denial regarding the possibility of a death of a terminal parent and continues the defense even after the parent dies. Denial may also relate to an individual's lifestyle or core convictions when conditions or experiences are denied despite the existence of contrary objective information (Bishop, 1991). A client, for instance, maintains an ingrained conviction since childhood that he is inconsequential and that other people are rejecting. As an adult, when he is responded to as a valued person, the client denies his feelings and perceives the interactions as dismissive and manipulative.

Context. Consideration of situational variables, such as when and where a person uses denial, assists in determining the appropriateness of client defenses. There are occasions when denial provides an understandable respite from overwhelming circumstances, whereas in other instances, the employment of denial clearly represents maladaptive functioning. Kübler-Ross (1969) views denial as a commonly occurring initial stage when individuals experience terminal illness, the loss of a loved one, or other temporarily incapacitating life crises. It is reasonable for a person to employ denial when initially responding to painful transitional experiences, but in other situations, individuals may use denial in avoidant ways. For instance, a client refuses to acknowledge her culpability after being involved in an accident while driving under the influence. Cultural aspects should also be considered when differentiating contextual qualities of denial. A Native American client, for example, refutes the personal importance of a serious setback and insists that he is more concerned about its effect on members of his tribe or family. A counselor may misconstrue the individual's statements as a denial of personal relevance, when the client's primary concern is centered on the welfare of others. In research studies with college students, the defense of denial was found to be more frequently employed by women in comparison with men (Cramer, 1991; Ihilevich & Gleser, 1995).

Types of Denial

Anna Freud (1936/1966) identified three types of denial observable primarily in young children in their fantasy, verbal expressions, and actions. Freud considered denial to be a normal function of early childhood and in the occasional fantasy of adults. Others (Sjöbäck, 1973; Sperling, 1958) categorized denial into two types: meaning and existence. A person employing denial of meaning acknowledges the occurrence of an experience but offers various self-protective interpretations to explain phenomena. Denial of existence rejects the occurrence of an experience. Samuel Breznitz (1983) postulated a particularly useful model of seven levels or types of denial in a sequential schema. The types of denial he proposed intensify in reality distortion as an individual responds to threat, concluding with a final level of indiscriminate rejection of information. Clarifying the type of denial employed by clients assists counselors in assessing the degree of reality distortion involved in their defenses.

Denial in Fantasy, Word, and Act. Freud (1936/1966) distinguished three types of denial, each involving a normal phase of development of the infantile ego during early childhood. A child may frequently enter the sphere of imagination through the reversal of real facts and the reverie of fantasy in solitary play and daydreaming. Individuals in later stages of the life span also may occasionally engage in related fantasies. In other instances, denial in fantasy occurs when painful conditions are converted to more tolerable representations through vivid images. A child may deal with daily parental separations, for example, by constructing a fantasy that she is carried in her mother's handbag when the parent departs from the family home. Other individuals engage in denial in word and act by directly including other people in their dramatizations. Children's play, games, and impersonations are among social fantasies involving peers and adults in interactive experiences. Because each type of denial manifests normal functioning by an individual, persons should be able to differentiate between constructions of their imagination and real-life experiences. Pathological conditions exist, according to Freud, when individuals are unable to separate imagined from objective conditions.

Denial of Meaning and Denial of Existence. Unlike Freud's conceptualization that clearly restricts the limits of normal denial, others categorize denial in meaning and existence by identifying the implications of each type for normal and abnormal functioning across the life span (Sjöbäck, 1973; Sperling, 1958). A client, for example, may deny the meaning or significance of poor report card grades and insist that there is sufficient time to improve his grades even when the marking period is coming to a close. Another client may deny the existence of unsatisfactory grades and refuse to participate in a discussion relating to the individual's report card. It is apparent from the examples cited that denial of meaning involves less distortion of reality than denial of existence.

Denial in a Sequential Model. Breznitz (1983) presents seven levels of denial in a cogent and instructive schema, with the first five categories relating to denial of meaning and the last two types implying denial of existence. Each category represents a progressively greater degree of reality distortion as a person attempts to ward off threat, although the sequence may be entered at any level. To clarify Breznitz's stratified types of denial, each level will be briefly described, including illustrations of counselor-client interaction regarding an individual's abuse of substances.

1. *Denial of personal relevance* occurs when specific threats to clients are perceived as unrelated to their functioning.

Counselor: It seems that you hurt the people whom you really care about with your drug use.

Client: Hey, I'm not hurting anybody. They can take care of themselves.

2. *Denial of urgency* relates to situations that are perceived by clients as less pressing.

Counselor: Is it possible that your drug use has gotten out of control?

Client: I can stop whenever I want to.

3. *Denial of vulnerability or responsibility* involves clients' lack of acknowledged threat or accountability in regard to experiences.

Counselor:	Maybe you have to look at what your drug use is doing to you.
Client:	I'm young and in shape. Nothing is going to happen to me.
Counselor:	What about the effect that your drug use is having on your job?
Client:	My problems on my job have nothing to do with how I spend my free time.

4. *Denial of affect* relates to clients' refusal to acknowledge their feelings regarding an experience.

Counselor:	You look anxious as we talk about your use of drugs.
Client:	I'm not worried about it.

5. *Denial of affect relevance* involves clients acknowledging their feelings about an experience but attributing benign or self-serving causation of the experience.

Counselor:	You look anxious when we talk about your use of drugs.
Client:	I've been uptight lately, and I'm worried about my father's health.

6. *Denial of threatening information* relates to how clients protect themselves from threat involved with new information.

Counselor:	It's difficult to avoid that your job is in jeopardy because of your drug use.
Client:	Why do you say that? I'm in trouble on my job because of my idiot boss.

7. *Denial of information* involves a pervasive response to threat by clients by indiscriminately rejecting information.

Counselor:	In a number of ways, your life is affected by your use of drugs.
Client:	I don't have those kind of problems, and I don't know what you're talking about.

PROCESSING DENIAL IN COUNSELING

Understanding theoretical aspects of denial is indispensable in guiding counseling practice as the counselor begins to collaboratively process client defenses through sequential stages and strategic interventions. Formulating a model for modifying denial by progressing from a lack of awareness to adaptive control provides a direction for client development through the counseling process. In the initial or relationship stage of counseling, clients gain an awareness of their defensive posture when responding to painful feelings of threat. The middle or integration period focuses on comprehension of how and why individuals employ denial in threatening circumstances. In the final or accomplishment stage, clients attempt to control denial and assume more adaptive levels of functioning.

Relationship Stage

Initiating a counseling relationship with clients becomes progressively more difficult when they minimize or refuse to acknowledge pertinent issues or conditions, thus essentially impeding the counselor's efforts to focus on critical issues. In response to client resistance, various interventions are available to promote understanding and trust, fostering less guarded and constricted communication. Reflection, assessment methods, and counselor self-disclosure are selected techniques that offer a potential to involve clients in a therapeutic alliance within a reasonable time allocation. The duration of the relationship stage typically involves several counseling sessions, although more resistant persons may require additional time for this initial period.

Reflection. Since Carl Rogers first introduced the term, reflection has evolved into two types—feelings and meaning (Ivey, 1994; Raskin & Rogers, 1995). Reflection of feelings acknowledges individuals' more explicit communication by focusing on feelings. Reflection of meaning involves more implicit communication by abstracting the essence of client disclosures. A counselor, for example, uses reflection of feelings in response to a client's denial of substance abuse: "You feel angry because despite what everyone says, you don't believe that you have a problem with drugs." At a later point, the counselor employs reflection of meaning: "The accusations about your having a drug problem attack your belief that you are a good parent." As the counselor captures the perceptions of clients in denial, the counseling relationship is enhanced as clients feel supported and understood. Contesting clients' denial early in counseling may only intensify their perceptual distortions and lead to further engagement of the defense.

Instances of denial by clients occur frequently. The examples below are illustrative of vast possibilities:

- A patient in a coronary care unit rejects the personal relevance of following a recommended diet.
- As the school year comes to a close, a student dismisses the urgency of making up incomplete grades.
- In counseling for instigating frequent fights with peers, an adolescent insists that he is not responsible for any of the fighting.
- After receiving a report of excessively high cholesterol levels, an over-weight client disputes the importance of the test results.
- In counseling for spousal abuse, a client refuses to admit that there is anything wrong with his behavior.

In response to each of the examples, the counselor should attempt to process client perceptions in a way that reduces threat while clarifying individuals' awareness of their denial reactions. The following suggests how the counselor may use reflection with a 10-year-old child who is denying feelings about his parents' separation.

Counselor:	You were saying that your dad moved out of your house a few weeks ago.
Client:	Yes, but it doesn't bother me (stated with tears in his eyes). I've got a lot of friends.
Counselor:	You find that staying busy helps you keep your mind off your parents' separation.
Client:	Yeah, I'm on a baseball team, and I collect baseball cards.
Counselor:	It helps you to keep doing things that you enjoy.
Client:	I keep busy, and I don't have time to worry about my father.
Counselor:	It also helps because you don't want to think about the way it used to be.
Client:	Well, my dad and I used to do a lot of things together, and it isn't the same anymore.
Counselor:	That makes you feel sad, and it is hard to talk about.

Client:	I miss him so much (now crying), and I think about him all the time.

Assessment. Establishing individuals' use of denial involves three types of corroboration: client behavior, collateral sources, and projective techniques. Client behavior may be inconsistent and reveal the occurrence of denial through client statements or actions. Denial becomes evident, for example, through repeated client statements that contradict objective information or conditions. Collateral sources encompass data available to the counselor that may be inconsistent with individuals' assertions, including written reports and records, teacher or employer observations, parental or spousal statements, and related considerations. Projective techniques are another potential resource that may contribute to the understanding of client behavior, including the discernment of denial.

Clients' behavior may suggest that they are using denial through demonstrated inconsistencies between statements and nonverbal expressions, previous statements, actions, and objective conditions. A person may also employ denial by omitting comment on significant issues that warrant discussion, such as the death or divorce of a parent. The following presents examples of a high school student using denial in counseling:

1. *Statement:* I'm not worried about my schoolwork.
   Nonverbal expression: Tense and apprehensive.

2. *Statement:* I'm improving in all my subjects.
   Previous statement: I've missed a lot of school lately.

3. *Statement:* I've just got a little homework to make up.
   Action: Incomplete in numerous homework assignments.

4. *Statement:* I can get a good job if I quit school.
   Objective condition: High unemployment among school dropouts.

5. *Statement:* Things are OK outside of school.
   Omission: Client's parents are going through a bitter divorce.

Collateral information, such as school records or psychological reports, may also be available to the counselor when assessing individuals' use of denial. Contradictions between the manifest data and client behavior may also suggest the employment of the defense. An adolescent, for example, insists that his academic grades have been "fine," yet his scholastic records indicate that he was unsatisfactory in the majority of his subjects in his 2 years in high school.

Projective techniques offer another method for assessing the occurrence of denial when individuals respond to relatively nonthreatening and stimulating tasks. The interactive structure of projective devices provides an alternative in counseling that is frequently appealing to less verbal clients. Selected instruments constituting a relatively brief assessment include early recollections, human figure drawings, and sentence completion tasks (Clark, 1994a, 1995d). The Rorschach test and the Thematic Apperception Test may also be used in assessing client defenses but require a more extensive and time-consuming evaluation (Bellak & Abrams, 1997; Schafer, 1954). The questionable psychometric qualities of the cited projective techniques, including marginal validity and reliability and imprecise scoring systems, are of less concern if the devices are used as informal methods for generating hypotheses relating to client defenses that may be confirmed or rejected through corroboration with other sources, such as observations of a parent or a spouse (Clark, 1995d).

Early recollections as a projective technique suggest a client's core assumptions and various personality indicators (Bruhn, 1984; Clark, 1994a, 1995d), including the use of defense mechanisms. An evaluation of a person's early memories, for example, reveals a conviction that perceived conditions in life are overwhelming and beyond her coping abilities and resources. Such assumptions contrast sharply with the client's statement to the counselor, "I'm doing very well and really have no problems," suggesting the possibility of denial as a defense. Similarly, the interpretive results of a client's human figure drawing may be compared with the individual's behavior or other corroborative sources to assess the employment of denial and broader aspects of personality functioning (Cummings, 1986). A middle school student, for instance, states that rejection by his peers "doesn't bother me" and subsequently draws a human figure with arms raised high and reaching out, revealing a need for social acceptance and a denial of contextual circumstances (Machover, 1949).

The sentence completion tasks complement early recollections and human figure drawings in a relatively brief personality assessment battery. Written protocols with scoring systems are available, or incomplete sentence formats may be constructed by a counselor for specific populations (Hart, 1986). Table 2.1 provides a sentence completion form that I have used for many years with children and adolescents. The format may be adapted for various clients across the life span.

Responses or a pattern of responses to sentence stems may be compared with an individual's expressed statements, collateral sources, and other projective data for detecting denial. An older client, for example, states, "For my age, I'm doing fine," but in response to the sentence stem "I suffer . . . ," he writes, "from so many problems." The individual's written response differs markedly from his oral statement, suggesting the operation of denial. In another instance, an adolescent with a history of unsatisfactory grades in school completes the sentence "I failed . . ." with "nothing."

Self-Disclosure. The counselor may choose to disclose personal experiences or perspectives to enhance the counseling relationship and to clarify client defense mechanisms. Disclosures by the counselor frequently increase communication in counseling because the client begins to perceive the counselor as less threatening and remote (Watkins, 1990). At the same time, a counselor's disclosures may be perceived as intrusive and threatening and induce guarded and defensive client reactions. A counselor, for example, relates her early work failures with individuals who are experiencing current related problems. One client responds positively to the disclosures and is encouraged by the counselor's perseverance despite failure. In contrast, another client denies the counselor's experience as personally irrelevant and becomes even more defensive. Establishing guidelines is essential as a therapist discloses on content variables related to success or failure, the past or present, and similarity or dissimilarity in relationship to client experience (Cormier & Cormier, 1998). Counselor self-disclosure may also involve the counselor's reactions to a client's behavior in counseling, referred to as self-involving statements (Watkins, 1990).

TABLE 2.1 Sentence Completion

Name: _____ D.O.B. _____ D.O.T. _____

1. I feel _____
2. I regret _____
3. Other people _____
4. I am best when _____
5. What bothers me is _____
6. The happiest time _____
7. I am afraid of _____
8. My father _____
9. I dislike to _____
10. I failed _____
11. At home _____
12. Boys _____
13. My mother _____
14. I suffer _____
15. The future _____
16. Other kids _____
17. My nerves are _____
18. Girls _____
19. My greatest worry is _____
20. School _____
21. I need _____
22. What pains me is _____
23. I hate _____
24. Whenever I have to study, I _____
25. I wish _____

Specific qualities of judicious disclosures by the counselor may promote the counseling relationship while clarifying client defense reactions. Pertinent counselor experiences and perceptions may be disclosed that relate to a client's denial. As an example, a client denies the urgency of conducting a job search on graduating college, and the counselor recounts his experiences in seeking employment. Realistic therapist disclosures may increase awareness of a client's denial by clarifying viable choices. A client, for instance, may deny the existence of crucial health information. In response, the counselor might appropriately reveal how she once perceived the health issue in a similar way as the client but now sees things differently. Timely self-disclosure by the counselor occurs when a client is not distracted or agitated, when the client is able to cognitively focus on the disclosure, and the counseling relationship has developed beyond a minimal trust level. Using the same guidelines for self-disclosure, the counselor may express self-involving statements in reaction to a client's denial responses. A counselor states, for example, to an adult client who is denying affect relevance, "I find it hard to talk to you about how you really feel about your job when you joke around about its importance."

Integration Stage

With the foundation of a sound counseling relationship, counselors may begin to challenge individuals' use of denial in the middle or integration period of counseling. The operation and purpose of clients' denial are scrutinized, as they are encouraged to reconcile inconsistencies and conflicts inherent in the mechanism. Confrontation, cognitive restructuring, reframing, and interpretation are selected techniques that allow for an in-depth and purposeful clarification of client behavior. The duration of the integration stage largely depends on the intensity and related psychopathological dimensions of clients' denial and related defenses.

Confrontation. Various types of denial involving inconsistent and conflicted client behavior may be clarified through the technique of confrontation. Inconsistencies recognized during the relationship stage between clients' statements and nonverbal expressions, previous statements, actions, objective conditions, and omissions now become a focus of counselor confrontations. It is essential that counselors express a confrontation in a supportive, descriptive, and nonjudgmental style (Ivey, 1994), avoiding a harsh, accusatory, or attacking tone.

The following examples of client denial illustrate a counselor's use of confrontation by responding to various types of client inconsistencies.

1. *Statement—Nonverbal Expression*

Client: I'm just not going to follow that crazy diet for my heart condition. What's the point of living if you can't even eat?

Counselor: You'd love to just chuck your diet, but your tone of voice seems uncertain about this.

2. *Statement—Previous Statement*

Client: The other kids in the class are such jerks. I feel like pounding some of them every time I see them.

Counselor: Just in seeing the kids you react strongly. You said before, though, that you're not the one who starts trouble.

3. *Statement—Action*

Client: I've got plenty of time to make up my incomplete work.

Counselor: Time does not seem to be a problem, but you haven't completed any assignments this week, and the quarter ends next Friday.

4. *Statement—Objective Condition*

Client: The test for cholesterol levels is a waste of time. I shouldn't have bothered with it.

Counselor: You're upset with the results of the report, but you took the test on the advice of a doctor whom you have trusted for many years.

5. *Statement—Omission*

Client: So I guess that's about all I have to talk about today.

Counselor: We have talked about a number of things, but you haven't mentioned the battering charges brought against you by your wife this week.

The practice of confrontation is more effective in combination with other counselor interventions, particularly reflection, as individuals begin to clarify their inconsistent behavior. In the following example, a late adolescent client demonstrates symptoms of anorexia nervosa while employing denial.

Client: My parents and some of my friends are always after me to gain weight, and I'm sick of it. I wish people would get off my case and stop telling me what to do.

Counselor: It's very important for you to feel that you can make choices on your own.

Client: I'm not a fool. I watch my calorie intake and make sure that I get enough nutrients.

Counselor:	When you say that, you don't have much conviction in your voice.
Client:	Well, recently I've been having dizzy spells, but I think that I've been working too hard.
Counselor:	You want to believe that your eating habits are not causing you problems.
Client:	It's the one thing that I can control, and I have to do what makes sense to me.

Cognitive Restructuring. Although confrontation clarifies the operation of individuals' denial or related defenses, other counselor interventions may be necessary to change ingrained client perspectives relating to the mechanisms. Core assumptions that clients maintain about life frequently relate to their employment of defense mechanisms, and generating alternative beliefs contributes to therapeutic gain. The counseling technique of cognitive restructuring focuses on transposing negative and self-defeating cognitions to constructive and purposeful assumptions (Cormier & Cormier, 1998; Meichenbaum, 1977). Core assumptions or convictions about how individuals construe life may be revealed through self-verbalizations conceptualized as basic mistakes (Adler, 1931/1958; Dinkmeyer et al., 1987), irrational ideas (Ellis, 1995), and cognitive distortions (Beck & Weishaar, 1995). In a counseling example, a client expresses a basic mistake, "I never do anything right," while simultaneously denying the personal relevance of clear instances of demonstrated competency.

Cognitive restructuring involves identifying negative and self-defeating assumptions and schemas, constructing alternative frames of reference, and practicing purposeful self-statements, both in and outside counseling (Cormier & Cormier, 1998). In the following example, a client denies the degree of physical abuse inflicted by her husband, and the counselor begins to use cognitive restructuring. The person's denial of abuse, although contradictory to actual conditions, relates to her core assumption schemas of self-devaluation and dependency on others.

Client:	I'd rather put up with the fights from time to time than be without him. It's not that bad, and I'm a nobody without him.
Counselor:	I'm a nobody without him?

Client: Well, sure. If I didn't have him, I'd just about have nothing going for me.

Counselor: I'm going to say something that is really a different way of looking at yourself. It seems that you often think that you are not a valued person on your own merit. Is it possible for you to change that around in a major way and begin to see yourself as a somebody or as a person of worth?

Client: I've always had someone to rely on and to be there for me.

Counselor: It does feel kind of unnatural to you, but this is just the change that you have said that you would like to make, to feel worthy of respect.

Although this example suggests that the client stays in her relationship because of low self-esteem, the prevalence of domestic violence is culturally based and clearly extends beyond esteem issues. Harway and Hansen (1993) report in their survey on the scope of domestic violence that one of every six wives has been hit by her husband during her marriage.

Reframing. Related to cognitive restructuring, reframing is another counseling technique that focuses on transforming the meaning of individuals' perspectives, including the operation of denial. Reframing broadens client frames of reference and schemas in a positive direction through semantic change (Cormier & Cormier, 1998). For example, a coronary care client continues to deny the importance of confronting painful thoughts and feelings. Through reframing, a counselor suggests a change in meaning in the client's perspectives, whereby the avoidance of conflicts has physiological costs and is a risk factor for continuing medical illness (Shedler et al., 1993). Several guidelines are helpful for the counselor to follow when using reframing with denial and related client defenses. Reframing should be plausible to a client; a perspective lacking viability is subject to outright rejection. Reframing presented in a supportive and inviting tone and as an option for a client to consider is more likely to be accepted. In the following example, a counselor reframes a client's denial of responsibility in connection with her husband's alcohol abuse problem.

Client: More than anyone else, I understand the problems that Bill has in his life.

Counselor:	It seems that you are always there to support him when nobody else cares.
Client:	Everyone else but me has just about given up on Bill.
Counselor:	Yet with all your understanding, Bill's drinking seems to have gotten worse.
Client:	That's true. Sometimes, I wonder what more I can do because he's so desperate.
Counselor:	You try all you can and even now believe that you can do more to protect Bill from himself. I'm going to say something that may offer you a different way to look at this problem. Are you up for this?
Client:	Well, nothing else seems to be working.
Counselor:	Perhaps what you are actually doing is that by being patient and supportive, you are enabling him to continue drinking.
Client:	I'm not sure what you mean.
Counselor:	It is Bill's responsibility to control his alcohol abuse. Could it be that the support that you offer Bill is a means of denying an awareness to be more forceful with him?

Interpretation. Reframing is a type of interpretation whereby the counselor attempts to modify clients' frame of reference by changing the meaning of pertinent experiences or perspectives. In addition to this semantic aspect of interpretation, an interpretation of a propositional aspect relates to the counselor explaining causal relationships in the life of individuals (Levy, 1963). Many clients need to explore motivational factors inherent in denial and other defenses, including a causal framework that explains, rather than merely describes, their behavior. Although the psychodynamic tradition emphasizes propositional aspects of interpretation in treatment, the technique is also prevalent in various other counseling orientations, including Adlerian, rational-emotive, transactional analysis, and some types of family therapy (Clark, 1995a). Through a propositional aspect of interpretation, a counselor suggests causal referents involving clients' denial for them to more fully understand and control the defense.

Several guidelines assist the counselor in collaboratively using interpretation in counseling. Interpretations may be expressed in a tentative or approximate way ("Is it possible that . . ."), slightly discrepant from the client's frame of reference, and at a time when the client is able to cognitively process the technique (Ivey, 1994). An interpretation also requires follow-up discussion and clarification for a person to assimilate its meaning. In the following interaction, which continues the example involving the reframing of the woman who enables her husband's alcohol dependency, the counselor decides to use a propositional aspect of interpretation to focus on the client's motivation at a core assumption level.

Client:	I know that I shouldn't try to rescue Bill all the time, but I still do it. I must be a weak person.
Counselor:	I don't think you are weak at all because you show a lot of determination in trying to help Bill and other people, too.
Client:	Well, I do, but things have gotten worse because of it.
Counselor:	It seems that you have a really difficult time in letting people try to take care of themselves.
Client:	That's true, but people like Bill really need me.
Counselor:	Could it be possible that you have learned that you must take care of people to feel useful and significant?
Client:	What do you mean?
Counselor:	Well, in your family, you have always been the one people rely on, and you choose to keep it this way.
Client:	You are saying that I try to help Bill and other people because I get something out of it, like feeling important.
Counselor:	Well, could it be that you are overlooking a key reason for rescuing Bill as a way to feel needed?

Accomplishment Stage

After the clarification of the functioning of individuals' denial and related defenses in the integration period, the counseling focus shifts to establishing more adaptive behavior. In the accomplishment stage of counseling, clients attempt to develop more purposeful actions and rely less on denial as a response to threat. For many persons who habitually employ the defense, however, attempting to control denial is challenging and difficult. To assist clients in this effort, action-oriented strategies provide strategic procedures. Considered next are two selected techniques from Individual Psychology, *catching oneself* and *acting as if* (Dinkmeyer et al., 1987), and a third procedure, *breaking it down*

(Clark, 1995f). The duration of the accomplishment stage largely depends on the progress that clients make toward controlling their use of denial and the acquisition of more purposeful behaviors.

Catching Oneself. Once clients make a commitment to control their use of denial, they may need support to avoid employing the defense. Through "catching oneself," individuals become aware of internal cues that trigger the occurrence of a denial response. At the critical point of engaging denial, clients deter actions related to the defense. As an example, a client named Al who formerly denied the value of a restricted diet for reducing high cholesterol levels makes a commitment to stay away from unhealthy foods. After being introduced to the technique of catching oneself, Al decides to try the procedure during the week between counseling sessions. A few days after meeting with the counselor, Al is about to purchase a large ice cream sundae but manages to catch himself and instead decides to buy a medium-size yogurt. In the next counseling session, Al reports the incident, and the counselor recognizes and affirms his self-control and determination.

In the following example, a client has progressed to the point of acknowledging his denial of abusing substances and indicates a desire to avoid chemical involvements.

Client:	I do want to stay away from drugs, but it is so easy for me to slip back into my old ways.
Counselor:	Let me ask you a question. What is the first thing that happens to you as you choose to get high?
Client:	Well, I usually start thinking about how good it will feel.
Counselor:	Does this happen all at once, or do you feel it coming on?
Client:	It kind of comes on me because it builds up inside until I can't seem to stop myself.
Counselor:	Well, let me suggest an idea. At the instant that you begin to think about getting high, try catching yourself and think about something else.
Client:	You mean like the second that I think about drugs, stop myself with another thought.
Counselor:	Does this make sense to you?
Client:	It does, but I'm not sure what I should think about.

Counselor:	Well, let's talk about that. What could you think about that might turn you off from wanting to get high at that moment?
Client:	It would probably be my wife, Ann, and my daughters, Marie and Angela.
Counselor:	To make it even better, could you carry a picture of your family with you and look at it as an alerting device when you think about drugs?
Client:	It might help some. Maybe I can carry it in my pocket.

Acting As If. Purposeful behavior that has been underused by clients because of the constricting influence of denial may need to be developed, particularly for those who have employed the defense for an extended period. "Acting as if " prompts clients to act how they would like to behave in an assumed and novel role. For example, a preadolescent who has acted aggressively toward his peers for months, while denying this fact, is unfamiliar or unpracticed with cooperative peer relationships. Once the behavior of a socially appropriate person is clarified, it is possible for the client to enact the role with his peers. An individual must also express the desire and possess the capabilities for performing actions inherent in a specified role. A client may also choose to role-play or rehearse certain actions prior to attempting them outside counseling.

In the following example, a late adulthood client has denied for an extended period the affect relevance of her husband's death and has attributed her prolonged depression to external conditions, such as a "long winter." By denying her feelings about her husband's loss during her depression, she has also been able to reject the role of being a widow.

Client:	It's really hard for me now to accept that Daryl is gone, and I miss him so much.
Counselor:	He was a very important part of your life for so long.
Client:	I tried not to admit that, and I even pretended that I was not a widow.
Counselor:	You needed some time to come to grips with the huge changes in your life.
Client:	That's right, but I'm not even sure how a widow should act. Daryl has been dead now for more than a year.
Counselor:	Maybe it would help if we talked about how a widow does act.

Client:	What do you mean?
Counselor:	Well, in your observation, what type of person seems to be doing best with her adjustment as a widow?
Client:	I think that women who get out of the house and have a chance to be around people do best.
Counselor:	We need to talk more about that, but what if you acted like, what shall we call them, perhaps "better adjusted widows," for a few days.
Client:	I know what you are saying. I need to do something to get myself going.

Breaking It Down. In a manner related to clients' employment of denial, clients may be reluctant to attempt previously avoided or inhibited actions because of their perceived magnitude. "Breaking it down" involves partializing actions into specific, smaller, and attainable parts. A client, for instance, may begin avoiding chemicals by remaining drug free for a day, and another individual starts a job search by reading classified advertisements in a newspaper. The technique emphasizes getting started and following through on actions; completing specific objectives contributes to feelings of accomplishment for clients.

In the following interaction, a high school student discusses difficulties that he is experiencing in finishing incomplete academic assignments.

Client:	I know now that I tried to tell myself that I was doing OK in school, but I wasn't getting the work done.
Counselor:	You're doing a lot better in dealing with your responsibilities instead of putting them off.
Client:	I can't believe how I used to try to fake out everyone. Now my problem is that I've got a ton of work that I'm trying to catch up on.
Counselor:	A ton of work?
Client:	Yeah, it's almost too much, and I feel like giving up.
Counselor:	You feel really discouraged when you think of all the work that you have to do. I'm wondering if you could look at it another way, though. What if you break the work down and try to do pieces of it?
Client:	Well, I need to do something. What was that again?

Counselor: I'm saying something like take one assignment, separate it
into sections, and finish one part at a time.

CONCLUSION

Denial is a prevalent defense mechanism that may be observed in its
various types in counseling with clients. For numerous clients, the use
of denial reduces intolerable affect and conflict. At the same time,
however, a rigid and stereotyped use of the defense restricts the potential
for individuals to establish more adaptive behavior. Denial involves
negating the meaning or existence of perceptions. Conceptualizing the
identification and modification of denial through the three stages of the
counseling process contributes to fostering and consolidating therapeutic change.

3

DISPLACEMENT

The man who can smile when things go wrong has thought of someone he can blame it on.

—Jones's Law

People frequently find it convenient and easy to place blame on others for their behavior, and this tendency becomes a compromising factor in understanding and clarifying client functioning in counseling. Various instances occur in the therapeutic experience in which a client shifts pent-up feelings toward other persons who are in vulnerable positions. For example, when ridiculed by his peers in school, a student goes home and picks on his younger brother and destroys furnishings in his home. In another instance, a young parent, feeling trapped in her small apartment, begins to take her feelings out on her two young children. Clients may also find relief from conflict by expressing negative feelings toward a counselor, who serves as a readily available substitute for a prohibited or inaccessible target. A client, for example, after describing hostile divorce proceedings with her ex-husband, who had moved to a distant state, verbally attacks an attentive and supportive therapist. Defining displacement as a defense mechanism emphasizes redirecting feelings to a vulnerable substitute.

THEORETICAL ASPECTS OF DISPLACEMENT

Emergence of Displacement

Late in the 19th century, Sigmund Freud (1894/1962b) referred to mental functions in the neuroses of defense as "a quota of affect or sum of excitation—which possesses all the characteristics of a quantity (though we have no means of measuring it), which is capable of increase, diminution, displacement, and discharge" (p. 60). In the same volume, Freud observed that displacement of one idea for another was a central dynamic in phobias and obsessions (Murray & Berkun, 1955). The operation of displacement in phobic behavior is clear in Freud's (1909/1955a) classic case of Little Hans, a 5-year-old boy whose extreme fear of horses was connected to his fear of his father. Freud also extensively explored the function of displacement in dreams (1900/1953a) and jokes (1905/1960). During this period, he specifically defined displacement: "I propose to describe it as 'displacement,' since its essence lies in the diversion of the train of thought, the displacement of the psychical emphasis on a topic other than the opening one" (p. 51). It is evident from these writings that Freud extended the role of displacement beyond that of a mechanism of defense to include diverse displacement activity across various behavioral manifestations.

Anna Freud (1936/1966) did not identify displacement as a defense mechanism in *The Ego and the Mechanisms of Defense,* but many years after the publication of this volume, she commented on the proposition of displacement as a defense mechanism. Freud observed that she did not include displacement in her original list of defense mechanisms partly because she viewed it as relating largely to the primary process that is distinct from the secondary process of the ego (Sandler & Freud, 1985). Further, Freud stated that her list of defense mechanisms was not definitive: "I remember that I was very reluctant to say there were nine mechanisms, because I had the feeling that if I said there were nine there might by then be ten. One should never count these things" (Sandler & Freud, 1985, p. 113). Despite Freud's hesitancy to determine a set of defense mechanisms, others have often detailed specific defenses, and displacement is commonly placed on such lists (American Psychiatric Association, 1994a, 1994b; Gladding, 1996; Swanson, 1988).

Psychopathology and Displacement

Age Adequateness. As with other defenses, the relative age of a client employing displacement partly determines its appropriateness. Developmentally, younger children are more likely to express feelings directly and, as a consequence, may be less apt to use displacement. As individuals advance in age, they generally begin to express negative feelings indirectly at vulnerable targets, particularly when the source of conflicted feelings is inaccessible or prohibited. As an example, a 5-year-old child expresses hostile feelings directly at a parent, whereas an adolescent deals with the same feelings by threatening her peers. This example of an adolescent's functioning may be age-inappropriate if the individual is capable of finding a constructive outlet for expressing her negative feelings, rather than relying on displacement. In an extension of this example, a 30-year-old client may be expected to be sufficiently autonomous to communicate more directly with his parents and be even less reliant on displacement. It is essential, however, when considering these examples, to distinguish client use of displacement from the culturally ingrained tendency among girls to modulate their "voices" when they enter adolescence (Brown & Gilligan, 1992). Strong feelings are frequently devalued and dismissed because girls feel pressured to conform to a restricted gender role in authentic communication.

Balance. Relying primarily on displacement to ward off threat and deal with intensifying affect produces a repetitive and inflexible quality to persons' behavior. Rather than confronting conflictual issues inherent in displacement, individuals engage in stereotyped interactions. The obsessive quality identified by Freud in his early analysis of displacement of affect is evident in the rigid and compelled manifestation of displacement as a defense mechanism. The immediate measure of tension relief that displacement provides is strongly reinforcing as clients vent their feelings on vulnerable targets. In a case of spousal abuse, a client expresses feelings of resentment and hostility toward his wife that are identifiable in repeated instances of assaults. Increasing intolerable feelings are discharged through a displacement defense, but the threatening source of conflicted feelings remains essentially unaddressed. The counselor must also be alert to becoming a target of a client's displacement; a tolerant and accepting therapist may be perceived as weak and assailable.

Intensity. Reliance on displacement as a means of avoiding conflict and intolerable affect can also occur through excessive use. The habitual employment of displacement may reach a frequency rate that begins to distort an individual's perception of reality. This intensity level is consistent with Freud's view of a compulsive quality inherent in displacement of affect. In instances of high occurrence of displacement, a client's avoidance pattern often becomes evident to a counselor. In a counseling example, an acting-out adolescent repeatedly defies her mother's attempts to control her behavior. On the basis of assessment information, the counselor hypothesizes that the source of the individual's hostility possibly relates to her stepfather, who no longer lives with the family. The counselor also becomes aware of a history of sexual abuse perpetrated by the stepfather early in the client's life. As long as the adolescent continues her intense pattern of displacing hostility, she also avoids examining unresolved issues relating to her victimization.

Reversibility. An individual initially employs displacement to control threats existing at particular times and places. Yet for some, the habitual use of displacement persists long after perceived dangers are nonexistent. Rather than adapt to changing conditions, a person maintains an outmoded interaction that is no longer relevant to personal circumstances. Consider the counseling example of a parent, Mildred, who displaces hostile feelings on her children, when the primary source of her rage relates to the abuse that she endured as a child. Although Mildred no longer experiences the abuse, she continues to discharge intolerable feelings on vulnerable and innocent targets. Many years have passed since Mildred was victimized, and the perpetrator may even be deceased, yet her instilled pattern continues. Displacement that endures despite changing environmental conditions suggests the relationship of the defense to a person's lifestyle or core convictions. In the example cited, Mildred may believe that she must aggress against weak and vulnerable individuals to feel safe in a threatening world.

Context. In attempting to understand a client's use of displacement, it is essential for the counselor to evaluate social and cultural contexts. Social interactions in diverse environments influence an individual's behavior and the use of displacement as a defense mechanism. Consider the following counseling example (Axelson, 1993). A client raised in an authoritarian and punitive family environment frequently experienced parental reprisals for expression of emotion. Almost any demonstration of anger resulted in withdrawal of love and affection by the client's parents, and, subsequently, he developed a pattern of displacing anger at others outside his family. Differentiating emotions relating to their actual source is also a consideration in the event that a client expresses sudden resentment and hostility toward minority groups. Individuals perceived as inferior and incapable of retaliation may serve as vulnerable targets in the place of prohibited or inaccessible sources that elicit negative feelings. In research studies considering gender conducted with college students, displacement as a defense was found to be more prevalent among men than among women (Cramer, 1991; Ihilevich & Gleser, 1995).

PROCESSING DISPLACEMENT IN COUNSELING

Relationship Stage

When a client expresses negative feelings toward other people or objects, the counselor can only begin to surmise the possibility of the operation of displacement. Selected counseling techniques in this period—reflection, assessment methods, and counselor self-disclosure—promote more open communication and trust.

Reflection. Displacement response typically involves a substantial degree of affect, and reflection use by the counselor acknowledges the expression of client emotion. As a counselor intervenes with reflection of feeling, both the intensity of affect and the guardedness of a client often begin to diminish. To illustrate, a counselor responds to a middle school student, Kevin, who expresses hostile feelings relating to an inexperienced teacher, "You feel angry with her because she doesn't control the kids in the class." It is possible for the counselor to contest or even refute the client's perspective at this point, but this approach would likely intensify Kevin's anger and defensiveness. Reflecting a client's feelings enables the counselor at a later point to use reflection of meaning to affirm the implied meaning of the person's communication. To continue with the example, the counselor states to Kevin, "You are also worried because you believe that you won't get a decent grade from her." This comment prompts Kevin to finally vent his anger at an intimidating classmate who incites other students to misbehave in the teacher's class, "I can't stand the kid, but he really scares me."

Clients often use displacement as a defense in counseling. The examples below illustrate various possibilities:

- In counseling for child abuse, a mother continues to express anger and resentment toward her two young children. She has been persuaded by her spouse not to work and is often left alone with the children while her husband is working or out with friends.

- Observing that a 10-year-old African American student is periodically ridiculed by his peers and that he eats by himself in the cafeteria, the school counselor asks the boy to meet with him. In counseling, the client admits that he is afraid of the kids who tease him and that he thinks about them a lot. The counselor learns from the client's mother that the boy has been picking on his younger brother and has destroyed a number of toys in the home.

- A middle-aged man living in the inner city enters counseling experiencing feelings of hostility and discouragement. He expresses a central conviction of having been cheated in life and a sense of bitterness about not having been more successful. The client blames minorities in his neighborhood for his living conditions and for making his situation so unpleasant.

- A Hispanic American man is controlling and abusive toward his wife. He dismisses his behavior as "no big deal." The client's work situation is unpleasant, and his supervisor criticizes him quite often.

◆ An early adolescent client rarely expresses her feelings about her parents' constant arguments and their bitter divorce proceedings. In school, the client recently destroyed several of her classmates' drawings from an art class.

In response to each of these examples, a counselor's use of reflection enables clients to begin to clarify their defensive feelings and perceptions relating to displacement. The following illustrates a counselor's interactions involving reflection with a client who physically abuses his wife.

Client:	My wife makes me furious. When I get home, I expect her to be there, not chasing all over the town.
Counselor:	You're angry because she doesn't do what you expect her to do.
Client:	Hey, I work all day, and the least she can do is be around when I get home. Sometimes, I have to knock her around a little for her to get the message.
Counselor:	You contribute your share, and you feel this should allow you to strike her to make her do what you want.
Client:	It isn't that big a deal. I don't hit her very much, and that's the way I was raised. Nobody gets upset about it where I come from.
Counselor:	It's important for you to believe that occasionally striking your wife is just something that husbands do. This is what you have come to expect as you have grown up.

Assessment. The use of displacement involves appraising client behavior, considering collateral sources, and administering projective techniques. The behavior of individuals may reveal inconsistencies that suggest the employment of displacement. Consider the following examples relating to various clients' possible employment of displacement in counseling:

1. *Statement:* I don't really mind that my husband is gone so much; the kids keep me busy.
   Nonverbal expression: The client's face muscles are tightly clenched.

2. *Statement:* When I get home, I remember the kids in school, and I get ticked off just thinking about them.

Previous statement: It doesn't bother me that much—so what if they don't like me?

3. *Statement:* The way I treat my wife has nothing to do with my job; it's just the way it is between us. I have to keep her in line.
Action: The client's spousal battering primarily occurs when he returns home after a day on his job.

4. *Statement:* Those minorities are ruining the neighborhood. They're either criminals or unemployed. They're wrecking things for all of us.
Objective condition: The unemployment and crime rates are approximately equal between the white and minority populations in the individual's neighborhood.

5. *Statement:* My parents are getting a divorce, but I try not to let it get to me.
Omission: The client recently destroyed several of her classmates' art projects in a rageful episode.

Collateral sources available to the counselor, such as written or verbal reports, may also suggest a client's use of displacement. For example, a parent of an elementary school client discloses to a counselor that her son has been hitting his younger brother for no apparent reason. In school, the student is frequently teased by several of his classmates, and the social worker infers the possible operation of displacement. In another instance, the adolescent children of a man in counseling for abusing his wife report that their father batters their mother. This disclosure differs markedly from the client's insistence that his wife provokes him, and again the therapist considers the possibility of displacement as a client defense.

Selected projective techniques provide the counselor with another method for assessing client use of displacement. Early recollections also assist in determining clients' core convictions while enabling the counselor to clarify the dynamics of their use of displacement. Consider, for example, a client named Jim who discloses an early recollection occurring in the first grade when another child asks to borrow a crayon. Aware of the teacher's rule that he cannot leave his seat, Jim pushes a crayon across the floor to the other student. The teacher, observing this action, throws a large box of broken crayons on the floor and demands that Jim pick them up. Jim, feeling humiliated and resentful, collects the crayons around the feet of his classmates. This memory, and two others like it, suggests that Jim perceives authority figures as unfair and punishing, and his use of displacement directed at alternative, vulnerable targets becomes more comprehensible.

Human figure drawings and sentence completion tasks may also be used to infer the operation of client displacement. For example, a client's full human figure depicts a large person (average size is approximately 7 inches long), with well-defined teeth and closed fists. This drawing suggests that the individual maintains hostility that is subject to displacement (Hammer, 1958). The sentence completion, in a complementary function, is often helpful in clarifying to whom or to what a client's feelings may be directed. In particular, sentence stems "Other people . . . ," "What bothers me . . . ," "My father . . . ," "Boys (men) . . . ," "My mother . . . ," "Other kids (adults) . . . ," "Girls (women) . . . ," "What pains me is . . . ," and "I hate . . . " tend to elicit displaced client feelings toward others or objects. Often, however, the sentence completions reflect the vulnerable or overt target of a client's displacement because individuals tend to omit sentence stems relating to highly threatening sources of conflicted affect. In a counseling example, a 10-year-old client completes the sentence stem "I hate . . . my younger brother," when the eliciting source of his feelings is several tormenting classmates. In response to the sentence stems "Boys . . . " and "Other kids . . . ," the client leaves them blank.

Self-Disclosure. Counselor self-disclosure is another counseling technique with potential for enhancing the counseling relationship and for clarifying a client's use of displacement. In this regard, it may be possible for counselors to relate their use of displacement to a similar or dissimilar employment of the defense by a client. For example, a counselor discloses, "Sometimes, when pressures build up in my life, I take my feelings out on other people." In other instances, counselors may be able to disclose past or present experiences relevant to a client's use of displacement. A therapist, for instance, in working with a child who is ridiculed by his peers, states, "I remember in the sixth grade when a big kid picked on me a lot. I felt really angry, but I was too scared of the kid to fight him. Sometimes, I would go home and punch the wall in my bedroom." Therapists may also be able to identify personal success or failure experiences relevant to a client's displacement. In a continuation of the example, the counselor says, "It took me a while before I could admit how scared and angry I was at the kid who teased me." Counselor disclosure through self-involving statements may also be helpful in acknowledging a client's interactions in the counseling experience. In the conclusion of the presented example, the counselor states to the client, "Just admitting that you are scared of the kids who tease you and that your feelings get all bottled up inside takes courage."

Integration Stage

With the establishment of a counseling relationship, the counselor may begin to challenge inconsistencies and conflicts inherent in a client's use of displacement in the middle or integration stage of counseling. Selected counseling techniques of confrontation, cognitive restructuring, reframing, and interpretation assist in clarifying the function and purpose of displacement during this period.

Confrontation. Contradictory client behavior recognized during the initial stage of counseling now becomes an appropriate focus of scrutiny. As a counseling technique, confrontation clarifies inconsistencies between a client's statements and nonverbal expressions, previous statements, actions, objective conditions, and omissions. Displacement as a defense is evident because the primary source of an individual's conflicted affect is avoided. In the following counseling examples, the counselor employs confrontation to respond to inconsistencies relating to a client's use of displacement.

1. *Statement—Nonverbal Expression*

   Client: I don't really mind that my husband is gone so much; the kids keep me busy.

   Counselor: You continue to tell me that it doesn't bother you that much, but your facial expression appears tight and tense while you are talking.

2. *Statement—Previous Statement*

Client: When I get home, I remember the kids in school, and I get ticked off just thinking about them.

Counselor: You feel angry when you think about the kids, but a little while ago, you said that it doesn't upset you that much if they don't like you.

3. *Statement—Action*

Client: The way I treat my wife has nothing to do with my job; it's just the way it is between us. I have to keep her in line.

Counselor: You don't think that your abuse of your wife has anything to do with your job. Yet from what you and your wife have told me, most of the abuse occurs after you've had a bad day at work or when something in your life is going wrong.

4. *Statement—Objective Condition*

Client: Those minorities are ruining the neighborhood. They're either criminals or unemployed. They're wrecking things for all of us.

Counselor: You believe that the minorities in your neighborhood are to blame for poor living conditions. Yet it is widely reported that the unemployment and crime rates are fairly equal between both white and minority populations around you.

5. *Statement—Omission*

Client: My parents are getting a divorce, but I try not to let it get to me.

Counselor: It's important to you not to let your parents' divorce bother you that much. Although you are able to say this, you haven't mentioned that you recently destroyed several student art projects.

A counselor's descriptive and nonaccusatory style in using confrontation is essential to avoid increasing a client's defensiveness even further. In the following example, a counselor employs confrontation with a client accused of spousal abuse.

Client: Look, I've told you before, it's not that big a deal. It's just the way things are in my family.

Counselor:	You think your treatment of your wife is no different from how things are often done in your family, but I remember your telling me that your two brothers don't abuse their wives.
Client:	Well, they're different. They just let their wives lead them around by their noses.
Counselor:	It's important for you to feel that you are in control of things in your home.

Cognitive Restructuring. Although confrontation assists in clarifying discrepant client behavior, an individual's core convictions may also be associated with the displacement defense. At the core level, a person maintains a cognitive organization involving schemas, developed early in life, relating to certain unquestionable and ingrained assumptions about oneself, the world, and life (Adler, 1931/1958; Liotti, 1987). The technique of cognitive restructuring focuses on actively constructing alternative perspectives relating to an individual's lifestyle. In a counseling example, a client holds the perspective toward others, "People should serve and care for me." In maintaining this conviction, the client frequently encounters conflicts with people who refuse to conform to his expectations. In particular, authoritarian or domineering individuals tend to reject the demands of the client to be served. Consequently, the client becomes angry and takes his feelings out on vulnerable and submissive targets.

In the following example of the use of cognitive restructuring, a client is in counseling for abusing her two young children. The individual's core convictions involve perceiving herself as a victim and other people as rejecting and worthy of rebuke. Therefore, life is bleak with little hope for improvement.

Client:	I get so sick of things the way they are, and I'm beginning to realize that I sometimes take it out on the kids.
Counselor:	At the same time, you had a chance to get away last weekend when your sister offered to take your children, but you didn't want to go.
Client:	Oh yeah. If I went, she would expect me to pay her back somehow.
Counselor:	I wonder if more is going on here than we are even talking about.

Client:	What do you mean?
Counselor:	In our beginning talks, you said you were dissatisfied with your life long before you met your husband or had kids.
Client:	Well, there's nothing I can do about that.
Counselor:	The way you look at things suggests to me that you are convinced you cannot improve your situation.
Client:	You got that one right. Why bother trying? It won't make any difference.
Counselor:	That's exactly what I mean. You appear to be telling yourself over and over again that nothing will improve, so you might as well give up. I know it's only words right now, but what if you begin telling yourself that you can make a difference in improving your life?
Client:	I don't see how that can help. I'm just not happy with things.
Counselor:	It would be only a start because this seems so unfamiliar to you. For so long, you have thought things will not get any better regardless of what you do.
Client:	I'm not even sure where to begin.
Counselor:	Well, let's talk about certain assumptions you seem to have about how you view life and try to evaluate them.

Reframing. As an intervention related to cognitive restructuring, reframing also focuses on constructing alternative perspectives. Through a semantic change process, clients broaden their frames of reference in constructive and purposeful directions. Specifically, relative to displacement, individuals are capable of revising the meaning of their defense pattern. As an example, if a client who values strength and control begins to perceive his spousal abuse as a sign of weakness, his displacement use may take on a new and adverse meaning. To continue with the example of the client in counseling who uses the defense of displacement in abusive interactions with his wife, the counselor employs reframing.

Counselor:	It's important for you to see yourself as a strong person.
Client:	Well, I mean . . . I guess so.
Counselor:	Sometimes, though, you take your strength out on your wife.
Client:	As we talked about, once in a while things build up, and I lose it.

Counselor: I'm wondering if it is possible for you to think that a strong person is someone who is more ablto control his feelings and not take them out on people who are less able to defend themselves. When you think of individuals you know who are truly respected, isn't it true that they are straight with people and are not out of control?

Interpretation. To gain increased control of displacement, it may be necessary for some clients to explore motivational considerations that explain patterns of their functioning. Through a propositional aspect of interpretation (referred to here as interpretation), clients examine causal referents relating to displacement and, when appropriate, their core convictions. In the following example with a client in counseling for abusing her children, the counselor tentatively expresses an interpretation to the individual whose displacement functionally relates to her lifestyle.

Client: I guess it's just the way life is. My mother went through the same things; she was unhappy and couldn't seem to change her life. She died at a fairly young age.

Counselor: So, in essence, you expect the same things in life as your mother.

Client: Well, it seems so, doesn't it?

Counselor: We have already talked about your resentment toward your mother for being a victimized person and taking it out on you.

Client: I'm still working on that.

Counselor: Could it be that in similar ways you are subjecting your own children to the same hurt that you felt with your mother?

Client: Well, maybe, but I don't think I do it intentionally.

Counselor: It may be like a cycle, perhaps? You can't get angry at your mother because she's not alive, so you possibly take it out on your children.

Client: I never thought about it just that way.

Accomplishment Stage

In the final or accomplishment stage of counseling, the emphasis shifts from a behavioral focus on comprehension and meaning to one of client action. Habitual patterns of displacement do not yield easily, even when an individual is receptive to change. Action-oriented strategies may be effective in breaking the repetitive cycle of displacement and for establishing more adaptive client behavior.

Catching Oneself. Once clients decide to try to control their use of displacement, "catching oneself" may be useful for limiting the employment of the defense. As individuals are about to use displacement, they attempt to resist the action through a cued reminder. A client, for instance, who makes a commitment to stop abusing her children uses catching oneself when she feels her anger building up to a point of losing control. At this critical point, the client takes a picture of her two smiling children out of her shirt pocket and thinks about how innocent they are.

In the next example, an African American early adolescent who displaces his anger generated by peer ridicule attempts to control the source of his feelings.

Counselor:	It seems now that the kids know that you will get angry when they tease you, and this only makes it worse.
Client:	I know. We've talked about that. I shouldn't let them know that it gets to me, then maybe they'll go bother someone else. It didn't stop Dr. Martin Luther King Jr. when he was called names.
Counselor:	Well, what about doing something such as picturing his face inside your head when you are teased, and this will help you avoid getting steamed up. Then you can quickly try to get away from the situation.
Client:	I sort of know what you mean. It would be like a stop sign in my mind. It might work.

Acting As If. Individuals who have used displacement for extended periods may have underused adaptive behaviors because of the constrictive influence of the defense. As a counseling strategy, "acting as if" enables clients to assume novel roles in purposeful capacities. In the following example, a client has responded to his wife in abusive ways for so long that he is at a loss as to how to relate to her as a more caring husband.

Client:	I realize that I sometimes take my frustrations out on my wife. I do treat her rough once in a while, but it's been that way for so long that it seems the natural way to do things.
Counselor:	You don't know what it means to be a gentle and caring husband.
Client:	That's right. That's it. So many of the men that I know are like me. I know that I need to be able to talk about what is bothering me so that I can get my feelings out without always taking them out on her.
Counselor:	Can you think of any men who treat their wives as you've decided you would like to?
Client:	Yeah, I can think of a few men I know who seem to be very good to their women. They talk about what is happening with them, and they tell me how open and honest they are with each other.
Counselor:	We could spend some time talking about how they act toward their wives, and maybe by doing that you could get an idea of where you can go from there.
Client:	What would I do? I'm not sure.
Counselor:	I guess what we are talking about is that you begin to act like a husband who talks to his wife in an open way and avoids taking his anger out on her. This would seem really different for you when you first try it.
Client:	You're right. It would be different for me, but I think I could give it a shot.

Breaking It Down. Establishing a sequence of specific actions toward decreasing the use of displacement is the focus of "breaking it down." In a concluding example, the counselor suggests an attainable plan for a client living in the inner city to deal with what he perceives are overwhelming problems.

Client:	I would like to be able to say what is on my mind and to talk about all the problems in my neighborhood, but there is so much going on that I don't know where to begin. When I think about all of it, and how hopeless it seems, I start looking for someone to blame.
Counselor:	You're finding it hard to sort out so many things in your head all at once.

Client:	That's true. There are so many things that I need to work out that everything gets jumbled up.
Counselor:	Why don't we spend some time talking about all the problems that you are facing? Once you've expressed what you're thinking in regard to each of them, we could look at whatever you feel are the most important. You could then decide which one you would like to start working on first.

CONCLUSION

Displacement for an individual involves redirecting an emotional response to a vulnerable substitute. In counseling, a client's use of displacement is often directed at persons who are perceived as weak and less able to retaliate. The source of a person's emotional reaction may be prohibited because of threat or inaccessibility. Displacement may be identified and modified through the three stages of the counseling process: relationship, integration, and accomplishment.

4

IDENTIFICATION

But I identify myself, as always,
With something that there's something wrong with,
With something human.

—Randall Jarrell, 1965, p. 45[1]

The particularly human tendency of individuals to identify with other people commonly occurs both as a developmental process and as a defense mechanism. Developmentally, interactions with various persons in an individual's environment during sustained periods have a significant impact on shaping one's personality. Related to this universal phenomenon of identification as a primary developmental process is the defense mechanism of identification. As a more circumscribed construct, its application involves identifying with others as a response to threat and conflict. Consider, for instance, the marginalized adolescent who joins a gang and revels in the perceived power and authority inherent in the group membership. In another example, a child is so endangered by the emotional and physical abuse inflicted by his father that he identifies himself with his aggressive parent as a means of resolving intolerable conflict. In yet another instance, after a promotion, a heretofore amiable employee abruptly begins to act in a demanding and controlling manner, much like his supervisor whom he admires. In these examples, and others like them, the counselor can begin to recognize the significant influence of others on the behavior of clients, on both an immediate and a long-term basis. Defining identification as a defense mechanism emphasizes assuming desired attributions of another person through fantasized associations.

THEORETICAL ASPECTS OF IDENTIFICATION

Emergence of Identification

Sigmund Freud (1921/1955d) explicated identification in three ways. First, Freud viewed identification as an earliest form of a shared emotional tie with another individual. He termed this undifferentiated, initial interaction as a type of primary identification. Second, Freud saw identification as a means to replace a much desired lost or abandoned libidinal relationship. This exchange was referred to by Freud as a type of secondary identification, involving identification with a person with differentiated, separate boundaries. Third, Freud recognized identification as a tendency for an individual to share common perceptions with another person. In particular, this related to the formation of the ego ideal as an aspect of the superego. Relating to the defense mechanism of identification, Freud (1915/1957a) construed "turning round upon the subject's own self" (p. 126) as a means of resolving conflicted feelings of aggression felt toward another person by redirecting the feelings inward. In her enumeration of defense mechanisms, Anna Freud (1936/1966) listed this construct as "turning against the self" (p. 44).

Turning against the self occurs as individuals experience feelings of aggression or hostility toward another person but are manifestly afraid of expressing those feelings because of fears of retribution and excessive guilt. As a means of dealing with this conflict, individuals identify with the threatening person and turn aggression or hostility inward through pronounced self-rebuke and self-accusations (Sandler & Freud, 1985).

In addition to clarifying turning against the self, or identification with the victim, Anna Freud focused on another construct relating to identification. Through identification with the aggressor, persons control and manage fears of domination evoked by an aggressive person by becoming like him or her (Blum, 1987). As the individuals assume aggressive attributes, they are transformed and emerge with a perceived equivalent power of the feared person (Freud, 1936/1966). Although Freud devoted an entire chapter in *The Ego and the Mechanisms of Defense* to identification with the aggressor, she did not include it as one of the defense mechanisms in this volume. Years later, however, Freud clarified this choice, "I didn't list it here because I thought only of the recognized defense mechanisms, and I felt modest about this new one. I didn't think it had a claim to be introduced yet" (Sandler & Freud, 1985, p. 100). Since Freud's early conceptualizations, both turning against the self, or identification with the victim, and identification with the aggressor have subsequently been considered within the broader construct of identification as a defense mechanism (MacGregor, 1991).

Psychopathology and Identification

Age Adequateness. Because identification is both a developmental process and a defense mechanism, the distinction between the two points of reference is not always clear (Koff, 1961). Consequently, the relative age of a client becomes a significant consideration in determining the normal-abnormal dimensions of both conceptualizations. Identification as a defense involves a response to emotional conflict, and children are especially susceptible to the use of the mechanism. In a counseling example, an 8-year-old client who is abused identifies with an adult perpetrator in an attempt to resolve the intolerable conflict inherent in an intensely threatening relationship. In this instance, the victimized child possibly lacks the resources or experience to seek out protection and instead resorts to an identification defense. The experimental period of adolescence, with shifting variations in speech, attire, opinions, values, and related behaviors, involves inevitable change (Clark, 1995f). Again, the counselor must evaluate if such variabilities are due primarily to developmental or to defensive functions. Consider the example of an adolescent who is experimenting with self-denial by manifesting a somewhat common ascetic adolescent behavior. This pattern may represent a developmental stage function, or the same actions may possibly involve a client's identification with the victim in the form of punishment and self-abasement. Identification increases during middle childhood and once again during middle adolescence (Cramer, 1991). Beyond adolescence, an individual's identification is relatively stable within life span stages, and marked changes may suggest identification as a defense mechanism. In a counseling example, a 40-year-old client assumes an identification with celebrity figures representing a youth culture to stave off an intolerable conflict associated with growing older.

Balance. An individual using identification as a defense mechanism tends to emulate behaviors in ways that are like those of another person or persons on the basis of perceived commonalities (Abend & Porder, 1986; Sanford, 1955). Identification may also be employed in rigid and stereotyped patterns that prohibit more versatile and flexible responses. Further, a client may become dependent on identification, rather than making situational adjustments when dealing with conflict and threat. In a counseling example, a sixth-grade student, Melinda, assumes characteristics of a film star as a means to gain approval and recognition. To resemble the celebrity, she begins to dress and talk in similar ways to the admired person. It may be that her identification use developed and expanded subsequent to a period when Melinda was ostracized by her peers. The lack of balance in pursuing more adaptive behaviors, even including the employment of other defenses, becomes increasingly evident as she becomes further involved in a consuming identification with the actress. A pervasive pattern of identification further restricts attempts by Melinda to develop her own unique qualities that ultimately may make her more appealing and attractive.

Intensity. As an individual develops a pattern of frequently using identification, an increasing intensity level can begin to undermine more purposeful social adaptation. An excessive engagement of identification may be observed when a client habitually relies on the defense to deal with emotional conflict. For example, an early adulthood client experiences an inability to improve conditions in her life, and, in addition to feeling depressed, she perceives herself as a victim. When the client is faced with challenges and uncertainties, she typically withdraws and passively incurs a variety of difficulties and failures. The client's core convictions suggest that she believes, regardless of her efforts, that inevitable pain and sorrows will be inflicted on her. For this person, the use of identification as a victim is intrinsic to her lifestyle.

Reversibility. In many instances, identification is evoked by threatening situations, and clients employ the defense for a time until personal challenges recede or pass. With changing circumstances and a diminution of threat, individuals may no longer continue to engage or persist with their use of identification (Sanford, 1955). For others, however, identification is not as easily subject to reversibility, and the defense continues to be employed long after a threat or crisis passes. Instead of adjusting to new conditions, clients maintain an inflexible and out-of-date response. As an example, a client named Anna demonstrates a pattern of identification for several years in a marital relationship with a spouse batterer. Under these highly threatening and volatile circumstances, Anna employs identification with her aggressor husband to gain some measure of perceived security and stability. Yet months after Anna extricates herself from the abusive relationship with her spouse, she continues to use the defense of identification and acts in hostile and aggressive ways.

Context. Social and cultural contexts frequently have a significant impact on identification, both as a developmental process and as a defense mechanism. Involvement in diverse groups influences the beliefs and values of individuals, and the meaning of identification is embedded in its environmental context. As an example, an adolescent may assume an identification with a powerful and flamboyant professional wrestler. This same admired personage, however, may offer less appeal and attraction to a late adulthood client. Thus, some level of similarity and attachment between the behavior of a person and the object of identification may be assumed by the counselor (Bieri, Lobeck, & Galinsky, 1959). By examining the contextual setting of clients' identification, the meaning of their defenses becomes clearer. At the same time, the counselor must be cautious not to overemphasize social and cultural forces and make stereotyped assumptions about individuals who may or may not employ identification as a defense. An Asian American client, for instance, behaves in passive and submissive ways to the point of assuming a victimization role. The counselor stereotypically surmises that the meaning of the client's behavior relates to a particular social milieu and fails to consider the possibility of the employment of identification as a defense.

Types of Identification

As a defense mechanism, identification is broadly conceptualized in the literature and, as a type, has variously been related to the aggressor, the victim, the rescuer, the comforter, the love object, and the lost object (Blum, 1987). In the instance of a lost object, a person assumes characteristics of someone or something lost to diminish or prevent emotional pain. Although identification as a defense may represent one of several variations, only two types have received particular prominence: identification with the victim and identification with the aggressor.

Identification With the Victim. Initially referred to as "turning against the self" by Anna Freud (1936/1966, p. 44), identification with the victim has emerged as a major type of identification with significant implications for counseling. Aggressive feelings elicited by a person are prohibited or blocked, and a client redirects the hostile affect inward through pronounced self-accusations and self-depreciation. In effect, the client becomes a protective substitute for another person, and, to some extent, the interaction mitigates conflicted feelings for wishing harm to someone (MacGregor, 1991). In a counseling example, a client employs identification with the victim with her husband, who abuses alcohol. Although the client experiences hostility toward her spouse, she redirects her aggression inward and blames or censures herself for her husband's abuse of alcohol despite the multiple and complex cultural forces involved in his drinking pattern. An even more disturbing example involves an individual who identifies with the victim to the extreme of attempting suicide (Sandler & Freud, 1985).

Identification With the Aggressor. Anna Freud (1936/1966) formulated the concept of identification with the aggressor:

Here, the mechanism of identification or introjection is combined with a second important mechanism. By impersonating the aggressor, assuming his attitudes or imitating his aggression, the child transforms himself from the person threatened into the person who makes the threat. (p. 113)

Theoretically, identification with the aggressor involves threat by a fearful or terrorizing person, and an individual subsequently models similar aggressive behavior. Adopting characteristics of the threatening person enables an individual to gain a perceived sense of power and control in what otherwise would be a vulnerable and helpless position. In counseling, the construct is intrinsic with traumatically abused children and terrorized adults who become abusive toward others (Blum, 1987). As an example, an 8-year-old is emotionally and physically abused by the child's parent and consequently demonstrates a pattern of assaulting other children. In a less distressing instance, a classroom teacher acts in hostile ways as a consequence of identification with an aggressive and intimidating school principal. Research studies conducted with college students found that identification with the aggressor as a defense mechanism was employed more frequently by men and that identification with the victim was more common among women (Cramer, 1991; Ihilevich & Gleser, 1995).

PROCESSING IDENTIFICATION IN COUNSELING

Relationship Stage

In the initial stage of counseling, selected techniques promote client trust and understanding. Reflection, assessment methods, and counselor self-disclosure assist persons in becoming aware of their defensive reactions relating to identification.

Reflection. Client use of identification typically evokes a marked degree of affect, as individuals associate with various attributes of another person. Clients generally employ identification on occasions that elicit threat and emotional conflict, and reflection as a counseling technique acknowledges their subjective experiencing. For example, a high school student expresses strong feelings toward a number of his classmates who have been ridiculing him. Although the client does not state that he is being taunted for acting like Elvis Presley, he is visibly upset, and the counselor uses reflection of feelings, "You feel angry and embarrassed when the kids make fun of the way you act." Although the counselor may recognize the object of the identification, it is generally premature at this point to confirm this possibility because the client may be threatened even further. After the counselor affirms individuals' feelings, it becomes therapeutic to explore the meaning of their communications. In the same example, the client states, "I'm sick of being a nobody around this school and having everyone ignore me." In response, the counselor uses reflection of meaning, "You are telling me that you would like to be recognized as a person who matters and have a little attention paid to you."

Periodically, the counselor may observe client use of identification in counseling. The following examples suggest various possibilities:

- An inner-city youth has recently joined a gang. Her mother has been raising the client and her four siblings since the father walked out on them 5 years ago. The client has been required to attend counseling by the courts after being arrested for vandalizing local businesses.

- A middle adulthood man has joined a motorcycle club. He spends most of his time with the members and has been neglecting his family and his job. He is in counseling because his wife has threatened to leave him if he does not attend.

- For more than 2 years, a woman has endured an abusive relationship with her highly volatile husband. Although she has threatened to leave him after episodes of physical and emotional abuse, the client has repeatedly decided to give her husband another chance to change his hostile behavior.

- A kind and gentle African American man has started to emulate the behavior of his manipulative and controlling supervisor. He has become demanding with employees under his supervision and is no longer liked by his coworkers.

- A middle school client has threatened and has attacked small children. The counselor learns that the individual was physically abused by his father for a lengthy period as a young child.

As a response to each of these examples, the counselor may use reflection to acknowledge a client's feelings involving identification. In the following counseling example, a client begins to clarify defensive functioning relating to identification as a defense. A middle adulthood client who had previously demonstrated tolerant and supportive qualities in his relationships with coworkers begins to demonstrate aggressive behavior that is characteristic of his supervisor. The client emulates the dress, speech, and abrasive mannerisms of the supervisor in a large organization. The supervisor had been applying intense pressure on the client to become more demanding and assertive and even referred him to an employee assistance counselor. This example suggests a cultural imperative of the stereotyped male role that sanctions aggression and control and devalues affiliative relatedness (Levant, 1995).

Client:	I'm not at work to make friends. I need to be a strong and effective leader if I ever want to move up in the company.
Counselor:	So it doesn't really bother you that some people at work are not very pleased with you right now.
Client:	No, not really (with uncertainty). My supervisor has been very successful, and he's always managed people this way.
Counselor:	You admire your boss because he is valued in the company although he is not well liked by many workers.
Client:	That's just the way it is in corporate work.

Assessment. Appraising the use of identification as a defense mechanism includes consideration of client behavior, examination of collateral sources, and the use of projective techniques. Inconsistencies in individuals' behavior may suggest the use of identification, and the following examples indicate the possible employment of the defense in counseling:

1. *Statement:* Being in the gang means a lot to me. They're the only ones I can count on right now.
   Nonverbal expression: The client appears tense when she talks about the gang.

2. *Statement:* I like the guys in my motorcycle club. They're a lot of fun, and there is no one I would rather be with right now.

Previous statement: I haven't been spending that much time at home, and I guess somehow that has got to change.

3. *Statement:* I told my husband I will leave him if he hurts me again, and I mean it.
   Action: The client has repeatedly told her husband that she will leave him if he continues his assaultive behavior, but she has never followed through on this ultimatum.

4. *Statement:* I need to be more aggressive at work. The people below me need a boss who takes control.
   Objective condition: The client was previously successful and popular when he was a kind and friendly supervisor.

5. *Statement:* Nobody ever pushes me around. I don't take anything from anyone.
   Omission: The client fails to acknowledge the history of abuse from his father.

Evaluation of collateral sources, such as written psychological reports available to the counselor, may also suggest client use of identification. For example, a student's file is found to include an anecdotal report that the individual demonstrated some type of identification with an illustrious figure in an earlier grade in school. In another case, a client's probation record documents a history of abuse as a child, and the counselor hypothesizes a relationship to the individual's current aggressive behavior and identification as a defense.

Projective techniques, including early recollections, human figure drawings, and sentence completion tasks, may also contribute to the assessment of client use of identification as a defense mechanism. Early recollections provide perspectives on individuals' core convictions that may relate to their employment of identification. As an example, Jason, a high school client, relates an early memory of raising his hand in a second-grade classroom and being ignored by the teacher. Relating to the recollection, Jason reports feelings of frustration and resentment. The memory, and two others like it, suggests that Jason believes that he will be overlooked despite reasonable efforts to be noticed. The identification defense supports Jason's lifestyle conviction that conventional behavior will not bring him the recognition that he seeks and that more dramatic action is necessary. In this assessment context, the counselor learns from a collateral source that Jason has been emulating Elvis Presley.

The graphic images portrayed by an individual may represent aspects of the artist and some other person in the environment who is real or fantasized (Levick, 1983). A client, for instance, who identifies with a celebrity or an illustrious person reflects features of this object in a drawing of a person. In another instance, a client draws a figure associated with an identification with the aggressor. The drawing may include hostility indicators of teeth emphasis, closed fists, and exaggerated size (Hammer, 1958). Sentence completion responses may also suggest possible identification figures. As an example, employing the defense of identification with the aggressor, the client, who has been physically abused by his father, may indicate the object of the aggression. In this context, the client completes selected sentence stems as follows: "I am afraid of . . . my father." "My father . . . has hurt me." "I hate . . . my father." It is also possible that specifying directly the objects of the identification with the aggressor may be so threatening that pertinent sentence stems may be left incomplete. In another case, a client with an identification with the victim completes revealing sentence stems, "I feel . . . like a failure." "I failed . . . so many things." "I suffer . . . due to my own stupidity." "I hate . . . so many things about myself."

Self-Disclosure. Various dimensions of counselor self-disclosure such as personal success or failure experiences may be relevant to a client's use of identification. For example, a counselor discloses to an adolescent, "There were times when I was in high school that I wanted to be anybody else but me." In other instances, the counselor may discuss similar or dissimilar experiences with a client that relate to identification. A counselor, for instance, discloses to a middle adulthood client with a manifest identification relating to youth culture figures. The counselor, a 45-year-old woman, states, "I find aging difficult sometimes, too, because our society places so much emphasis on youth." It is also possible for a therapist to focus on past and present experiences relating to a client's use of identification, as is the case with the counselor who discloses, "There have been times in my life when I tried to be like someone else when I was afraid of that person." A counselor may also employ self-involving statements as a reaction to a client's behavior in counseling. As an example, in response to an individual who uses identification with the victim, the counselor supportively states, "You continually put yourself down, and I find this painful."

Integration Stage

With the development of a counseling relationship in the initial stage of counseling, emphasis in the middle period of counseling shifts to clarifying client perspectives and motivations relating to identification. Selected counseling techniques, including confrontation, cognitive restructuring, reframing, and interpretation, focus on reducing client contradictions and conflicts.

Confrontation. Inconsistencies in clients' functioning observed in the initial stage now become a focus of inquiry through the counseling technique of confrontation. Clarifying discrepancies relating to identification clarifies individuals' use of the defense. The following counseling examples include contradictions in the behavior of various clients and the counselor's use of confrontation.

1. *Statement—Nonverbal Expression*

   Client: Being in the gang means a lot to me. They're the only ones I can really count on.

   Counselor: The gang is very important to you, but you have a concerned look on your face as you describe this relationship to me.

2. *Statement—Previous Statement*

   Client: I like the guys in the motorcycle club. They're a lot of fun, and there is no one I would rather be with right now.

   Counselor: They mean a lot to you, and you enjoy being with them, but I also heard you say that you need to spend more time with your family.

3. *Statement—Action*

Client: I told my husband I will leave him if he hurts me again, and I mean it.

Counselor: You seem determined to leave your husband if he abuses you again, but you have already warned him a number of times about this before.

4. *Statement—Objective Condition*

Client: I need to be more aggressive at work. The people below me need a boss who takes control.

Counselor: You are convinced that you need to be very direct to succeed in your new position, but I have the impression you were popular as a supervisor who had allowed people a reasonable amount of freedom to work independently.

5. *Statement—Omission*

Client: Nobody ever pushes me around. I don't take anything from anyone.

Counselor: We have talked a lot about your determination not to be pushed around by people, but you rarely mention your abusive relationship with your father.

The impact of a confrontation on a client is difficult to predict, and variations occur in response to a counselor's intervention. In the following counseling example, an early adolescent appears confused in reacting to the confrontation by the counselor. It is evident that further therapeutic examination is needed to clarify discrepancies involving the individual's aggression and the defense of identification.

Client: The kids here at school are such jerks. They get me ticked off on purpose, even when I have told them they're going to get it.

Counselor: So you think they have it coming to them because they should know better than to get you upset in the first place.

Client: Well, even when they know what'll happen, they give me trouble anyway (pauses). I don't think it's any big deal; I don't really hurt them that much.

Counselor: You don't see any reason to make a fuss about it, but you also said earlier that you are sick of getting in trouble for going after other kids.

Client: I don't know. I feel really mixed up about the whole thing.

Cognitive Restructuring. In challenging clients' use of identification as a defense mechanism, it may become necessary to scrutinize their lifestyles. Cognitive restructuring as a counseling technique contributes to the development of more adaptive life perspectives that may also alter identification use by an individual. In a counseling example, a 35-year-old client with three young children appears to use identification as a defense as she is victimized in an abusive relationship with her husband. In response to the client's self-reproach, the counselor attempts to broaden her perspective by implicating larger cultural forces that suggest why it is sometimes easier for a woman to remain a victim rather than attempt to change a situation that threatens her with isolation, condemnation, and a lack of alternatives (Miller, 1986). By the counselor's expanding the client's awareness that her beliefs and feelings must be understood in a societal context that frequently subjects women to gender inequities, the client is able to understand her functioning in a more objective and empowered way.

In another counseling example relating to cognitive restructuring, an adolescent client known for bullying other students employs the defense of identification. The counselor introduces an alternative schema to the client's aggression-related identification.

Client:	No one really cares what I do anyway. Even my mother doesn't care if I get into trouble. So I don't see what the big deal is.
Counselor:	Because no one at home seems concerned about what you do, you don't see any reason you should get worked up.
Client:	Yeah. All the other kids I know do what they want to, so why shouldn't I?
Counselor:	I'm wondering if it is possible for you to look at your situation in a different way. Because it seems that nobody particularly cares what you do, could you see yourself as having the freedom to make your own choices? You are free to become what you would like to be.
Client:	Maybe. At least I don't have anybody on my back telling me what to do.
Counselor:	With this freedom, is it possible for you to choose to become somebody that you can feel good about?

Reframing. As a counseling technique related to cognitive restructuring, reframing emphasizes modifying client maladaptive perspectives. Through semantic change, individuals transform the meaning of their behavior, including the use of identification as a defense mechanism. The following exchange continues the counseling example with the adolescent demonstrating a pattern of aggression and the defense of identification.

Client:	This is the way things are for me. Fights happen. I've gotten used to it at home. People sort of expect me to be like this anyway, so what's the point in trying to change now?
Counselor:	It seems to me that because of the violence you experienced when you were younger, you don't think things can be any different. But you are your own person, and you're the only one who can choose what your life will be like.
Client:	I've always just accepted that I'd end up like my dad. But sometimes I don't like things that he does.
Counselor:	Maybe you could look at it in a different way. Is it possible for you to be strong like your father but use this strength in ways that work better for you?

Interpretation. A propositional aspect of interpretation focuses on motivational considerations, and for some clients, it is necessary to explore past referents to their current behavior to enhance their self-understanding relating to the use of identification. In a continuation of the example of the adolescent client who demonstrates a pattern of aggression and the use of identification, the counselor presents an interpretation in a tentative and inviting style.

Client:	It did hurt when my dad pushed me around, and I couldn't do anything to stop him. It's probably the same for kids that I hit. I know it should bother me that I do this, but it doesn't, really (confused).
Counselor:	For some reason, it's hard for you to stop pushing around other kids, although you went through it yourself.
Client:	I like having them be afraid of me. I know that sounds stupid, but it's true.
Counselor:	I'd like to suggest something for you to consider that may help make some sense out of this. You've said before that the

worst thing about the way your father used to treat you was that you had no power or control over any of it. You were not big enough to fight back.

Client: No, I wasn't. I hated having to just stand there and take it from him.

Counselor: Could it be possible that although you talk about how much you hate the way your father treated you, you admire the power and control that he had in his life? And so you've been acting the same way with kids in the school because you feel stronger when you go after them.

Client: I don't know. I can't believe that I want to be like him, but I guess I am in some ways.

Accomplishment Stage

After clarifying inconsistencies and conflicts relating to clients' use of identification, the final stage of counseling focuses on action change. For many individuals, breaking an entrenched pattern of identification is challenging, and selected counseling strategies assist in this pursuit.

Catching Oneself. As clients strive to control their use of identification, they often need strategic assistance to follow through on this effort. For some individuals, their identification pattern has been intense, and a counseling strategy that assists in breaking a repetitive cycle can be therapeutic. "Catching oneself" enables clients to interrupt identification use through a cuing tactic as they are about to engage the defense. A client, for example, maintaining a long-term use of identification with the victim, decides to memorize two lines from a poem by Elizabeth Barrett Browning (1844/1974):

> I strive and struggle to deliver right
> That music of my nature, day and night.
> ("The Soul's Expression," p. 98)

She recites the line to herself at a critical point when she is about to assume a victimized role and attempts to act more assertively.

Client:	I don't know. I know that I shouldn't pick on other kids, but I'm so used to it by now.
Counselor:	What happens to you just before you go after somebody?
Client:	I'm not sure. I guess that I just feel like it.
Counselor:	Do you feel bad about it at that second?
Client:	I guess that I do, but then I get into it and lose it.
Counselor:	I'm wondering if there is anything that you could do to catch yourself and stop bullying other kids just at the second before you lose yourself?
Client:	Well (pause), I could tell myself not to do it.
Counselor:	Do you think that would work?
Client:	Probably not (pause). Maybe I could just pinch myself when I get the feeling.
Counselor:	That sounds good. How will it work?
Client:	Well, when I feel like going after someone, I can pinch myself hard on my hand and tell myself to stop.

Acting As If. As clients begin to control their use of identification, they may need to develop alternative and more purposeful behavior. Some individuals may be unpracticed in adaptive actions because of their extensive employment of the defense or because they lack awareness. "Acting as if" addresses this need by enabling clients to deliberately act in the manner they would like to behave by emulating the actions of another person. In the next example, a client who had identified with his aggressive supervisor recognizes that his behavior was inappropriate but still would like to make adaptive changes.

Client:	I know now that I had been way too domineering at work. I was really afraid of my supervisor and the control that he had over me and my future. I was so glad when he was fired last month. He was a tyrant.
Counselor:	That was a big relief for you, but you were already making changes to distance yourself from him.
Client:	As we have talked about quite a bit, I hated him but, at the same time, felt drawn to him. I have thought about it a lot, though, and perhaps he had a point that I need to be somewhat more assertive with people on the job.
Counselor:	It seems that after all you have been through, you would like to take away some positive gains from this.

Client: I would like to effect more of a balance between a leader who is both friendly and respected.

Counselor: I'm wondering if there is someone in management who demonstrates these qualities?

Client: Well, there is a woman I used to work with before she got promoted. She related to people well, but she still demanded and got respect from those around her.

Counselor: Why don't we spend some time talking about what kind of a person she was as a boss and as a coworker? Perhaps you could get an idea of things that might work for you, and you could try them out.

Breaking It Down. As clients attempt to control identification and establish more adaptive behavior, some individuals find the perceived magnitude of change daunting. Focusing on incremental progression and following the principle of not trying to do everything at once engender more manageable and attainable objectives. In the following counseling example, a 40-year-old client employs "breaking it down" as a counseling strategy to begin work on specific tasks.

Client: I have been pretty irresponsible lately. I know I need to spend more time with my family, but I don't want to give up the motorcycle club. I get so much pleasure from being with those guys.

Counselor: We've talked before about the reasons you like being a part of the club: the respect and attention you're given and the excitement and freedom you feel when you're on your bike.

Client: Those things are all really important to me. I try to think about what could give me these things so I don't have to be with the guys all the time, but I don't know where to start.

Counselor: I have an idea that might make things easier to deal with. What about considering the problem one step at a time? We could start by looking at the most important part of the club, what you receive from being with them that means the most to you.

Client: I'd have to say it's the freedom I experience when I'm on my bike. I don't feel that free very often.

Counselor: Why don't we look at some ways that could give you a sense of freedom and still be with your family more often? After you've dealt with this, we could move on to the rest, one at a time.

Client: It sounds like it might work. I'm willing to try it and see because I have to do something.

CONCLUSION

Identification has been conceptualized both as a developmental process and as a defense mechanism. Identification with the victim and identification with the aggressor are specific types of the defense. Identification for an individual involves assuming desired attributes of another person through fantasized associations. The counselor may conceptualize therapeutic change of identification through the three stages of the counseling process.

NOTE

1. Excerpt from "The Lost World" (p. 45), by R. Jarrell, in *The Lost World*, by R. Jarrell, 1965, New York: Macmillan. Copyright © by the Estate of Randall Jarrell, care of Rhoda Weyr Agency, Brooklyn, New York. Reprinted with permission of the Rhoda Weyr Agency.

5

ISOLATION

We know the truth not only through our reason but also through our heart.

—Blaise Pascal, 1662/1966, p. 58

It is not unusual for individuals to blunt the impact of painful events by muting their emotional reactions for a time. People are also able to talk about the occurrence of hardships and traumas in subdued tones that belie the sorrow or even terror of their experiences. In many instances, this ability to separate reason from emotion may be adaptive by enabling individuals to survive conditions and not be overwhelmed by their ruling passions. At the same time, it is also possible for persons to come to rely on a pattern of avoiding affective responses to painful encounters that are inevitable in life. Emotions represent essential aspects of human behavior, and sustained exclusion of affective expression generally results in constricted personality functioning that lacks integration. Consider, for example, in an initial counseling session, a client who engages in an intellectualized discourse about the societal implications of adolescent drug abuse while minimally addressing his son's arrest for dealing drugs the previous day. In another counseling instance, a client discusses with a flat affect sexual assaults she experienced as a preadolescent but makes no emotional connection of the abuse to her tormenting dreams. Defining isolation as a defense mechanism emphasizes severing verbalized cognitions from associated affect.

THEORETICAL ASPECTS OF ISOLATION

Emergence of Isolation

Sigmund Freud (1894/1962b) initially described the intrapsychic effect of isolation, "if the ego succeeds in *turning this powerful idea into a weak one,* in robbing it of the affect—the sum of excitation—with which it is loaded" (p. 48). Through an isolating process, persons separate distressing affects from their associated cognitions. It is also possible within the context of an intense focus on obsessive thinking and compulsive action for individuals to avert or impoverish the affective domain of their behavior. In a well-known case history, "The Rat Man," Freud (1909/1955e) described the dynamic course of isolation in the treatment of an obsessive-compulsive patient. Years later, Freud (1926/1959) specified the functioning of isolation in obsessional neurosis: "The experience is not forgotten, but, instead, it is deprived of its affect, and its associative connections are suppressed or interrupted so that it remains as though isolated and is not reproduced in the ordinary processes of thought" (p. 120).

Anna Freud (1936/1966) also recognized the connection between obsessional neurosis and the process of isolati, and she listed the construct among the mechanisms of defense. She postulated that the meaning of isolation involved the ability to tolerate an idea in an individual's consciousness because the associated affect had been removed (Sandler & Freud, 1985). Freud rejected the theoretical possibility that isolation related to separating two ideas or cognitions that belong together and maintained that the original meaning of the term is limited to the withdrawal of emotion from an associated thought (American Psychiatric Association, 1994b; Sandler & Freud, 1985).

Freud recognized that isolation became manifest when a patient discussed what are usually considered emotionally laden issues with a relative absence of feeling.

Psychopathology and Isolation

Age Adequateness. The capacity to restrain the expression of feelings generally expands as persons develop across the life span. Young children tend to express feelings directly. With advancing age, individuals become increasingly able to modulate affect control. With the use of isolation, however, persons constrain feelings in situations beyond the level that is developmentally appropriate. Consider the counseling example of an 8-year-old child who is repeatedly teased by his peers. Instead of expressing fear, anger, or some other legitimate emotion, the client states to the counselor in a muted tone, "It seems to me that some of the time those kids do upset me." In another instance, an adolescent who also endures peer ridicule says to the counselor in a constrained and intellectualized voice, "Persons of that caliber are not worthy of my consideration of their folly." Even with the propensity of some adolescents to intellectualize experiences, the adolescent example exceeds reasonable expectations of reserve and restraint. In another counseling example, immediately after learning that his spouse is having an affair, a client states to the counselor in a subdued voice, "It happens, and I guess it hurts." The client's passive reaction and use of a qualifier contradicts the customary expectation for the individual to express feelings of betrayal or related affect.

Balance. Clients may employ the defense mechanism of isolation as a repetitive and rigid response to threat. By withdrawing from the emotional impact of a conflict, individuals are able to endure what otherwise might be an intolerable experience. In counseling, clients using isolation typically demonstrate a pattern of discussing personal or intimate topics in a bland tone devoid of feeling. Rather than examining issues in a more integrated sense, individuals repeatedly verbalize ideas with a minimal expression of emotion. Consider, for example, the client in substance abuse treatment who articulates his regret over the pain that his irresponsible behavior has caused his wife and children. Although the individual expresses sentiments of shame and anguish in his personal accounting, he does so in a manner that essentially conveys an emotional vacuum. Consequently, the full and profound impact of the client's substance abuse remains unassimilated at a vitally felt emotional level.

Intensity. As a defense mechanism, clients may use isolation to an excessive degree as a means of dealing with emotional conflict. Obsessive-compulsive qualities also become recognizable when clients employ isolation in an intense manner. The intensity pattern of individuals' use of isolation inhibits spontaneous affective responses in those situations in which most people experience a variety of affective reactions. This lack of what might be considered socially appropriate emotional behavior may also result in interpersonal difficulties. Peter, for example, is an early adulthood client who exhibits marked inhibitions in expressing feelings on almost any topic involving the disclosure of preferences or needs. The counselor also learns that Peter has had few close friendships or relationships in his life. In this instance, isolation may be intrinsic to Peter's lifestyle or core convictions that relate to distrust and suspicion of other people. The isolation defense appears to be integral with his assumptions about life while serving to maintain a distance from other people who cannot be trusted. Peter's use of isolation in this case is representative of Alfred Adler's (1936) safeguarding tendency of *hesitating attitude,* an evasive pattern that protects an individual's self-worth from perceived threat.

Reversibility. For some individuals, the pattern of separating affect from associated cognitions has been of such long duration that the two psychological domains are no longer experienced as belonging together (Killingmo, 1990). Feelings relating to conflicted material are blunted and lack integration, even when the source that elicited the severance of the elements may no longer be a threat. Despite experiencing evidence to the contrary, clients may continue to maintain the use of isolation and not adapt to changed circumstances. This condition of a lack of reversibility may result when particularly traumatic events prompted the employment of isolation or when persons have assimilated the defense into their lifestyles. In a counseling example, Mina, a college sophomore, speaks in a reserved and subdued tone, even at points that would typically provoke an emotional response. Specifically, Mina discusses a pattern of preadolescent sexual abuse perpetrated by her stepfather. Yet even during this disclosure of trauma, she appears emotionally expressionless. Although the stepfather presently lives hundreds of miles from the college campus and is no longer involved in her life, Mina continues to mute the affect relating to the sexual assaults. Mina's employment of isolation may have been of service to her during the abusive episodes, but the defense currently restricts her potential of working through past trauma and the development of more integrated behavior.

Context. Social and cultural contexts must be appraised to evaluate the question of what is a normal or appropriate level of emotional arousal in relation to the question of isolation use. In a counseling situation, an Asian American client may experience disapproval and rejection from his or her peers or elders for expressing anger, hostility, or disappointment (Axelson, 1993). Without considering cultural factors, a counselor's determination that the client employs isolation may be inaccurate. In a contrasting direction, a counselor may make assumptions about a client's lack of spontaneity and constricted affect and inaccurately attribute a person's behavior to specific environmental factors. Consider the example of a late adulthood client who demonstrates emotionally constricted behavior, resulting in the counselor's assumption that these tendencies are a product of social conditions relating to personal losses or illnesses (Brezin, 1980). Yet it is possible that the client experiences emotional conflicts beyond those that are immediately apparent in an environmental context; in such instances, the source of the individual's isolation requires further scrutiny.

Types of Isolation

An essential quality of isolation involves an individual's verbal statements that are largely devoid of affect. Intellectualization, as a type of isolation, represents a similar function but with an additional component that incorporates the expression of abstract, analytical, and precise verbalizations. Although intellectualization is considered by some theorists as a discrete defense mechanism (Sharf, 1996), its dynamic properties are inclusive of isolation, and it is sometimes difficult to distinguish between the two conceptualizations in counseling practice. As a type or subcategory of isolation (Killingmo, 1990; Mahl, 1969), an individual's use of the defense involves a detached emphasis on objective judgment and technical knowledge, accompanied by a preoccupation with words and abstractions. For example, the counselor asks a 50-year-old client named Stuart about his feelings relating to a recent termination from a professional position as the result of corporate restructuring. In a rational and logical tone, Stuart responds, "The organization has a pertinacious view entailing an insoluble dilemma. There is a corporate perception that downsizing augments fiscal yield in a free market, yet invariably these forces cannot be precisely regulated." Through a constellation of words, Stuart disconnects the emotional impact of his employment loss, but his behavior also precludes the expression of constricted feelings that may ultimately enable him to pursue more adaptive actions.

PROCESSING ISOLATION IN COUNSELING

Relationship Stage

The initial stage of counseling emphasizes expanding client awareness of feelings. This period is particularly challenging when individuals employ isolation with a minimal or impoverished expression of affect. Reflection, in combination with assessment methods, assists the counselor in understanding and acknowledging clients' experiencing relating to the defense. Another counseling technique, counselor self-disclosure, enables counselors to relate personal experiences that are pertinent to clients' use of isolation.

Reflection. As an intervention in counseling, reflection elicits and clarifies client feelings and perceptions. Persons who use isolation, however, attempt to inhibit the expression of affect. For individuals employing isolation, expressing feelings evokes a sense of disequilibrium, and the counselor must accurately acknowledge the experience of clients in an understanding and supportive way. Rick, for example, is an early adulthood client who discusses events in his life in a detached and shallow fashion. In reaction to the loss of a job, in which Rick had been employed for several months, Rick says, "Well, it just happened. That's the way it is." The counselor, attempting to reflect Rick's feelings, states, "This must be a terrible blow to your confidence." In response, Rick relates, "No, not really." In this example, the counselor uses reflection of feelings from her subjective perspective and makes assumptions about Rick's perceptions. In actuality, Rick experiences a muted level of emotion, and an alternative reflection of feeling may be closer to his frame of reference. The counselor responds to Rick, "Your feelings seem neutral or subdued about your job loss." By avoiding too rapid a pace in using reflection and by deliberately acknowledging the subjective functioning of the client, the counselor invites and encourages an expression of feelings. Subsequently, the counselor may clarify the meaning of an individual's experience. In the conclusion of the cited example, the counselor, using reflection of meaning, says to Rick, "It is important for you to control your feelings because some of the things that you have to deal with seem overwhelming to you."

Various instances of client isolation occur in counseling. The following examples suggest diverse possibilities:

- A middle school client is referred to the school counselor by his teacher. In class, the student has difficulty staying on task and frequently stares into space, rarely finishing his work. In discussion with the counselor, the client becomes animated when he talks about rockets but is relatively emotionless at other times.

- A client who has left her husband because he abuses her is living temporarily in a shelter for battered women. She talks to the counselor in a restrained tone about her spouse's abusive behavior.

- After a recovery of 2 months, a 40-year-old client who abuses alcohol speaks to a counselor in a detached manner, devoid of affect. The client's husband has threatened to leave her if she begins to drink again, and it is a matter of record that she was arrested earlier in the week for driving while intoxicated.

- An African American client speaks to a counselor in an emotionally sterile way about his adolescent son who was recently arrested for dealing drugs.

◆ After acknowledging being raped by her stepfather during preadolescence, a young adulthood client discusses the sexual assaults in a calm and affectively bland tone.

The counselor may consider employing reflection in response to each of these examples. The following illustrates the technique with the middle school student with a strong interest in rockets, who also happens to be teased by his classmates.

Client:	I'm really into rockets and space travels (excitedly looks off into space).
Counselor:	It sounds as if you're so interested in outer space and rocketry that sometimes you feel you can't get enough of it.
Client:	Yes, for sure. So it really doesn't bother me when the other kids laugh at me or push me around.
Counselor:	You are telling me that being picked on by the other kids doesn't get to you that much.
Client:	No, not really. Can we get back to talking about outer space (eager, pained expression on his face)?

Assessment. Evaluating isolation as a defense mechanism focuses on appraising client behavior, analyzing collateral sources, and using projective techniques. The behavior of clients may indicate inconsistencies relating to their use of isolation, and the following examples suggest employment of this particular defense in counseling:

1. *Statement:* It doesn't really bother me that the other kids try to make fun of me.
   Nonverbal expression: The middle school client often appears unfocused in class and on the playground, and he infrequently smiles or laughs.

2. *Statement:* It's not that bad; my husband usually just pushes and shoves me around. I think I can handle it.
   Previous statement: Perhaps I can't deal with being afraid anymore.

3. *Statement:* I guess it could be seen as a setback (deep sigh).
   Action: The 40-year-old client who abuses alcohol was recently arrested for driving under the influence.

4. *Statement:* Like other youth in his age range, my son has a propensity for reckless action, and for this he was apprehended.
   Objective condition: A relatively small minority of adolescents are arrested for dealing drugs.

5. *Statement:* I guess you could say that I must have been frightened by the assaults.
   Omission: A college-age woman discusses her experience of sexual assaults as a preadolescent only when the topic is raised by the counselor.

Collateral source information, such as teacher, parental, or employer observations, may also be available to the counselor when appraising a client's use of isolation. Inconsistencies between outside data and the client's behavior in counseling may suggest employment of the defense. Consider the example of the middle school student who demonstrates muted affect in counseling other than at times when he talks about rockets. In a report to the counselor, the client's teacher states that the student is emotionally withdrawn in the classroom during activities that normally excite and interest other students. The counselor should also be aware, however, when assessing bilingual clients, that those individuals speaking in their nondominant language may appear to be emotionally withdrawn, speak at a slower rate, and use longer pauses (Marcos, 1980). The cognitive demands of a person's expression in a less familiar language may result in the counselor's inaccurately identifying isolation as a client defense mechanism.

A counselor may also find that selected projective techniques assist in assessing clients' use of isolation. Early recollections contribute to understanding of individuals' lifestyles and may also clarify their employment of isolation as a defense. The core convictions of clients may intrinsically relate to constricted affect inherent in isolation. Consider the counseling example of a middle adulthood client who recalls an early memory of an incident that occurred when he was about 6 years old. The client remembers being on his hands and knees wiping up milk that he had spilled on the floor, while his father stood over him yelling that he had better clean up every drop and keep his mouth shut. He further states feeling scared and shameful in the memory. The central feature of the recollection involving prohibited expression of affect clearly relates to a dynamic quality of isolation. In this instance, the individual appears to maintain a core conviction that feelings must not be expressed to prevent even more dire consequences from occurring.

In addition to early recollections, human figure drawings and sentence completion tasks may also clarify a client's use of isolation. In drawing a picture of a person, an individual can take an excessively long time in completing the figure and provide intricate details. The obsessive-compulsive aspecwts of this behavior may have clinical significance (Chandler & Johnson, 1991) and possibly relate to isolation as a defense. Another possible indicator of isolation use occurs when a client draws an image of a person in pain or emotional duress and verbalizes no emotion in relation to the drawing (Levick, 1983). Sentence completion tasks may also suggest possible leads relating to an individual's use of isolation. A client's responses to sentence stems may be bland and colorless, indicating a minimal degree of affect expression. As an example, in completing the sentence "I feel . . . ," an individual writes "that there are a variety of possible emotions that people have everyday." In completing the sentence "I hate . . . ," a client comments, "I guess you could say I hate my sister." In yet another example, a client completes the sentence stem "What bothers me . . . " with "It is possible that one of my supercilious classmates will gain undue recognition." Individuals may also be emotionally noncommittal and leave sentence stems blank, such as "I feel . . . ," "My greatest worry . . . ," and "What pains me . . . ."

Self-Disclosure. Various dimensions of counselor self-disclosure potentially assist clients in gaining an awareness of their use of isolation. In this regard, a counselor's successes and failures pertinent to isolation may serve as instructive experiences for clients. As an example, a counselor shares her failure in being terminated from a job and how difficult it was for the counselor to express her feelings following the discharge. This experience parallels a situation relating to a client's loss of employment and his use of isolation as a defense mechanism. A counselor may also disclose past or present experiences involving isolation. In a counseling session, for instance, with an early adolescent who is teased by his peers, the counselor discloses that for a time he was ridiculed as a teenager and experienced great difficulty in expressing his feelings about the taunting. Experiences that are similar or dissimilar to those of clients may also provide purposeful discussion directions in counseling. A therapist, for example, discloses a long-existing pattern in his family whereby members rarely expressed their feelings. Sharing this common childhood background with a client who has a similar family history and who employs isolation as a defense advances communication and understanding in counseling. A counselor may also express self-involving statements relating to a client's behavior in counseling. A counselor, for instance, comments to a client who is abused by her spouse and who expresses a minimal degree of affect relating to the assaults, "I believe that you are in a lot of pain and that you find it really hard to talk about it."

Integration Stage

With a foundation of trust and understanding developed in the relationship stage, counseling emphasis now shifts to a more challenging posture. In the middle period of counseling, confrontation, cognitive restructuring, reframing, and interpretation are central interventions in fostering therapeutic change.

Confrontation. An individual employing isolation typically demonstrates discrepancies between what is appropriate or expected in emotional expression and what becomes manifest. The following examples illustrate client use of isolation through various statements and a counselor's challenge presented through confrontations.

1. *Statement—Nonverbal Expression*

   Client: It really doesn't bother me that the other kids try to make fun of me.

   Counselor: You want me to understand that it doesn't disturb you that much when the kids tease you, but you have an unhappy expression on your face when you say this.

2. *Statement—Previous Statement*

   Client: It's not that bad; my husband usually just pushes and shoves me around. I think I can handle it.

Counselor:	It is important for you to believe that your husband's treatment of you is tolerable, but when I first saw you a few weeks ago, you told me you couldn't handle being struck anymore.

3. *Statement—Action*

Counselor:	You say that you can control your drinking, but you were arrested on Monday for driving under the influence.
Client:	I guess it could be seen as a setback (deep sigh).

4. *Statement—Objective Condition*

Client:	Like other youth in his age range, my son has a propensity for reckless action, and for this he was apprehended.
Counselor:	You believe that your son is like a lot of other adolescents who get into trouble, but only a small percentage is involved with dealing drugs.

5. *Statement—Omission*

Client:	I guess you could say that I must have been frightened by the assaults.
Counselor:	It seems that you address the topic of your sexual assaults only when I bring up the subject.

Even when the counselor attempts to state a confrontation in a nonaccusatory and descriptive way, its effect on individual clients often varies. In the following counseling example, a client acquiesces to a counselor's confrontation by responding with a minimal degree of enthusiasm and emotional involvement.

Client:	Yes, I had a major heart attack 6 months ago, but that is past. I am fine now. These things happen.
Counselor:	You're glad it's over with and satisfied that it's all behind you now.
Client:	Life goes on, and it's nothing to worry about (looks fretful).
Counselor:	Although you are telling me that you are not worried, you seem to be having difficulty convincing yourself this is true.
Client:	I guess you may have a point.

Cognitive Restructuring. Isolation may relate to an individual's core convictions, and it may become necessary to address lifestyle perspectives to establish more adaptive levels of client functioning. The technique of cognitive restructuring focuses on altering maladaptive client schemas that possibly involve the employment of isolation. As a counseling example, a client who evinces a pattern of isolation perceives himself as emotionally vulnerable to torment in intimate relationships. As a consequence of this core assumption, the individual uses isolation as a defense to ensure that feelings are contained in threatening situations. Unless the counselor addresses this central assumption of the client, the likelihood of change at the intermediate level of the isolation defense becomes remote.

In the following counseling example, a counselor uses cognitive restructuring with an early adulthood client who was sexually abused by her stepfather as a preadolescent.

Client:	Well, I'm not sure what you want me to say. It just happened. I was 10 years old, and he moved out of my mother's house just after my 12th birthday.
Counselor:	Although it is not easy to express your feelings about the rapes, you are able to talk about some of the details. People probably tell you that you should express your feelings about it.
Client:	I've been told this over and over, and, in some ways, I'm rather sick of it.
Counselor:	Maybe you can begin to see yourself as a survivor and understand that the way you kept yourself going was to keep your feelings under very careful control.
Client:	(pause) What a relief to hear you say that!
Counselor:	I am sure you will express your feelings when you are ready, just as you are doing now.

Reframing. As a counseling technique, reframing expands client frames of reference by transforming personal meanings of experiences and perspectives in purposeful directions, including the use of isolation as a defense mechanism. In a counseling application of reframing, clients who employ isolation occasionally report experiencing feelings of anger or other strong emotions at times that are inappropriate for a specific context (Mahl, 1969), and reframing may be useful in altering individuals' perspectives of this interaction. In counseling, when clients describe this experience, they typically do so with hesitancy because they are concerned about its psychopathological implications. As an example, a client states that he occasionally experiences hostile feelings toward a friend and feels like punching him in the face. After acknowledging the client's bewildered feelings, the counselor reframes his perspective by suggesting an alternative view, "Perhaps your response is an indication that you have unexpressed pent-up feelings that have nothing to do with your friend."

In another counseling example, a middle adulthood African American client named Tyrone acts in compulsively productive ways with a minimal degree of affect expression.

Client:	I had a lot of catching up to do. As a minority, I was brought up to be goal oriented. Since my heart attack, I find functioning at my present slow pace frustrating and inhibiting.
Counselor:	You are accustomed to strict schedules and making things work with a fair degree of precision.
Client:	Yes. I don't know what to expect from myself any longer, and I can't get things done as I have for years.
Counselor:	This is frustrating for you, but I'm wondering if there may be a different way for you to look at things. Now that the pressure is off, you no longer need to feel you must perform at a certain rate or level. You believed that you had to work extra hard, but now you can slow down. It's as though you have caught up and no longer are required to run.

Interpretation. Related to reframing, interpretation provides new perspectives involving the meaning of clients' behavior, but the technique also focuses on motivational considerations. Through interpretations, individuals clarify causal linkages between their current and past functioning, including lifestyle implications and the use of isolation as a defense. With the cognitive emphasis of interpretation as a counseling technique, however, clients who use the defense of isolation may merely assume the validity of a counselor's interpretation rather than fully examine its impact for personal relevance (Schlesinger, 1994). As an example, a client responds to a counselor's interpretation with a simple "perhaps" or "possibly" without additional comment (Eissler, 1959). Attempts by the counselor to use interpretation when a client responds with a minimal degree of emotion will likely be counterproductive. In these instances, shifting to another counseling intervention, such as reflection or counselor self-disclosure, may be timely. In the continued example of the middle adulthood client with compulsively productive strivings, a counselor uses interpretation to clarify the function of Tyrone's lifestyle and related employment of isolation. In this instance, Tyrone reacts on an emotional and cognitive level to the counselor's interpretation.

Counselor:	You seem to push yourself quite a bit and keep your feelings to yourself.
Client:	I'm achievement oriented and perhaps what you call a "Type A" personality. And I'm not one to express myself emotionally that much. I'm accustomed to fast-paced deadlines.
Counselor:	This has been a pattern you have maintained for a long time.
Client:	Since I was a little kid, I have had to prove myself.
Counselor:	It seems that part of proving yourself was keeping your feelings to yourself.
Client:	My dad used to say to me, boys and men don't cry, and he would get angry with me if I did.
Counselor:	Could it be that it is difficult for you to express your emotions because you received messages in growing up not to give expression to your feelings?
Client:	It's possible (pause). I've thought about this myself lately. This was especially important in my family, because as African Americans, we had to deal with discrimination and not be viewed as weak.

Accomplishment Stage

Clarifying conflicts and contradictions relating to isolation prepares clients for the final stage of counseling. In the accomplishment stage, individuals focus on pursuing adaptive actions, including more purposeful control of isolation. Counseling interventions involve clients in action-oriented strategies designed to promote affective expression.

Catching Oneself. Although individuals may choose to control their patterned use of isolation, the mechanism has a strong reinforcing quality. "Catching oneself" provides a cue to a client to avoid using isolation at the moment the person is about to engage the defense. As an example in counseling, a client decides to wear a leather necklace with a smooth stone attached. As the person is about to trigger an isolating response, he rubs the stone to remind himself to express his feelings. In another counseling example, a client who has verbally committed herself to change still persists in assuming the role of a victim and employs isolation to mute her feelings.

Counselor:	Changing is important to you, but it can be difficult. I'm wondering if it would help if you had some way to remind yourself how far you've come and the changes you are continuing to make.
Client:	What do you have in mind?
Counselor:	Is there something, a picture or a news clipping, that might remind you to continue thinking about the way you are changing?
Client:	Well, I have a plastic card with Mother Teresa's picture on it that she actually signed. It also has a few inspiring words that are helpful.
Counselor:	Is this something you could carry with you, and when you find yourself holding in your feelings, look at her picture and the caption?
Client:	Yes, that's a good idea. It will remind me that things don't have to be the way they were and that I should stand up for myself.

Acting As If. As individuals gain increased control over limiting their affect constraint, they also may need assistance in understanding how persons appropriately express themselves in various situations. Clients may be emotionally constricted after a lengthy period of avoiding affect release, and identifying a person or a model who expresses feelings more spontaneously may be beneficial. In this regard, "acting as if" is a counseling strategy that focuses on emulating the constructive actions of other individuals. In the following counseling example, a middle school client who has experienced rejection and ridicule uses the procedure to clarify the actions of a student who is socially accepted.

Client:	As long as I remember, I have been ignored or made fun of.

Counselor:	You have been hurting for a long time.
Client:	I guess. I just want the kids to like me more.
Counselor:	Are there people in your class who have friends and act in ways that you would like to?
Client:	Yes. I can think of a few I like who have lots of friends and get good grades. They seem to know how to talk to other kids.
Counselor:	Maybe we could look at how they go about making friends and doing well in school.
Client:	Well, I'm not sure what they do that makes other kids like them.
Counselor:	Perhaps if you select one person as a model, we can talk about how he acts around other kids.

Breaking It Down. Individuals demonstrating a pattern of isolation may experience difficulty expressing feelings because the change required is perceived as excessively demanding. Clients who are involved with an intensive use of isolation may be receptive to strategies that make change more manageable. "Breaking it down" emphasizes segmenting tasks into small attainable steps, including attenuating isolation use. In a concluding counseling example, a middle school student seeks a means to avoid withdrawing emotionally to sustain adaptive change.

Client:	You know, I do want the kids to like me, and I want to do better in school, but I find myself slipping back into drawing rocket ships to avoid thinking about it. I sometimes feel like giving up.
Counselor:	It is not easy breaking out of a habit that has been so comforting for you.
Client:	It seems so hard to change all at once.
Counselor:	I'm wondering if you are trying to accomplish too much of it all at one time. What if you break it down and just think about changes you are making today?
Client:	What do you mean?
Counselor:	Well, you can focus on what you are trying to do today and don't think about any more than that.
Client:	Oh, I get what you are saying. I could change a little at a time—kind of like taking baby steps.

CONCLUSION

Isolation as a defense mechanism enables individuals to exclude intolerable conflicted feelings, and there is an integral relationship of the mechanism to obsessive-compulsive behavior. Intellectualization is a type of isolation that emphasizes abstract and precise verbalizations. Isolation for a person involves the severance of verbalized cognition from associated affect. Conceptualizing isolation change through the three stages of the counseling process assists the counselor in evaluating client progress from awareness to adaptation.

6

PROJECTION

Such as everyone is inwardly, so he judgeth outwardly.

—Thomas à Kempis, 1441/1864, p. 88

The capacity of an individual to accurately appraise the experiences of other people is an essential component of empathy and sound human relationships. The attribution of certain qualities to others as a result of one's own subjective functioning contributes to identifying and understanding mutual perspectives. At the same time, however, an individual's perceptions may be distorted to such an extent that judgments about others may lack accuracy. When using the defense mechanism of projection, a person's assumptions about the motivations of other people may proceed more from avoiding threat than attempting to communicate objectively. Conflicted behavior is essentially disowned and attributed to others, who are then viewed as responsible for creating difficulties or problems. Take the high school client, for example, who blames numerous students for harboring hostile and distrustful feelings when, in actuality, the primary source of the affect emanates from the client. In interactions with the students, the client is predisposed to encounter hostility and suspicion. Defining projection as a defense mechanism emphasizes attributing intolerable behavior to others that is characteristic of oneself.

THEORETICAL ASPECTS OF PROJECTION

Emergence of Projection

At the end of the 19th century, Sigmund Freud (1896/1962a) explained the function of projection as a defense, "In paranoia, the self-reproach is repressed in a manner which may be described as *projection*. It is repressed by erecting the defensive symptom of *distrust of other people*" (p. 184). Lack of trust is a central quality of projection as the motivations of others become suspect in various encounters. Freud recognized the disruptive effect that projection may create in normal interpersonal activity, such as jealousy in a marriage relationship, but he tended to focus on abnormal dimensions of the defense in his clinical writings. As an example, in the well-known Schreber case, Freud (1911/1958) discussed the role of projection in controlling homosexual wishes that reached delusionary levels of suspicion. In a succinct comment on projection, Freud (1920/1955b) clarified dynamic qualities of the construct in pathological processes:

> If a particular way is adopted of dealing with any internal excitations which produce too great an increase of unpleasure: there is a tendency to treat them as though they were acting not from the inside, but from the outside, so that it may be possible to bring the shield against stimuli into operation as a means of defense against them. (p. 29)

According to Anna Freud (1936/1966), when the concept of projection was first introduced, its pathological properties were emphasized as primary process activity relating to psychotic states. Freud also recognized the use of projection by young children when they attribute a range of unwanted fears and anxieties to external figures in the environment. In the instinctual life of psychotics and young children, Freud (1965) detailed projection interactions of possessiveness, extreme jealousy and competitiveness, and impulses to kill rivals and frustrating figures. Freud also focused on more normal functions of projection, but she designated this form with the term *altruistic surrender.* Through altruistic surrender, individuals attribute their instinctual impulses to another person and then vicariously identify with the person. As an example, a young adult experiences substantial anxiety involving the expression of intimate emotions and, in turn, attributes the feelings to his older brother. Subsequently, the individual demonstrates a great deal of concern about the romantic life of his brother, to the point of encouraging him to marry. Altruistic surrender relates to the concepts of attributive projection in which an undesirable trait of an individual is consciously projected onto a target person. A substantial amount of research supports the stress-reducing effect of this interaction (Sherwood, 1981).

Psychopathology and Projection

Age Adequateness. Anna Freud (1936/1966) found support for projection as a normal process for young children, but as persons advance in age, their use of the defense should progressively diminish. Prior to latency, children may periodically employ projection to place blame, fear, or hostility on other people rather than assume responsibility for conflicted feelings. A young child, for example, attributes fear and distrust that she experiences to strangers that she encounters on a fam- ily vacation. Although the child's parents are concerned about the girl's behavior, they recognize that children at 5 years of age may experience misplaced and unsubstantiated emotions. In a similar situation, however, when an adolescent consistently maintains suspicious and fearful responses on encountering strangers, the behavior may be age-inappropriate and involve the defense mechanism of projection. Projection is more characteristic during late childhood and early adolescence (Cramer, 1991). Relatedly, projection has been viewed as a prominent defense in acting-out behaviors with adolescents (Blos, 1979). As an individual advances in age beyond adolescence and develops a more stable and inte- grated identity, the use of projection may be less frequently employed. In another counseling example, a middle adulthood client repeatedly blames people at his place of employment for creating problems and difficulties for him. For a mature adult in chronology, the avoidance pattern of protestations and of blurring of boundaries between the client and his coworkers is inappropriate regarding age expectations.

Balance. Some persons employ a rigid and inflexible pattern of projection to stave off intolerable conflict (Murstein & Pryer, 1959). Rather than adapt to varying conditions, individuals engage projection in a stereotyped way with a minimal degree of versatility in responding to threat. Qualities of distrust and suspicion as noted by Freud in his initial depiction of projection are often inherent in client use of the defense (Magid, 1986). In a counseling example, a late adulthood client states that other residents in her community center constantly gossip about her and that she finds it impossible to trust any of them. The repetitive use of projection also involves disturbances on an interpersonal level. In the example cited, the residents resent being accused of talking behind the back of the client, and, as a consequence, arguments and disputes frequently result. A client may incite hostility, resentment, or other adverse reactions in other people and actually engender states that the individual accuses others of maintaining. The presence of projection is prominent in the clinical presentation of the characteristic symptoms of paranoid schizophrenia and in paranoid personality disorder, with the essential features of unwarranted suspiciousness and distrust of others (American Psychiatric Association, 1994a).

Intensity. Excessive use of projection may become apparent when persons repetitively employ the defense to reduce threat in interpersonal situations (Sherwood, 1981). When used at inordinate frequency levels, individuals almost invariably maintain an accusatory and fault-finding posture toward other people and rarely critically evaluate their role in instigating disruptive social interactions. Craig, for example, expresses hostility toward a relatively large number of high school classmates and teachers, who he states are "out to get me." Craig cites several recent incidents in which he believes that individuals in the school are gossiping about him. Although the counselor realizes that he may be accurate in his depiction of the interactions, the high frequency of the adverse exchanges and the lack of admitted culpability by Craig suggest the possibility of projection as a defense. The counselor may also evaluate the relationship of individuals' pattern of projection in the context of their lifestyles. In the present example, after completing assessment procedures, the counselor hypothesizes that Craig perceives himself as vulnerable and other people as malevolent. For Craig, the use of projection supports his core convictions as he assumes an aggressive defensive stance in anticipation of hostile responses from others.

Reversibility. As a response to threat, projection may be invoked by individuals until perceived dangers diminish. Some persons, however, tend to employ projection long after conditions that initially elicited the defense have changed or become nonexistent. Consider the counseling example of a middle adulthood client named Angel, who voices caustic and condemnatory statements relating to the actions of others. Through the assessment process, the counselor learns that Angel experienced a history of paternal reproach and contempt as a child. During this developmental period, she established a pattern of using projection to ward off intolerable conflicted affect. Although Angel has not been subjected to her father's psychologically injurious behavior for many years, she persists with her use of projection. In instances in which perceived diminution of threat in the environment is not assimilated, projection may become intrinsic to an individual's lifestyle. In the example cited, Angel perceives herself as loathsome, and this intolerable core conviction becomes evident in her use of projection in threatening interpersonal experiences.

Context. Social and cultural contexts influence individuals' use of projection and are essential considerations in appraising client employment of the defense. Evaluating diverse developmental histories and current conditions in the lives of clients assists in clarifying the etiology and function of projection. For example, an adult client's distrust and suspicion when encountering authority figures become more understandable when the counselor learns that the individual experienced parental abuse as a child. In another counseling case, a client currently lives in a violence-prone home located in a dangerous neighborhood. The person's guarded and fearful responses within and outside the local environment are more comprehensible given the real potential for harm. In both counseling examples, projection may be a response to perilous conditions that existed or exist in each person's social and cultural experience. By differentiating environmental variables, the counselor is able to clarify if a client's perceptions involve distortions at a particular time and place and result in the use of projection. In studies conducted with college students regarding gender, researchers found that projection as a defense mechanism was used more frequently by men in comparison with women (Cramer, 1991; Ihilevich & Gleser, 1995).

Another defense mechanism, projective identification, relates to projection and can emerge rapidly in diverse social contexts, including the counseling experience (Goldstein, 1991). Projective identification involves a three-phase sequence of attributing undesirable qualities to another individual (Ogden, 1982). First, a person or projector attributes shame, contempt, hostility, or other unwanted characteristics to another individual or recipient. Second, the projector provokes the qualities in the recipient through a manipulative and intense encounter. Third, the projector vicariously identifies with the recipient and persists with the provocations through a circular dynamic. In contrast with the defense mechanism of projection, whereby the projector almost always feels repelled by and estranged from the target of the projection, with projective identification, the projector feels profoundly drawn to and connected with the recipient. This active exchange also differs from the defense of identification, in which the idealized person is involved only passively in the process.

In counseling, the counselor may become entangled in collusive projective identification interaction that can undermine the therapeutic relationship. Unlike exchanges involving a client's use of projection that are foreign and unrepresentative of the counselor's experiencing, with projective identification, the counselor feels incited and induced to conform to the client's manipulations. Consequently, when a client persists with provocative behavior, the counselor should maintain an empathic response and avoid succumbing to an individual's contentious projections. Further processing of a client's employment of projective identification may involve a sequence like that of other defense mechanisms through a three-stage modification process in individual and group treatment (Clark, 1995c, 1997).

PROCESSING PROJECTION IN COUNSELING

Relationship Stage

Because clients using projection tend to be distrustful and suspicious of the motives of others, establishing a trust relationship in counseling typically presents a challenge for the counselor. Selected counseling techniques, including reflection, assessment methods, and counselor self-disclosure, assist in providing client support and understanding in the initial period of counseling.

Reflection. Intrinsic to an individual's use of projection are variations of emotional expression that can reach intense levels. To respond effectively to client affect such as suspicion, hostility, and repulsion, the counselor may employ reflection of feelings. Consider the example of a client in a college counseling center who vehemently insists that a large number of students continually provoke arguments and disputes with him. In response, the counselor states, "As I hear you describe the situation, it seems that for no good reason, a number of people apparently enjoy agitating you, and this makes you angry." Although the individual may provide only minimal documentation of the maliciousness of others, disputing the client's perspectives at this point may only incite further hostility and jeopardize the counseling relationship. In addition, when clients project strong feelings relating to the objectionable and antagonistic behavior of others, they typically reject efforts by the counselor to explore how they may be contributing to the occurrence of the disturbances. After their feelings have been acknowledged, however, individuals are often more receptive to an examination of the implied meanings relating to specific feelings and perceptions. In the present counseling example, the client continues, "I'm sick of people talking behind my back. They never ask me to do anything with them." In response, the counselor employs reflection of meaning, "It hurts to be a target of gossip, and because the talk doesn't seem to end, you are convinced they will never accept you."

Various instances of projection occur in counseling. Examples of diverse possibilities follow:

- A student with behavioral conflicts is referred to the school psychologist. The student emphatically blames other people for his difficulties, saying that they are out to get him.

- A woman is in counseling for personal and marital issues. She often belittles people and tells them how worthless they are.

- In a college counseling center, a client states that many of the students in his dormitory frequently provoke arguments with him. He expresses an urgent mix of anger and fear toward a relatively large number of students who reside in a facility known for its openness toward diverse views and beliefs.

- A man tells a counselor that his coworkers are trying to undermine his success at the office by frequently talking about him and reporting his mistakes to his supervisor.

- Soon after moving into a community residence center, a late adulthood client meets with a counselor and complains about other residents in the facility. The client insists that other persons are constantly talking about her and trying to make her life miserable.

The counselor may consider using reflection as a response to each of these examples to enhance communication. The following illustrates a counselor's use of reflection with a client who experiences persecutory feelings in response to interactions with other employees at his work site.

Client:	Whenever I turn my back at work, they start in on me. No matter what I do right, they still try to tear me apart.
Counselor:	So they're never pleased with you and can't wait to talk about things you do wrong.
Client:	That's right. How can I feel good about what I do there, if everyone is always cutting me down? I sit there feeling like the center of attention, with everyone watching me.
Counselor:	You feel uncomfortable and insecure because some people at work talk about you so often. It's as though you don't measure up.
Client:	That's true. It's as if I can't make even a minor mistake without them making a big deal out of it.

Assessment. Evaluating multiple sources enables the counselor to more accurately appraise a client's use of projection. Synthesizing information derived from observations of client behavior, collateral sources, and projective techniques provides a more comprehensive view of an individual's functioning. As represented by the following examples, a client's behavior in counseling may reveal inconsistencies and omissions that suggest possible employment of projection.

1. *Statement:* I don't get angry until someone starts in on me. I wish they'd all get off my back.
   Nonverbal expression: The client's fists are clenched in a tight grip.

2. *Statement:* My husband is so worthless; I can't believe I ended up with someone like him.
   Previous statement: Last week I was sick, and my husband was a big help with the house and kids.

3. *Statement:* I can't stand it. I'm constantly belittled for no reason at all on my part.
   Action: According to the client's dormitory director, he constantly provokes arguments with other students.

4. *Statement:* I know people at work have been talking about me to my boss. They all talk about me over there.
   Objective condition: The client's supervisor provides a report stating that individuals at work have actually been fairly supportive of the person.

5. *Statement:* For no reason, the residents in the center give me a hard time and start in on me.
   Omission: The counselor has access to information indicating that the client started two arguments the previous day in her community residential facility.

Collateral sources, such as information available from oral or written reports, may provide data relating to a client's use of projection. Collateral material may be inconsistent with an individual's behavior and suggest engagement of the defense. A late adulthood client, for example, contends that other residents in her residential facility continually provoke arguments with her. The counselor, however, has access to documentation indicating that the client recently started several arguments with individuals in the center. In the case of a late adulthood client who exhibits distrust, suspicion, and related behaviors inherent in the defense of projection, a counselor should also consider the possibility of neurological disorders.

Selected projective techniques may also contribute to the assessment of client projection. Early recollections provide perspectives on individuals' core convictions that may relate to their employment of projection. Joe, for instance, a young adulthood client, discloses the following early memory:

> When I was in the first grade, I was standing in line in the school nurse's office for a physical examination. The nurse asked us to take off our shoes, and when I did, one of the kids noticed that I had holes in my stockings. The other children and the nurse laughed at me, and I felt so humiliated that I covered my face.

An assumption derived from this memory is that Joe perceives himself as inferior and other people as malevolent and capricious. When he interacts with others, Joe anticipates that they will embarrass and hurt him. To stave off this conflicted affect, he frequently reacts in hostile or retaliatory ways in various encounters with others. In this example, Joe's use of pro- jection provides a protective measure against a threatening environ- ment, and the defense becomes assimilated into his lifestyle. From a perspective of transactional analysis, Joe's script decision is main- tained by his employment of projection (Chang & James, 1987).

As clients complete the early recollections procedure, in addition to human figure drawings and the sentence completion tasks, it is essential for the counselor to observe individuals' behavior. Client interactions with the counselor may suggest the use of projection through such behaviors as speaking and acting in suspicious or contemptuous ways and insisting that the counselor is distrustful or worthy of rebuke. Such behavior may indicate that clients attribute negative feelings to the counselor that, in actuality, are not representative of the counselor's subjective functioning. Individuals' drawing of a person may also be suggestive of their feelings that become manifest in perceived attributions of other people. As an example, feelings of inadequacy of a client may be represented by a diminutive human figure drawing (Oster & Gould, 1987). In turn, a client may attribute these same feelings to the counselor or to others. The counselor may also make inferences relating to clients' use of projection through the sentence completion tasks. In the following sentence completion examples, a counselor hypothesizes that an individual projects various feelings onto others: "Other people . . . are worthless." "What bothers me . . . is that I can't trust anyone." "I am afraid of . . . the way people look at me." In other instances, clients may specifically identify individuals through sentence completions, and their untenable responses may indicate the employment of projection. For example, a client completes the following sentence stems: "I feel . . . every teacher in this school hates me." What pains me . . . is that everyone at work talks about me all the time." "At home . . . my parents and my sisters are all out to get me."

Self-Disclosure. Discussion of a counselor's success or failure experiences relating to projection may demonstrate a degree of understanding of a client's employment of the defense. For example, a high school student contends that many students continually provoke arguments with him and talk behind his back. After acknowledging the client's feelings of hostility and isolation, the counselor discusses a period in her adolescence when she was a target of gossip. Although it seemed to the counselor at the time that almost all the students in her school were talking about her, it was only when she was able to more objectively appraise her situation that she realized that perhaps only three or four persons actually participated in the gossip. Recounting past and present experiences by the counselor may also provide support to a client who is demonstrating a pattern of projection. A client, for instance, expresses resentful feelings toward coworkers who attempt to undermine her success. The counselor, in response, details a period in his life when he felt that "everyone was against me" and how difficult it was for him to begin to believe that anybody actually cared about him.

It is also possible for a counselor to disclose similar and dissimilar experiences with a client employing projection. Consider the example of the counselor working with a late adulthood client who insists that a number of other residents in her community living center dislike her for "no good reason." The counselor responds by discussing an experience in her life when she joined a social club and felt ignored by most of the members. After attending several meetings without any apparent change in the attitude of other members, the counselor was prepared to drop out of the organization. Unexpectedly, she was approached by a person who befriended her. This individual sometime later told the counselor that she initially appeared "aloof and difficult to get to know." Observations relating to a client's use of projection in counseling may also be expressed through self-involving statements. For instance, when a client accuses a counselor of acting in hostile and distrustful ways, the counselor may say something such as, "I feel disappointed that you find it difficult to trust me and see me as working against you, particularly when I feel that I have been consistently supportive."

Integration Stage

Although a counselor may emphasize developing client trust and understanding in the initial stage of counseling, an individual employing projection may continue to question the relationship quality of a counselor's interactions. In the middle or integration period of counseling, a counselor may use selected counseling techniques, including confrontation, cognitive restructuring, reframing, and interpretation, that focus on scrutinizing a client's behavior in a supportive context.

Confrontation. As generally construed, clients' use of projection involves a contradictory interaction of attributing behavior to others through an exchange that does not actually represent their immediate experiencing. The counselor may confront clients as projection becomes apparent through inconsistencies that surface when individuals' statements are measured against nonverbal expressions, previous statements, actions, objective conditions, and omissions. The following counseling examples present instances of client employment of projection and confrontations by the counselor.

1. *Statement—Nonverbal Expression*
   Client: I don't get angry until someone starts in on me. I wish they'd all get off my back.

Counselor: You are saying that other people trigger your anger, yet your fists are tightly clenched right now, although no one has been bothering you.

2. Statement—Previous Statement

Client: My husband is so worthless; I can't believe I ended up with someone like him.

Counselor: You feel strongly about this now, and yet you also told me what a good job he did taking care of the house and the kids while you were sick recently.

3. Statement—Action

Client: I can't stand it. I'm constantly belittled for no reason at all on my part.

Counselor: You feel that other students ridicule you for no apparent cause, but your resident director reports that you seem to provoke arguments with a number of people in your dormitory.

4. Statement—Objective Condition

Client: I know people at work have been talking about me to my boss. They all talk about me over there.

Counselor: You believe that your coworkers are trying to undermine your work, yet your supervisor says that the other employees have been fairly tolerant of your behavior.

5. Statement—Omission

Client: For no reason, the residents in the center give me a hard time and start in on me.

Counselor: You're saying that it doesn't make sense for people to criticize you when you haven't done anything wrong, but I have a resident's report stating that you started four arguments last week.

Although the counselor should express a confrontation in a descriptive and nonjudgmental way, a client employing projection may react to the intervention with varying degrees of acceptance. In the following counseling example, an employee assistance counselor confronts a client about an allegation the individual makes and a lack of substantiation of the assertion. In this instance, the client rejects the counselor's initial confrontation.

Client:	Here I am talking to you about all this, when I don't feel I can trust you any more than anyone at work.
Counselor:	It seems that you see me in the same way as you describe people at your office, out to get you as soon as you turn your back.
Client:	If I ever let my guard down, I'd really get it from all of them, and probably from you, too.
Counselor:	You are saying that you have problems in trusting me and that I'm out to get you, but you haven't talked about what I have done to make you feel this way.
Client:	I can tell how you feel about me. I can see it in your eyes when you look at me.

Cognitive Restructuring. An individual's patterned use of projection may relate to core convictions that the person maintains about life. In a counseling example, a client maintains a lifestyle assumption that people are malevolent and untrustworthy, and this belief becomes manifest in her employment of projection. Unless this schema is modified, however, the potential for the development of more adaptive interpersonal behavior may be limited. Cognitive restructuring involves transforming faulty and self-defeating beliefs that may also include projection use by a client. In a counseling example, a college sophomore's engagement of projection is evident in disturbed relationships with other students in his dormitory. To broaden the perspective of the client, the counselor makes reference to the cultural tendency among men to behave aggressively to establish and gain their own ends (Levant, 1995).

Client:	As I told you before, people are always starting things with me, and I make sure that I get to them first.
Counselor:	So, since you've decided that you can't expect a fair deal from anyone, you make sure you go after people before they get to you.
Client:	Well, they just want to get on my back for no reason.
Counselor:	I'm going to say something that is a different way of looking at your situation. For a male in our society, your aggressive behavior is not unique.

Client:	What are you saying?
Counselor:	The point that I'm trying to make is that anger is one of the few feelings that boys and men are sanctioned to express on a social level.
Client:	It almost sounds as if you are trying to make an excuse for my behavior.
Counselor:	What I'm saying is that how you act is affected by broader forces in culture.
Client:	I'd rather make decisions for myself about how I feel.
Counselor:	In that case, does it make sense to you to begin to look at people in more discriminating and possibly more tolerant ways?

Reframing. Reframing is another counseling technique that enables clients to broaden their frames of reference in more constructive directions. Through a semantic change, individuals gain a new perspective relating to their use of projection. Consider, for example, a client who repeatedly belittles her husband for his perceived lack of confidence. Using reframing, a counselor suggests to the client that her actions may be understood as a capacity to empathize with persons who possibly feel less capable than others. Conceptualizing the client's attribution functioning as an aspect of empathy may engender a more purposeful perspective as to how she perceives her own behavior and also that of others. In another reframing example, a counselor provides an alternative perspective to a college sophomore client relating to his projected anger. The counselor alludes to the gender role strain paradigm (Pleck, 1995), suggesting that traditional gender roles have negative cultural consequences, particularly for men.

Client:	We have talked about how I seem to get angry in my dealings with a lot of people. I just kind of act this way, and trying to open myself up to more sensitive feelings is hard.
Counselor:	It seems difficult for you to express yourself in ways that perhaps you see as vulnerable or even weak.
Client:	I'm just used to acting in a certain way.
Counselor:	I'm wondering, though, if it is possible that how you act is even more difficult for you in pressure and strain.
Client:	What do you mean?

Counselor:	Well, if you restrict your behavior to a limited way of expressing yourself, this creates tension because you can never reveal your more vulnerable or even caring side.
Client:	I think I see where you are coming from, but . . .

Interpretation. As a counseling technique, interpretation entails change in the meaning of client perspectives but also involves motivational and causal considerations. Regarding projection, the counselor tentatively presents an interpretation to explain why clients attribute various feelings and perceptions to others that actually represent aspects of the individuals' own functioning. In the following counseling example, the counselor associates a client's pattern of projection with his persecutory feelings and developmental history.

Client:	I don't care if no one believes me because people don't like me regardless what I do.
Counselor:	From everything you've said, you think people are against you, and you never get a break.
Client:	Well, it's been this way a long time.
Counselor:	We've talked about your older brother and how your parents seemed to give him anything he wanted while you got whatever was left over. You said that you felt so alone. Is it possible for you to see a connection between that and the way you feel about people at work?
Client:	It was bad when I was growing up because I always got a raw deal in comparison with my brother. In some ways, it is the same at work.
Counselor:	Could it be that you've come to expect people to be against you? You have become so used to it in your family experiences that maybe you've stopped expecting anything different from people, and, as a result, you strike out at them before they have a chance to hurt you.

Accomplishment Stage

After clients clarify the dynamics of their projection use, counseling emphasis begins to focus on regulating the employment of the defense. Action-oriented interventions emphasize reducing habitual patterns of projection and establishing more purposeful behavior in the final stage of counseling.

Catching Oneself. As a counseling strategy, "catching oneself" enables individuals to control their employment of projection at that critical point when they are about to trigger the mechanism. Through a cued reminder, clients alert themselves to avoid using projection in various social contexts. Take, for instance, the late adulthood individual who is attempting to regulate her habitual use of the defense in a community residence center. Through discussion with the counselor, the client decides to employ as a signaling device an Italian phrase that she learned as a young girl but had not used for many years. Whenever she is about to act on the unwarranted assumptions about the malevolence of others, the client repeats to herself, *"No dice niente."* This phrase, "Don't say anything," and an accompanying pause allow the client to interact with others relatively free of presumptions about their hurtful intentions. In another counseling example, a client, realizing that she projects her undesirable feelings onto her husband, identifies a tangible cue to alert herself when she is about to use projection as a defense.

Client:	I really do care about my husband, and I know that I criticize him sometimes when I feel bad about myself. When I feel that way, I find it hard not to start in on him.
Counselor:	Maybe we could devise a way to stop yourself from attacking him when you are upset with yourself.
Client:	It's a habit, and I have been doing it ever since we were married, so I'm not sure.
Counselor:	It is, but what if you try to catch yourself when you start in on him? You would need to come up with an action or a thought that would remind you how you really feel about him, and this would stop you before you go too far. Do you have any ideas of something that might work here?
Client:	Well, maybe I could use my wedding ring to remind me. When I feel an urge to start in on him, I could touch my wedding band and remember what a good husband I have even if he's not always perfect.

Acting As If. Because some persons have used projection for extended periods, they may be unpracticed in alternative and more purposeful behaviors. The employment of "acting as if" enables clients to assume constructive roles in interpersonal exchanges that contrast with conflict-prone actions inherent in projection use. In the following example, a client wishes to change his lengthy pattern of projection that has been manifested in hostile and suspicious behavior at his place of employment.

Client: I'm starting to see that my own feelings of vulnerability have affected my judgment of everyone else. I'd really like to try to make my work situation better, but I'm afraid that I've turned everyone off. No one wants to be around me any more than they have to.

Counselor: So you'd really like to be accepted on the job, but at this point, other people aren't too eager to give you another chance.

Client: No. And I've given everyone such a hard time for so long, I'm not sure if I'd know how to act anyway.

Counselor: Are you able to identify coworkers whom everyone seems to like? There must be certain qualities about them that attract people.

Client: There are. I can think of a couple of popular people who are really a lot alike in how they act at work.

Counselor: Maybe you could look at things that they do, and you could try to model their behavior.

Client: You mean pretend that I'm like them?

Counselor: At first, it may seem as if you are "pretending," but if you act in ways similar to the type of person that other people like, maybe more people will give you a chance. Once they begin to feel more comfortable around you, you can do even more to improve the situation.

Breaking It Down. For some individuals, the prospect of attempting to control their habitual use of projection seems prohibitive because of the perceived difficulty required in effecting change. "Breaking it down" emphasizes modifying client employment of projection through small and incremental efforts. It is sometimes helpful for the counselor to use a metaphor to relate the technique to clients' personal life. A client with an interest in sports, for instance, may be interested in learning how some exceptional track athletes plan to run a 4-minute mile. To make the imposing feat less daunting, they segment the allotted time for the race into 240 seconds, rather than 4 minutes. In the following example with a middle school student, although the counselor does not use a metaphor, the focus remains on controlling projection use through manageable steps.

Client:	I'd like to make some friends. I hate not having anyone to talk to, but I just get so upset when I think that someone is going to start to criticize me.
Counselor:	It still takes a lot of effort to control yourself, and you are making a real attempt to hold yourself back.
Client:	When I think about always having to be nice to all of them, I don't think there's any way I can keep it up.
Counselor:	It is quite a big change. Maybe you could try it a little bit at a time.
Client:	What do you mean?
Counselor:	Well, what small, "bite-sized" steps could you handle now?
Client:	Maybe I can get through a few of my classes without losing my cool.
Counselor:	Perhaps you can start with four periods, and let me know how it's going.

CONCLUSION

Projection is a means that individuals use to avoid threat and subsequent self-reproach in interpersonal experiences, and distrust and suspicion are inherent qualities of the construct. Client use of the defense, which includes accusatory and fault-finding actions, almost invariably leads to disturbed interpersonal relationships. The employment of projection involves individuals attributing intolerable behavior to others that is actually characteristic of themselves. Conceptualizing projection change through the three stages of the counseling process provides a framework for therapeutic modification of the mechanism.

7

RATIONALIZATION

And oftentimes excusing of a fault
Doth make the fault the worse by the excuse.

—William Shakespeare, 1623/1990,
King John, act IV, scene ii, lines 30-31[1]

Making excuses for shortcomings and providing justification for one's particular faults are common human tendencies. People frequently attempt to protect their self-images by offering socially acceptable reasons for what may be considered objectionable or inappropriate actions. A guest, for example, on arriving late at a relative's celebration of the purchase of a new home, immediately begins to detail the extent of heavy traffic en route or the difficulty in locating the house. Attempting to save face under such circumstances is understandable, even when it is obvious to others that the person's explanations are false and unnecessary. In such instances, although individuals are quite aware that they are being deceptive, they will attempt to offer explanations that are reasonably plausible and perhaps difficult to refute. Rationalization is related to excuse making but with the essential difference that persons largely lack awareness that they are employing the defense. Further, clients using rationalization generally provide restricted explanations to justify their actions and resist efforts to explore their intentions and motives beyond those stated. In a counseling example, a high school client insists that her unsatisfactory grades in several subjects are due to inadequate teachers and irrelevant learning material and, even with prompting, refuses to examine her academic motivation and effort. Defining rationalization as a defense mechanism emphasizes justifying objectionable behavior through the use of plausible statements.

THEORETICAL ASPECTS OF RATIONALIZATION

Emergence of Rationalization

At the first psychoanalytic congress in Salzburg, Austria, Ernest Jones (1908) delivered a paper, "Rationalisation in Every-Day Life." Since Jones's introduction of what is now called *rationalization,* the term has gained wide acceptance both in therapeutic circles and in general use. Jones conceptualized rationalization as a means by which individuals justify their unacceptable behavior through the use of false explanations that have a "plausible ring of rationality" (p. 166). For rationalization to be effective, Jones believed that persons had to provide a connected, logical, and continuous account of their behavior. Individuals also had to lack awareness of the function of rationalization because of its self-serving nature and manipulative qualities. Additional dynamic aspects of rationalization involve the adamant refusal to question or analyze motivations of the defense beyond those stated. More often, individuals employing rationalization reiterate explanations that were originally tendered "for public consumption" (p. 166).

Although Sigmund Freud (1929/1961a) made only minimal reference to rationalization in his writings, he referred to the construct in relationship to psychoanalysis as an "important concept and an indispensable term" (p. 249). It is uncertain if Freud regarded rationalization as a defense mechanism, and a determination of this question depends on how his several scattered applications of the concept may be interpreted (Audi, 1988). In one of his works, for example, Freud (1909/1955e) clarified how obsessive-compulsive patients account for their consciously misunderstood behavior by rationalizing a secondary set of motives. Anna Freud (1936/1966) did not list rationalization among the defenses that she enumerated in *The Ego and the Mechanisms of Defense* and made only passing mention of the construct in this volume and in later writings. She related, for example, that rationalization played a role in transference by enabling patients to block awareness of objective discrepancies between cause and effect that are clearly apparent to an observer.

Psychopathology and Rationalization

Age Adequateness. As a defense component, a person's relative age may be used to justify either avoiding or pursuing certain behaviors. A child, for example, may avoid tasks by citing, "I'm only a kid." A late adulthood client may say, "You can't teach an old dog new tricks." In other instance, clients may support the initiation or continuation of particular actions, and the counselor's assessment of the developmental stage of individuals assists in clarifying the age appropriateness of rationalization. In the following counseling examples, clients at various stages of the life span employ rationalization to justify their misuse of alcohol.

Childhood:	Having a few beers isn't going to get me hooked on booze.
Adolescence:	Everyone that I know drinks. It's no big deal.
Early adulthood:	You've got to drink for a lot of years before there are any real health risks.
Middle adulthood:	I should have quit drinking years ago. It's too hard to stop at this stage of the game.
Late adulthood:	At this point, what difference does it make if I stop drinking? My liver is all shot anyway.

Balance. Some individuals employ rationalization as a predominant behavioral pattern and rigorously resist examining alternative motivations beyond those expressed in conjunction with the defense (Clark, 1995e). Threat involving intolerable conflicted affect is controlled through a reiteration of rationalization statements that set an end-of-discussion tone. In a counseling example, a client who abuses alcohol is not able to tolerate accusations that her excessive drinking is destroying her family and career. To reduce conflict incurred by her drinking behavior, the client relies on an entrenched and stereotyped use of rationalization. Variations commonly occur in relationship to rationalization explanations used by individuals, but essential themes tend to persist. Subsequent statements offering specific examples of rationalization as expressed by the client who is alcohol dependent include, "Who wouldn't drink with the problems I have?" "There are a lot of things worse in the world than having a few." "It helps me deal with the pressures in my life."

Intensity. Rationalization can be used by individuals at frequency levels that can escalate to excessive rates (Audi, 1988). Instead of acknowledging and evaluating a broader range of motivations, persons rely on less threatening explanations in support of their behavior. As suggested by Jones (1908), a common illusion of individuals is that by stating and restating evidence, eventually certain positions will be accepted as true. In counseling, clients frequently express constricted statements that justify their behavior and persist in repeating these fallacies. For example, a client in ninth grade states that school is a waste of time and that he plans to drop out within the year. In further support of this decision, the student offers the following justifications: "Plenty of people are successful without a high school diploma." "Most of the stuff you learn in school has nothing to do with real life." "I learn more outside school than I do in it." Although each of these statements has some degree of plausibility, the statements may also mask schemas at more complex and threatening levels. It is possible, for instance, in the example cited, that the student believes that he is intellectually inadequate and that academic demands are beyond his capabilities.

Reversibility. For some individuals, patterns of rationalization are employed long after the conditions that initially contributed to adopting the defense have changed. Persons may continue to rely on justifying their behavior, even when perceived threat becomes significantly diminished or nonexistent. Henry, for example, is a late adulthood client who initiated rationalization use as a child in response to highly demanding parents. Finding it extremely difficult to meet parental expectations, Henry began to express various reasons to justify his perceived deficiencies: "My teacher never really explains how to do things." "My leg hurts when I try to run." "The kids in my class fool around so much that I can't concentrate." As a child, Henry found that such avoidance statements were at least partially effective in justifying his less-than-superior accomplishments. In relation to Allport's (1961) concept of functional autonomy, it may be that Henry unconsciously recognized that rationalization was effective even beyond meeting parental demands in various situations throughout his life span. For example, at age 60, Henry is asked by a relative to attend a course with her at a local community college. In response, Henry states that he prefers not to sign up because "the instructor probably favors younger students" and "I have so many things on my mind that I couldn't possibly concentrate on taking a course."

Context. Social and cultural contexts affect an individual's use of rationalization and are primary factors in the development of defense patterns. The counselor is in a position to differentially evaluate a client's employment of rationalization in contrast to stating influential facts, as in the following two counseling examples. In the first instance, an adolescent acknowledges that he gets in frequent fights and arguments and attributes his aggressive behavior primarily to growing up in a home in which hostility was common. The counselor is aware of the violence-prone history of the client's family life. In another example, a Hispanic American adolescent also finds himself involved in numerous fights and arguments but attributes his aggressive tendencies primarily to his Latino heritage. In this instance, the counselor considers the existence of stereotyped perceptions of Hispanics as emotional and quick-tempered. In both cases, the counselor must evaluate past as well as current cultural forces that could affect either client in his use of rationalization. A client's employment of rationalization may also be directed at the counselor to discount or discredit the effectiveness of counseling. Consider, for example, the following client statements expressed to the counselor: "I know you are working hard for me, but my sessions with you just don't seem to be making that much difference." "Things are so complicated in my life, and I'm not sure if you are in the best position to help me." "You are a very nice person, but I think I need something more."

PROCESSING RATIONALIZATION
IN COUNSELING

Relationship Stage

In the initial stage of counseling, clients employing rationalization typically present somewhat credible and convincing justification for their unacceptable behavior. The counseling techniques of reflection, assessment methods, and counselor self-disclosure clarify client response to threat while establishing more open communication.

Reflection. Although individuals employing rationalization express delusive beliefs, initially a counselor may supportively acknowledge their experiencing through the use of reflection. In a counseling example, a college freshman named Anita, who exhibits diagnostic signs of anorexia nervosa, discusses her recent weight loss: "I work at keeping in shape, and I do look a little better." In response, the counselor employs reflection of feelings: "You feel relief when you find you are getting your weight down." Although at this point, the therapist could challenge her significant weight loss, in doing so Anita may insist further that her behavior is sensible or become irritated that the counselor questions her actions. After acknowledging Anita's feelings, the counselor is in a position to explore more implicit communication levels. Subsequently, after Anita reiterates her need to control her weight, the counselor uses reflection of meaning, "It's important for you to believe that you can make choices about your own life."

Numerous instances of rationalization occur in counseling. Diverse examples of client employment of the defense are listed below:

◆ The parent of an acting-out adolescent says that she doesn't even bother trying to discipline her son because he never listens to her anyway.

- A client on heart medication states that the treatment makes him drowsy, so he usually skips taking his pills.

- An adolescent who frequently gets in fights claims that as a Hispanic American, he is emotional and cannot stop himself once he loses his temper.

- A late adulthood client insists that she is too old to make changes and adjustments, concluding, "You can't teach an old dog new tricks."

- An unemployed client does not attempt to look for work, stating that the job market is so bad that she would never find anything.

In response to each of these statements, the counselor may consider using reflection to clarify client feelings and perceptions. In the following example, a middle school student uses multiple rationalization statements to justify his unsatisfactory progress in a history class.

Counselor:	You are telling me that history is just stuff from the past and not worth learning about.
Client:	Yeah, who cares what happened centuries ago? It's got nothing to do with what is going on today. I also get sick of Mrs. Jones being on my back all the time.
Counselor:	There are other things bothering you about the class.
Client:	Yeah, it's not fair the way she singles me out the way she does.
Counselor:	You don't see any reason for her to pay close attention to you, although your grades have dropped quite a bit.
Client:	(with resentment in his voice) Well, if she'd take the time to explain to me what she wants with the work in the first place, I would get more done.
Counselor:	It sounds as if you're having difficulty understanding what Mrs. Jones expects when she gives you an assignment.
Client:	Yeah (with some relief). I'm not always sure what she wants, so why bother wasting my time doing it all wrong?

Assessment. Without evaluating multiple sources relating to clients' use of rationalization, it would be difficult for a counselor to assess the accuracy of their assertions. Appraising client behavior, collateral sources, and projective material enables the counselor to consider defense engagement from different perspectives. In the following counseling examples, inconsistencies in client behavior suggest possible employment of rationalization:

1. *Statement:* I've been so busy with my job that I can't spend any more time dealing with all the messes my son gets into. Besides, nothing I do seems to help.
   Nonverbal expression: Perplexed and apprehensive.

2. *Statement:* My heart medication makes me feel so tired. I feel better when I'm not taking it.
   Previous statement: I do worry about having another heart attack.

3. *Statement:* I just can't help getting into fights. I guess it's my hot temper because of my Latino heritage.
   Action: Client provokes fights with peers without demonstrating feelings of anger.

4. *Statement:* I'm just too old to learn and change my ways.
   Objective condition: Most late adulthood individuals continue to develop and adapt.

5. *Statement:* I just can't seem to find suitable work. The job market is bad.
   Omission: The employment service informs the counselor that the client turned down two job interviews during the week.

   Teacher or employer observations are among a number of collateral sources that assist the counselor in corroborating an individual's use of rationalization. Data from third parties, although subject to inaccuracies, may be inconsistent with a client's behavior. A middle school teacher, for example, reports that a student appears to daydream in class and infrequently completes his homework. In counseling, the client states that the teacher and the subject are "boring." The counselor infers a question with clear rationalization implications: Would the student be bored in class if he paid attention and did his homework?
   Selected projective techniques, including human figure drawings, early recollections, and sentence completion tasks, contribute to assess-

ing client rationalization. The expressed statements of clients when completing human figure drawings in a cursory way may suggest rationalization use. An individual, for instance, states, "I'm too tired to draw, so I'll just do a stick figure," or "This is a waste of time, so I'll just draw it quickly." Early recollections provide perspectives on individuals' core convictions that may relate to their use of rationalization. In a counseling example, a late adolescent client who exhibits signs of anorexia nervosa reports the following three early memories: "When I was in the first grade, the teacher asked me to stand up to answer a question. I didn't know what to say, and I felt very embarrassed." "My mother told me that my grandfather died, and I cried." "I was playing a game with my older brother, and he laughed as he was beating me." The early memories provisionally indicate that the client perceives herself as vulnerable and helpless in a hurtful world. Through the employment of rationalization ("I work at keeping in shape, and I do look a little better"), the client provides herself a measure of control in what is perceived as a punishing environment.

Responses on the sentence completion tasks that explain or justify an individual's ostensible behavior may also suggest the employment of rationalization. The counselor may infer possible rationalization use from particular responses or from clusters of item reactions to sentence stems. Examples of individual sentence completions include the following: "My mother . . . keeps me from accomplishing anything." "I failed . . . at my marriage because of my fool husband." "The future . . . looks bleak because I never get a break in life." Various themes may also be identified through clusters of sentence completion responses. In the following examples, a high school client completes several sentences that suggest rationalization use relating to academic functioning: "I failed . . . three of my classes because the teachers didn't explain things." "School . . . is for losers, and I'm going to drop out." "Whenever I have to study, I . . . can't concentrate because I don't have a quiet place to study."

Self-Disclosure. Recounting instances of a counselor's success or failure experiences involving rationalization may prompt clients to become aware of their defensive functioning. In the following example, a 30-year-old counselor is working with a late adulthood client who states, "You can't teach an old dog new tricks." In response, the counselor acknowledges that it is not always easy to make accommodations with advancing age, and she recounts a period when she found herself using her age to justify avoiding change. Several years ago, the counselor relates that she accrued a high amount of charges on her credit cards while telling herself, "You're only young once." Past or present accounts of a counselor's use of rationalization may also demonstrate a level of client understanding. Take, for example, the case of a client who employs rationalization in avoiding taking prescription medication for his recent heart attack. "I find that the pills make me sleepy, so I skip taking them." The counselor hypothesizes that the client's noncompliance possibly relates to avoiding the acknowledgment of physical limitations. Accordingly, the counselor describes a recent occurrence in her life when, because of inflamed knees, she received medical advice to reduce her daily routine of 2-mile runs. Believing that her exercise was essential for conditioning, however, the counselor almost immediately resumed her running program. After a recurrence of physical problems, the counselor returned for medical treatment, and the physician stated that unless she reduced her daily running, future knee surgery would likely be necessary.

Similar or dissimilar patterns of client rationalization use may also be shared through counselor self-disclosure. Consider, for instance, the high school student who states that her chemistry class is a "waste of time, so I don't bother working in there." In response to this statement, which possibly conceals client feelings of inadequacy in the subject, the counselor discloses having had a somewhat similar experience in high school. In his biology class, after having been embarrassed by the teacher in front of other students, the counselor stopped doing his work in the subject for a lengthy time. Although he stated to his friends that the class was boring, his actual reason for not performing was his anger toward the teacher. A counselor may also use self-involving statements to disclose personal observations of a client's rationalization use in counseling. A therapist comment that may generally be useful is, "You seem to be working hard to convince me that the reasons for your behavior do not go beyond what you have told me."

Integration Stage

To challenge an individual to broaden perspectives relating to rationalization use, the counselor may employ selected interventions in the middle period of counseling. Confrontation, cognitive restructuring, reframing, and interpretation offer a potential for clarifying a client's functioning relating to the defense.

Confrontation. Clients employing patterns of rationalization typically reveal inconsistencies and omissions in their motivational functioning. Confrontation provides a descriptive and supportive approach for scrutinizing individuals' use of rationalization. In the following counseling examples, client statements suggest contradictory manifestations of behavior and subsequent confrontations by the counselor.

1. *Statement—Nonverbal Expression*

   Client: I've been so busy with my job that I can't spend any more time dealing with all the messes my son gets into. Besides, nothing I do seems to help.

   Counselor: You say that you can't deal with him anymore, but you have a troubled and uncertain look on your face.

2. *Statement—Previous Statement*

   Client: My heart medication makes me feel so tired. I feel better when I'm not taking it.

   Counselor: It makes sense to you not to take your prescribed medication, but you have also said that you are worried about having another heart attack.

3. *Statement—Action*

   Client: I just can't help getting into fights. I guess it's my hot temper because of my Latino heritage.

   Counselor: Once you lose control, you believe that you can't help fighting. The way you describe your fight today, though, you don't sound angry. It almost seems more as though you felt excited and enjoyed it.

4. *Statement—Objective Condition*

   Client: I'm just too old to learn and change my ways.

Counselor: You feel too old to change, but you are aware of a number
               of people in your age bracket who have managed to make
               quite a few changes in their lives.

5. *Statement—Omission*

Client: I just can't seem to find suitable work. The job market is bad.

Counselor: You're saying that it has been difficult to find a job, but the
               employment service reports that you turned down two job
               interviews this week.

In a counseling example with a client who abuses alcohol, a counselor uses confrontation to clarify an individual's furtive pattern of
drinking. In response, the client rejects the counselor's initial confrontation attempt.

Client: Things are going fine. I'm doing really well this week.

Counselor: It's important for you to feel that you are making progress.

Client: Well, I am, and it shows.

Counselor: At the same time, your family members report that you're
               experiencing double vision and blackouts. I can also see now
               that your hands are shaking.

Client: I know that I've been working too hard and drinking far too
               much coffee.

Counselor: You want to believe that your physical symptoms are related
               to something else other than abuse of alcohol.

Cognitive Restructuring. To effect more enduring therapeutic change
in individuals' employment of rationalization, it may be necessary for a
counselor to address their lifestyles. Consider, for example, the perspectives of clients who maintain schemas associated with learned helplessness: negative beliefs about oneself, lack of perceived control, and
expectation of future failure and futility (Peterson, Maier, & Seligman,
1993). In these instances, clients may use rationalization to justify
avoiding a multiplicity of experiences that predictably end in failure.
Challenging such persons to develop more efficacious core-level assumptions may also produce change at the intermediate rationalization
level. In the following counseling example, a counselor challenges a late

adulthood client to begin to develop alternative self-attributions by initiating a specific counterthought.

Client:	I'm just too old to change.
Counselor:	At this point in the game, you feel pretty set in your ways.
Client:	Well, yeah, but it's not like I'm dead yet.
Counselor:	Change is not easy, but you don't want to make like your life is over.
Client:	It's just that moving to another apartment is difficult for me. I used to be better about making changes.
Counselor:	What is it that you told yourself about change in those days?
Client:	I'm not sure if I told myself anything. I just looked forward to it.
Counselor:	Can you say that now when change is needed?
Client:	What, "I'm looking forward to it?"
Counselor:	What do you suppose would happen if you practiced this statement and used it when you need to make those changes?

Reframing. As a counseling technique, reframing involves changing the meaning of individuals' perspectives and developing new frames of reference. It is possible for a counselor to encourage clients to reconceptualize their use of rationalization in a way that transforms its perceived function. Considering one paradoxical approach (Seltzer, 1986), the counselor insists that a client should adamantly refuse to evaluate other behavioral explanations from anybody regardless of how sensible they may appear to be. Providing such an absurd dictum may reduce emotional threat inherent with rationalization and produce a paradoxical effect of establishing a receptive climate for evaluating alternative perspectives.

In another reframing example, the counselor employs the technique from an existential perspective with an adolescent client who engages rationalization to justify his acting-out behavior.

Client:	My parents don't care what I do, so why should I? If they expect me to be a bum, then what's the big deal if I am?
Counselor:	Since nobody expects anything of you, there's no point in trying.
Client:	Who cares what any of them think anyway?

Counselor: Things seem kind of mixed up to you. I'm wondering, though, if it is possible for you to look at this from another point of view?

Client: What do you mean?

Counselor: Well, maybe what you're saying about no one seeming to care also gives you the freedom to be whatever you want to be or can be.

Client: I'm not sure what you mean (pause). I guess you're saying that what I become in life is pretty much up to me.

Interpretation. An essential direction for persons who employ a pattern of rationalization may be to explore a broader range of motivations for using the defense. Interpretation enables clients to establish causal referents between current and past functioning, including lifestyle implications relating to rationalization. In a counseling example, an adolescent client with a diagnosis of anorexia nervosa uses rationalization to justify her weight loss because she is "fat." Through an interpretation, the counselor expands motivational purposes to include the possibility of gaining a sense of perceived control that the client has lacked in growing up in her family. In another counseling case with an adolescent, the individual has been using rationalization to justify his unsatisfactory academic progress.

Client: Well, maybe it isn't always the teacher's fault, and I need to do a little more work.

Counselor: This is not easy for you to say, and it takes some courage to admit it.

Client: I guess that I have been kind of looking for excuses for not doing better in school.

Counselor: Some things are harder to face than others, but I'm wondering if there is even more to your problems in school than we have talked about?

Client: What do you mean?

Counselor: Could it be that your lack of motivation in school relates to a belief that you developed as a child that you are less capable than other people?

Accomplishment Stage

After individuals clarify perspectives relating to rationalization use, counseling emphasis focuses on establishing more adaptive actions. In the final stage of counseling, specific strategies enable clients to institute more purposeful functioning that was previously avoided by employing rationalization.

Catching Oneself. With a commitment to reduce their use of rationalization, some clients need support in devising methods to control the defense. "Catching oneself" enables individuals to disengage from employing rationalization by using a cuing device just as they are about to enact the habitualized response. A cue that may generally be useful for modulating rationalization is for clients to touch their mouths as a signal to avoid engaging the response that is now consciously recognized as excuse making. In the following counseling example, a client who had been using rationalization to justify not seeking a job now wishes to control her patterned use of the defense.

Client:	I've been working now for 3 weeks, and although I like my job, I find myself starting to make excuses about why I can't get to work every day. I really don't want to do this.
Counselor:	This seems important to you. What is it about the job that seems worthwhile?
Client:	I really like doing something for myself. I got my first paycheck last week, and I was so excited that I had earned the money. I just sat there looking at it and smiling.
Counselor:	I'm wondering if you can use that paycheck to remind you how important the job is to you.
Client:	I'm not sure what you mean.
Counselor:	What if when you start to make excuses for why you can't get to your job, you could take out your first pay stub and look at it? It would be a reminder of all the benefits you get from work.
Client:	I guess that it would be easy enough to carry with me.

Acting As If. Some individuals maintain an entrenched pattern of rationalization use, and it is not an easy task for them to establish alternative actions. "Acting as if" enables clients to identify a person who employs direct and honest communication and who can serve as a model to emulate new patterns of behavior. In the following example, a high school student observes the difficulties that he is experiencing in redirecting his behavior.

Client:	It's hard to admit, but I've been goofing off and making excuses for so long that I have no idea where to begin to change.
Counselor:	It is a lot to think about to have to decide where you are trying to go.
Client:	The only thing that I know is that I want to do better in school for one thing and also be more straight with people and myself.
Counselor:	Whom do you know who is like this?
Client:	Not many kids that I hang around with, but there are a few.
Counselor:	What if you began to try to act like one of these persons?
Client:	I'd feel kind of stupid trying to copy someone else.
Counselor:	Of course, you would be yourself, but you would try to act like someone who does well in school and who doesn't make many excuses.
Client:	I think I'm getting what you mean, but it would still seem strange.

Breaking It Down. Change for some clients may also be difficult because of the imposing magnitude of the total effort that is required. "Breaking it down" emphasizes partializing actions through small incremental segments. The counseling strategy can be effective for attenuating client use of rationalization. In a concluding counseling example, a late adolescent client is experiencing difficulty in maintaining direct and honest communication.

Client:	I find I'm slipping back into making excuses again to avoid things, and this worries me.
Counselor:	You are making an effort, but you're concerned that your old pattern of excuse making may upset your progress.
Client:	Yeah, I really don't want to, but . . .
Counselor:	What if you concentrate on being honest with yourself simply one day at a time, rather than all at once? Try to focus on today, and don't worry about tomorrow.

Client: I know what you are saying. That might take the pressure off a little because it's a lot to think about all at once.

CONCLUSION

Rationalization is a commonly used tactic that individuals employ to justify unacceptable or inappropriate behavior. Ernest Jones introduced the term and emphasized how persons reiterate false but plausible explanations. In counseling, clients may present reasonably credible explanations of questionable behavior and resist exploring alternative positions. Within the three stages of the counseling process, selected interventions emphasize clarifying client perspectives and establishing more open communication and adaptive actions.

NOTE

1. Excerpt from *King John,* by W. Shakespeare (L. A. Beaurline, Ed.), 1990, New York: Cambridge University Press. Original work published 1623. Copyright © 1990 by Cambridge University Press. Reprinted with permission.

8

REACTION FORMATION

Virtue itself turns vice, being misapplied,
And vice sometime's by action dignified.

—William Shakespeare, 1595/1917,
Romeo and Juliet, act II, scene iii, lines 21-22

Most individuals wish to appear to be reasonably solicitous and scrupulous in their everyday interactions with other people. On a social level, expressions of kindness and honesty in word and deed represent essential qualities in civil and harmonious relationships. At the same time, persons may demonstrate oversolicitude and excessive conscientiousness in exchanges with others that mask or obscure their subjective intentions. In response to threat, individuals may employ the defense mechanism of reaction formation to fend off socially unacceptable or prurient tendencies through the expression of diametrically opposing behavior. Reaction formations also involve exaggerated and excessive responses of a person's effort to appear morally superior and beyond reproach. In counseling, for example, a client expresses highly critical and moralistic reactions toward society's preoccupation with sex. Subsequently, the counselor learns that this same individual purchases sexually explicit magazines. In another instance, a middle adulthood client, manifesting obsessive-compulsive tendencies, repeatedly condemns several relatives and neighbors for their "slothful ways." Subsequently, the individual revels with delight in recounting a personal experience in which she was able to be "lazy" for a couple of hours. Defining reaction formation as a defense mechanism emphasizes demonstrating exaggerated moralistic actions that are directly contrary to cognitive and affective functioning.

THEORETICAL ASPECTS OF REACTION FORMATION

Emergence of Reaction Formation

Sigmund Freud (1905/1953b) initially described reaction formation as a developmental pattern of behavior that evolves in response to feelings of shame relating to sexual preoccupations. Freud (1926/1959) observed that to avoid intolerable anxiety, individuals expressed opposite counterparts to prohibited impulses that were subsequently expanded to include aggression, in addition to libidinal forces. After developing during the latency period of childhood, reaction formations emerge at puberty through tendencies that appear to be exemplary from a moral perspective. Various expressions of reaction formation involve transformed responses that are verbalized in a manner exceeding normal expectations.

The excessive and exaggerated qualities of reaction formations were also observed by Anna Freud (1936/1966), and she recognized how evaded impulses may occasionally break through and be revealed through slips of the tongue (Sandler & Freud, 1985) and evidence of finding pleasure in dirt and disorder, exhibitionism, brutality, and cruelty to animals. More often, however, Freud found that commonplace trends that might ordinarily be viewed as within a normal range of functioning become excessive and thus suggest the employment of reaction formation. She cited the example of a mother who is overly concerned with the safety of her child as a result of a reaction formation against her own hostile impulses (Sandler & Freud, 1985). According to Freud (1965), other possible indicators of reaction formation, when carried to excess, include orderliness, cleanliness, obstinacy, punctuality, parsimony, indecisiveness, hoarding, and collecting.

Psychopathology and Reaction Formation

Age Adequateness. Reaction formations may be suspected by the counselor when individuals evince exaggerated and excessive moralistic patterns that are outside the norm for respective life span stages. Although reaction formation may become apparent in adolescence, occasionally younger children employ the defense, and the counselor must attempt to distinguish outward expressions of the mechanism from more developmentally appropriate behavior. In counseling, for example, an 8-year-old student insists that she does not wish to join in activities on the playground because she "hates getting dirty and looking like a pig." The client's mother informs the school counselor that her daughter is extremely neat and clean but periodically seems to delight in hiding soiled clothing and smelly objects in her room. During adolescence, individuals may demonstrate somewhat common patterns of self-denial and asceticism (Freud, 1936/1966), and again the counselor must differentiate reaction formation from more representative behavior depending on the relative age of a client. Consider the example of a 16-year-old client who is highly compliant and respectful in exchanges with a counselor. The client insists that his peers spend far too much time talking and thinking about sex and that he has "better things to do with his time." In this instance, the individual's exchanges in counseling and his expressed statements are atypical for an adolescent, and the counselor hypothesizes the engagement of reaction formation. In a middle adulthood example of a client's use of reaction formation, the person states, "My house must be spotless, or I simply can't live in it." The client also expresses revulsion when describing her neighbors' and relatives' lack of concern about cleanliness and propriety. In this example, although at some level the individual's behavior may be viewed as exemplary, most adults do not customarily maintain such judgmental and uncompromising positions.

Balance. Reaction formations may be adopted in rigid and stereo-typed ways to the point of becoming characteristic of individuals. When reaction formation is an entrenched pattern, persons may receive recognition for honorable or even virtuous behavior, and this degree of notice can have a strong reinforcing quality. At the same time, employing reaction formation as a predominant defense may inhibit clients' adaptation to perceived threat. In a counseling example, a client appears to use reaction formation as she belittles other persons in her life for their untoward behavior. The client continually relies on reaction formation in threatening interpersonal situations, and these exchanges prompt her to extend herself further by attempting to demonstrate even loftier personal standards. This pursuit becomes stressful and difficult to sustain as the individual strives to prove her purity and righteousness.

Intensity. Reaction formation can also be excessively engaged by individuals (Juni, 1981). Unlike an obsessive-compulsive disorder, however, in which clients find thoughts or impulses illogical and absurd (Maxmen & Ward, 1995), persons employing reaction formation generally perceive their responses as essential and imperative. An inordinate frequency of use of the defense may also result in interpersonal disturbances and cause individuals' behavior to be viewed as excessively ingratiating or arrogant. In a counseling example, a 60-year-old client repeatedly expresses comments to her relatives about her moral virtues while subjecting them to oversolicitous exchanges. As a consequence, most of the client's relatives avoid her, and only a sister and a son continue to visit. The intensity of clients' employment of reaction formation may also preclude examination of conflicted issues obscured by the defense. In the cited example, the client who persistently uses reaction formation with her relatives appears to maintain contemptuous core convictions toward others that become intolerable and are replaced with their opposite.

Reversibility. Some individuals maintain a pattern of reaction formation long after circumstances that may have prompted the employment of the defense have changed or no longer exist. Rather than adapt to new conditions, persons fend off conflicted affect by chronically attempting to demonstrate exemplary behavior. Consider the example of Sid, a middle adulthood client who proclaims that there is far too much emphasis on sex in society today yet is very interested in sex. When any mention of sexuality occurs, Sid appears to be embarrassed and reacts by professing moral condemnation toward others whom he believes are preoccupied with sex. As a child, Sid was raised in a family in which both his parents were stern and rarely expressed intimate feelings. His father was fervently moralistic, and any demonstration of interest in sex by Sid was met with harsh rebuke. Subsequently, in Sid's development, sexual feelings became associated with shame and emotional conflict. As a defense, reaction formations allowed Sid to deal with his conflicted feelings by replacing them with opposite outward expressions. Although this pattern of reaction formation provided a means for Sid to survive prohibitive and threatening circumstances in his family, many years had elapsed since he resided with his parents. Sid's current use of reaction formation is out-of-date in time and circumstances, yet he persists with habitual and ritualistic responses. It is also possible that Sid maintains a core conviction of himself as shameful, and reaction formation mollifies an awareness of this intolerable perception.

Context. A counselor's examination of the social and cultural forces influencing individuals contributes to understanding their use of reaction formation. In a counseling example, a 70-year-old client who is a member of a religious denomination zealously decries the excessive amount of gratuitous sex in the media today and states, "Sexual intercourse is an act of love and is a grievous sin outside marriage." As the counselor considers the possibility of defense mechanism employment, evaluating the influence of the values and mores of late adulthood and religious affiliation is essential in determining if the client's views are a function of cultural subgroup membership or a function of reaction formation. In another counseling example, a passive Asian American high school client repudiates the excessive focus on competition in her school at the expense of more cooperative pursuits. The counselor, in this instance, must consider the emphasis in Asian cultures on cooperation and humility and evaluate the influence of these values on the client's development that may be distinct from their excessive expression through reaction formation. In regard to gender, reaction formation was found to be more frequently employed by women than by men in research studies with college students (Cramer, 1991; Ihilevich & Gleser, 1995).

PROCESSING REACTION FORMATION IN COUNSELING

Relationship Stage

Addressing client defensiveness and establishing trust may be approached through selected therapeutic techniques. Reflection and assessment methods assist in clarifying excessive and exaggerated functioning of individuals who conceal antithetical feelings and cognitions. Self-disclosure of the counselor also provides the therapist a means to share pertinent experiences with clients relating to the defense of reaction formation.

Reflection. When clients employ reaction formation, various feelings such as shame, hostility, and resentment are obscured by the outward expression of opposite affects. When individuals demonstrate oversolicitude, self-righteousness, or other excessive conduct that possibly relates to the defense, the counselor may choose to reflect their explicit feelings. To illustrate, a college student interacts with a counselor in an obsequious manner in initial counseling sessions. After completing a human figure drawing, the client says to the counselor, "Here it is, sir. I hope that I did the drawing just as you would like it. Is there anything that I can do to improve it?" In response, the counselor reflects the individual's feelings, "You feel a sense of relief when you are able to please me by doing all you can to cooperate." The purpose of the counselor's reflection is to convey an understanding of the client's affective functioning and to promote more open communication. At a later point, the counselor may attempt to clarify the meaning and implications inherent in a client's statements. In the cited example, the client says with a subservient tone, "I hope that I completed these sentences fully and that they are of value to you in your important work." The counselor responds with reflection of meaning, "You seem to feel an urgency to be viewed as a conscientious and thoughtful person."

Reaction formation may be used in diverse ways by clients. Examples of the defense in counseling include the following:

- ◆ A middle school client who has been ridiculed and taunted by a small group of students states that he is not angry with them and refuses to fight back and defend himself. His mother has informed the school social worker that the client is experiencing recurrent nightmares relating to the teasing.
- ◆ An Asian American high school student is passive and nonaggressive. At the same time, the client is highly critical about the competitiveness of other students.
- ◆ A middle adulthood client frequently talks about the sexual promiscuity of today's young people. He is extremely critical of anyone who acts or dresses provocatively.
- ◆ A college student expresses disgust at how dirty and unkempt the dormitories are. The client often has run-ins with other students when he accuses them of being messy.
- ◆ Describing herself as a "workaholic," a 30-year-old impeccably dressed client discloses a vivid dream. The dream takes place in an open field adjacent to her corporate office where the client joyously rolls around in mud during a rainstorm. Although stating that on awakening she experienced unfamiliar feelings of freedom and a wanton sense of abandonment, the client insists that she is repulsed and distressed by the dream.

In each of these examples, clients express feelings and perceptions that may be responded to by a counselor's use of reflection. In the following example, the counselor employs reflection with a college student who appears to employ reaction formation.

Client:	I can't stand looking at anything that isn't clean and in order—the way my college dorm room is right now.
Counselor:	It is upsetting to you that your roommate doesn't feel the same way you do about cleanliness.
Client:	I talk to him about it all the time, but he dismisses everything I say about picking things up.
Counselor:	You feel frustrated because this means so much to you, and other people don't seem to take it seriously.

Client: (after a pause) They can live in squalor and act like pigs, but
I refuse to take part in such obscene behavior.

Assessment. Multiple assessment procedures contribute to accurately evaluating client employment of reaction formation. Data derived from observations of client behavior, collateral sources, and projective techniques enable a counselor to appraise the defense from different perspectives. Inconsistencies in individuals' behavior may suggest reaction formation use, and the following counseling examples indicate possible defense engagement.

1. *Statement:* Fighting is wrong, but I don't feel any anger toward the kids who tease me. It's always better to turn the other cheek.
   Nonverbal expression: Client's fists are tightly clenched.

2. *Statement:* Everyone is so competitive about grades. It's all so crass.
   Previous statement: They all think they're better than me, but I got one of the highest grades in the class.

3. *Statement:* I can't stand all the sex in advertising and in the media. It's absolutely disgusting.
   Action: The client's wife reports that he purchases erotic magazines.

4. *Statement:* My cleanliness doesn't hurt anyone, and somebody has got to speak out about filth.
   Objective condition: A significant amount of the client's time is spent cleaning, and residents in his dormitory avoid him because he is so adamant about everything being in its place.

5. *Statement:* The dream is so repulsive. I don't even know why I'm talking to you about it.
   Omission: The client called the counselor's office twice to tell her about the dream.

Collateral information may include observations and data obtained from outside sources, such as teacher or employer reports, that corroborate a client's use of reaction formation. Inconsistencies may be apparent between an individual's behavior in counseling and collateral material that points to the employment of the defense. In a counseling example, Jon, a middle school client, states that he refuses to defend himself against students who have been making fun of him because aggression is morally wrong. Although he has been having tormenting dreams about the peer ridicule, Jon insists that he is not troubled by the taunting. In contrast to this assertion, one of his teachers found a note written by Jon repeatedly stating, "They are all animals and deserve to die." The counselor is also aware that individuals employing reaction formation may overtly be quick to forgive even if treated unfairly (Sarnoff, 1960).

A selected battery of projective techniques may also contribute potential data relating to an individual's engagement of reaction formation. The elicitation of early recollections may also provide perspectives on a client's lifestyle that are integral to the moralistic views expressed through the defense. In a counseling example, a 19-year-old college student who demonstrates excessive cleanliness tendencies discloses the following early memory.

> I remember being in the kitchen in the house where I grew up, and I was smearing peanut butter and jelly on the floor and cabinets. Unexpectedly, my father came in the room and started yelling and put his hands on my shoulders and shook me. I felt so scared and ashamed of myself.

The client added that he experienced fear and shame in the memory. It is evident in the recollection that the client's messy behavior met with strong disapproval and harsh consequences. On the basis of a core conviction derived from this memory, and two others like it, the counselor hypothesizes that messiness is associated with adverse feelings, and the client's use of reaction formation provides relief from such conflicted affect.

A client's employment of reaction formation may also be inferred through human figure drawings and sentence completion tasks. With these and various other psychometric instruments, an individual may demonstrate an overcompliance with testing instructions, and this behavior may be associated with reaction formation (Schafer, 1967). For example, a client states when completing a human figure drawing, "I am trying to do this exactly as you told me to. Please let me know if you want me to change it in any way." In completing sentence stems, an individual says, "I hope that I have answered these with my true feelings. I do want to help you as much as possible with this." The human figure drawings may also reveal perceptions and feelings that are antithetical to a person's overt expressions and indicate possible reaction formation use. As an example, a client draws a profile of a human figure that possibly indicates evasiveness and opposition tendencies (Handler, 1996). Such characteristics are contrary to the person's expressed statement: "I want to cooperate fully with you and provide all the information that I can about myself."

Various sentence completion responses may reveal opposite tendencies to an individual's manifest functioning and possibly suggest employment of reaction formation. Consider the following examples of sentences completed by a client who exhibits excessively conscientious and fastidious behavior. "I feel . . . dirty sometimes." "Other people . . . disgust me." "I wish . . . I could let myself go once in a while." In another instance, a male client expresses extremely critical reactions toward male-male sexual activity in completing the following sentence stems: "I am afraid of . . . getting close to other men." "My greatest worry is . . . sometimes being attracted to another man." "What pains me is . . . thinking about a man being sexually intimate with another man."

Self-Disclosure. Success or failure experiences relating to reaction formation are among the various dimensions of counselor self-disclosure that may advance the counseling relationship. In counseling, for example, a client expresses strong resentment toward other college students for their lack of care about cleanliness in his dormitory. In response, the counselor discloses that she had also encountered difficulties with some students in her experience while living in residential facilities but had met with only limited success in persuading them to clean up after themselves. Past or present counselor experiences involving reaction formation may also prove to be pertinent with clients. Consider, for example, the client who reports a dream in which she acts in a reckless and abandoned way and experiences exhilarating and liberating feelings that seem foreign to her. The individual, who demonstrates obsessive-compulsive tendencies, says that she is repelled by the dream and embarrassed by her wanton conduct. The counselor responds by acknowledging that he analyzes dreams in his own life and finds that emotions expressed in dreams are especially important in clarifying blocked awareness or serving as a motivational impetus.

Self-disclosure by a counselor may also involve similar or dissimilar experiences that relate to a client's reaction formations. A middle school student, for example, is taunted by a small group of peers but refuses to defend himself. It is apparent, however, on a nonverbal level, that the client actually harbors feelings of anger and rage and that the defense of reaction formation may be operating. After acknowledging the client's feelings relating to the taunting, the counselor discloses that she also endured peer ridicule for a time in school but felt angry toward the students who made fun of her. Counselors may also use self-involving statements when providing feedback to clients about their behavior in counseling, including the use of reaction formation. Consider the example of a client who demonstrates a pattern of oversolicitous interactions with the counselor and expresses the following statement, "I want to be sure that I am doing everything I can to take advantage of the opportunity to work with you as my counselor." As a response, the therapist may say something such as, "When you compliment me, as you are doing now, I wonder if you sometimes have opposite feelings toward me that are also important to express."

Integration Stage

In the middle period of counseling, clients' conflicted behavior inherent in reaction formation becomes a therapeutic focus. Selected counseling techniques, including confrontation, cognitive restructuring, reframing, and interpretation, contribute to effectively processing a defense that involves exaggerated moralistic conduct.

Confrontation. Intrinsic to reaction formation is an outward expression of behavior that is inconsistent with individuals' internal functioning. In counseling, client statements may be disconnected from their nonverbal expressions, previous statements, actions, objective conditions, and significant material that is not expressed. A counselor may challenge clients' employment of reaction formation through confrontation. The following examples provide various illustrations.

1. *Statement—Nonverbal Expression*

   Client: Fighting is wrong, but I don't feel any anger toward the kids who tease me. It's always better to turn the other cheek.

   Counselor: You feel strongly about this, but your fists are tightly clenched. Could you help me understand this?

2. *Statement—Previous Statement*

   Client: Everyone is so competitive about grades. It's all so crass.

   Counselor: Trying to do better than your classmates doesn't make sense to you, yet last week you told me that you had one of the highest grades in your English class. The way you said it gave me the impression that it meant a lot to you.

3. *Statement—Action*

   Client: I can't stand all the sex in advertising and in the media. It's absolutely disgusting.

   Counselor: You are repulsed by the amount of sex in society today, but at the same time, I understand that you purchase erotic magazines.

4. *Statement—Objective Condition*

   Client: My cleanliness doesn't hurt anyone, and somebody has got to speak out about filth.

   Counselor: Although cleanliness is important to you, it seems that few people want to listen to you, and therefore you have to do most of the cleaning.

5. *Statement—Omission*

   Client: The dream is so repulsive. I don't even know why I'm talking to you about it.

   Counselor: You feel repelled by the dream, yet you called twice today wanting to talk about it.

A counselor's use of confrontation may be responded to at varying levels of perceived acceptance. In the following counseling example, a middle adulthood client employing reaction formation rejects the counselor's initial attempt to point out an overlooked discussion topic.

Client: I'm not saying that sex is such a horrible thing; it's a natural act of love between two married people. But the way it is portrayed in our society as a meaningless act makes my skin crawl.

Counselor: This troubles you a lot, and you believe that you must speak out about gratuitous sex.

Client: Well, I mean if things keep on going the way they are, this country will go down the drain.

Counselor: It seems that you frequently talk about sexuality on a societal level, but you rarely express how sex affects you personally.

Client: (pause) Well, I think that it's more important to focus on the broader effects of sex rather than on the experience of one individual person.

Cognitive Restructuring. Core convictions relating to fundamental perspectives on life may involve a person's use of reaction formation. To effect more enduring change in the operation of a client's reaction formations, it may be necessary to alter maladaptive cognitive schemas that undergird the defense. In the following example, a counselor uses cognitive restructuring to prompt a high school student to mollify her entrenched views involving competition with others. In this instance, the counselor integrates the client's interest in poetry with cognitive restructuring by quoting a verse from a poem by Alfred, Lord Tennyson (1898).

Client: As I said before, it's better not to get into all that competition that goes on around here. It's a waste of time.

Counselor: So you feel that you have better things to do than try to show how much better you are than your classmates.

Client: Yes, I do. It's a pointless game. So what if you're better than everyone else? Where does that get you? And what if you end up falling flat on your face? You look like a total fool. I bet those people never think about that happening (laughing).

Counselor: From what you've just said, I get the idea that you've decided that you're better off not to even try if failure is a possibility.

Client: Well, I hate to fail at things, but I'm no different from anyone
             else about this.

Counselor: (pause) I know that you like poetry and are probably familiar
             with the work of Tennyson.

Client: I like the British poets.

Counselor: In one of his poems, he wrote " 'T is better to have loved and
             lost, than never to have loved at all" (p. 182).

Client: (long pause) I know what you are saying. I guess Tennyson
             has a point here. What it means to me is . . .

Reframing. As a counseling technique, reframing expands the frame
of reference of individuals, including their use of reaction formation.
Through semantic change, it may be possible to modify rigid and
dysfunctional qualities of the defense. Consider, for example, the case
of the young adult client who demonstrates a pattern of obsessive-
compulsive cleanliness and appears to employ reaction formation in
conjunction with this behavior. The individual insists that he "must"
speak out against the messiness of other students in his dormitory. In
response, the counselor uses a reframe by suggesting to the client that
rather than assuming an imperative *must,* in actuality, he may *choose* to
act in a certain way. This semantic change focuses on a Gestalt language
approach emphasizing awareness and personal responsibility for one's
actions (Clarkson, 1989). In a related reframing example, a 30-year-old
client appears to habitually employ reaction formation as a means of
staving off a conflicted sense of shame and uncleanliness. After the client
discloses a reprehensible yet compelling dream, the counselor invites
her to consider an alternative and empowering perspective.

Counselor: Although you now say that you're repulsed by your dream,
             when you woke up from the dream, you felt great relief and
             a sense of abandonment.

Client: I know, but I just can't imagine myself rolling around in the
             mud in front of my corporate office.

Counselor: You are viewing the dream as a repugnant experience and
             find it threatening. I'm wondering if you could look at it
             differently.

Client: What do you mean?

Counselor: Are you able to view the dream as allowing yourself a completely reckless freedom and an absence of convention—feelings that are rare to you?

Client: Such feelings may be rare to me because there are certain ways a respectable person should act.

Interpretation. For some individuals, an exploration of their motivation for employing reaction formation is essential for therapeutic progress. Clarifying past and present referents through interpretation enables clients to gain increased understanding of why they behave in excessively rigid and moralistic ways. In the following example, a middle adulthood client persists in expressing morally zealous positions relating to sex in contemporary society. The counselor uses interpretation to clarify the condemnatory functioning manifested in the use of reaction formation.

Client: It really bothers me that our society places so much emphasis on sex. Sometimes, people act like such animals.

Counselor: You do feel strongly about this, but we have already talked about how you also have a clear interest in sex.

Client: (pauses) I can be such a hypocrite.

Counselor: You feel embarrassed, but you are trying to make sense of this conflict within yourself.

Client: I'm kind of messed up about this.

Counselor: It is confusing to you. I'm wondering perhaps if it could relate to how sex was viewed in your family.

Client: Well, as you know, my parents were very strict, and, well, sex was just considered wrong.

Counselor: Could it be that you feel shamed when sex is discussed in a personal way, and perhaps your way of dealing with this is to speak out about sexuality on a societal level?

Accomplishment Stage

As individuals develop more constructive perspectives involving their use of reaction formation, counseling emphasis shifts to regulating actions inherent in the defense. In the final stage of counseling, specific strategies focus on effecting action-change in patterns of moralistic functioning.

Catching Oneself. Once a person makes a commitment to change, "catching oneself" serves as an alerting strategy to limit the expression of exaggerated "exemplary" conduct. In a counseling example, a young adulthood client has developed a more balanced perspective toward accepting her physical and emotional functioning, yet she finds herself slipping back into rigid and constricted actions. Through discussion with the counselor, the client decides to place several children's toys on her desk at work and in different locations in her home. At critical points when the client feels that she is succumbing to excessively moralistic behavior, she picks up one of the toys to remind herself that she may choose to engage her less inhibited and judgmental side. In another counseling example, a client decides to employ a verbal cue to alert himself to avoid moralistic actions.

Client:	It's getting a little easier to talk about the shame that I feel about sex and about myself in general, and this is a relief. Our talks and the book you suggested that I read have helped quite a bit. One thing that does bother me, though, is that I find myself falling back into the old pattern of lecturing and criticizing people about their morality. It's hard to stop myself.
Counselor:	You've made clear gains, but you're finding that it's not easy to change your old ways.
Client:	That's the hard part, stopping myself before I offend someone.
Counselor:	There's an approach that may help in this type of situation. It's called "catching oneself." The way this works is that when you find yourself starting to say something offensive, you immediately use a cuing device to stop yourself.
Client:	I'm not sure what would work.
Counselor:	Is there something from the book *Healing the Shame That Binds You* (Bradshaw, 1988) that you could use to alert yourself when you find yourself getting too moralistic with people and acting from your own shame?
Client:	Well, what if I repeat to myself at those times, "Healing the shame that binds me."

Acting As If. Individuals employing patterns of reaction formation for extended periods may be unpracticed in responding to others with more restrained and tolerant interactions. "Acting as if" enables clients to emulate the actions of persons who model behavior antithetical to reaction formation expressions. In the following counseling example, a client has made therapeutic gains relating to obsessive-compulsive cleanliness but continues to have difficulties with interpersonal relationships. In response, the college counselor invites the client to consider using an action-oriented intervention.

Client:	I've gotten so used to hiding behind my neatness and not focusing on anything else that I'm having trouble relating to people about other things.
Counselor:	It's hard for you to approach people on a personal level because you have been out of practice.
Client:	Right. I guess my social skills aren't all that great (acts embarrassed).
Counselor:	You are struggling with this. I have an idea that might help.
Client:	I'd like to try something.
Counselor:	You would need to think about someone who relates effectively with other persons and attempt to model or imitate the individual's behavior.
Client:	It's funny that you should say that because I have some acting experience, but in this case, I'd be acting for myself. I'm not sure, but it's worth a shot.

Breaking It Down. Individuals employing patterns of reaction formation may also experience difficulties with achieving the extent of change required to progress to more adaptive actions. "Breaking it down" focuses on accomplishing specific and attainable objectives in developing alternatives to excessively moralistic functioning. In a concluding example, an early adulthood client discusses her current functioning and feels discouraged about maintaining behavior change.

Client:	I think that I have come a long way in accepting a part of myself that is more spontaneous and less judgmental. It still feels somewhat forced and artificial, though, to act this way, and I find myself slipping back into my old ways of trying to control everything and everybody.

Counselor: As much as it makes sense to you to strike a balance in your life between control and spontaneity, it is a challenge to keep changing.

Client: It's as if I know what to do, but I'm not doing it. I keep thinking about how to make this work.

Counselor: I'm wondering if it may be that you are forcing this into a control issue and making a strenuous effort out of it.

Client: In a sense I am. I'm really working at how to be less inhibited and moralistic.

Counselor: Perhaps it would help if you approach change in a less demanding way. What if you simply allow yourself to engage in one or two spontaneous activities each day, rather than trying to change all at once?

CONCLUSION

Reaction formation involves the outward expression of exaggerated "exemplary" conduct that belies persons' internal experiencing. Obsessive-compulsive tendencies are intrinsic to the operation of the defense mechanism. Excessive and exaggerated moralistic actions of individuals employing reaction formation are directly contrary to their cognitive and affective functioning. Clients using the defense in counseling frequently exhibit overcompliant and excessively conscientious interactions. Through the three stages of the counseling process, selected counseling techniques focus on effecting reaction formation change toward more integrated and purposeful behavior.

9

REGRESSION

All that is human must retrograde if it do not advance.

—Edward Gibbon, 1788/1932, p. 862

Although the trajectory of human experience understandably evokes praise when advancing, in some instances, the more adaptive course of development may prove to be other than simply forward strivings. Various experiences may occur in life when regressive tendencies can potentially serve growth-inducing purposes. Such universal phenomena as sleep, play, humor, dreams, and artistic creations entail essential qualities of childlike states, yet each offers activity that may be in the service of an individual (Kris, 1952; Schafer, 1958). More often, however, regression proper is linked to developmental reversions that clearly represent movement in less than constructive and purposeful directions. Situations involving trauma or stress, such as the divorce of a parent, a financial loss, or even a promotion at work, may trigger behavioral responses that are associated with an earlier period in a person's life that was more secure and stable. Regression involves a broad range of immature and intemperate behavior, such as avoidance of responsibility, attention seeking, and dependency. In a counseling example relating to this defense, an adolescent client manifests a marked maturational decline by crying or entering periods of prolonged silence when discussion focuses on completing academic projects and assignments. Defining regression as a defense mechanism emphasizes reverting to developmentally immature behavior.

THEORETICAL ASPECTS OF REGRESSION

Emergence of Regression

In the *Interpretation of Dreams,* Sigmund Freud (1900/1953a) introduced the concept of regression to account for regressive qualities that are characteristic of dreams. In subsequent writings, Freud (1905/1953b, 1913/1955c, 1926/1959) emphasized the impact of regression in neuroses and psychoses, as the concept assumed a significant theoretical role in understanding psychopathology. Freud (1905/1953b) noted the pathogenic influence of regression: "All the factors that impair sexual development show their effects by bringing about a regression, a return to an earlier phase of development" (p. 240). The temporal quality of regression gained increasing importance in Freud's clinical theory through his observation that individuals have a capacity to relapse to less complex, less advanced, and less organized stages of development (Jackson, 1969). In addition to temporal regression, Freud distinguished topographical and formal forms. Topographical regression relates to Freud's systemic model and involves a regressive shift in predominance from conscious to preconscious to unconscious functioning (Arlow & Brenner, 1964). Formal regression also involves more primitive methods of expression that may best be represented in the bizarre and archaic quality of dreams. In a paragraph added in 1914 to his seminal work on dreams, Freud (1900/1953a) recognized a correspondence among the three types of regression that are "one at bottom and occur together as a rule" (p. 548).

Anna Freud (1963, 1936/1966) also recognized regression as a mechanism of defense and identified regressive qualities in various defenses, such as denial, projection, reaction formation, and repression. In clarifying the three types of regression observed by Freud, Anna Freud (1963, 1965) considered each to be sufficiently distinct for discussion purposes, although she found that temporal regression was the most closely studied and examined in analysis because of its developmental implications. The temporal quality of regression was noted in the context of an individual's attempt to avoid intolerable conflict and stress by reverting to a mode of functioning that is characteristic of earlier developmental periods (Sandler & Freud, 1985). A child's development, according to Freud (1965), is not continuous and is subject to occasional relapses to more infantile behavior. Such varied activities as speech acquisition, bowel and bladder control, and manners may regress, particularly when a child is under stress. In her work with children in clinical treatment, Freud assessed the occurrence of regression through manifest behavior, such as lying, stealing, and bed-wetting, and suggested that the defense could be further discerned by consideration of an individual's fantasy activity as symptomatology.

Psychopathology and Regression

Age Adequateness. Evaluating the appropriateness of an individual's behavior depends in part on the relative age and certain underlying assumptions about the developmental stage of a person. What may be considered regressive and immature conduct by an adult, for instance, can be within normal expectations for a child. Further, a child's functioning may lack the stability and restraint that are more characteristic of advanced age. Consequently, by comparing clients within approximate age cohorts, a counselor may more accurately assess the possible employment of regression. In a counseling example, a 6-year-old client cries in daily meetings with a school counselor and begs to be allowed to go home. Although this mode of functioning is disturbing to the child and school officials, it is not extreme for a young child in the first few days of the first grade. In a similar situation, a 16-year-old client enrolled in advanced placement classes repeatedly sobs during several counseling sessions and pleads to go home. The counselor clearly recognizes the inappropriateness of the individual's infantile actions and infers the operation of regression as a defense mechanism. Although an adoles-

cent's behavior may involve discontinuities and reversals in development, the cited example is markedly immature for the client's age. In
another counseling example involving an apparent pattern of regression,
a 50-year-old client exhibits clinging and excessively dependent actions
in counseling, which sharply contradict the individual's prior level of
adjustment as a corporate executive and behaviors normally associated
with a mode of functioning of middle adulthood persons.

Balance. Regression frequently involves an aversion in attempting
to adapt to situational demands, and individuals can repeatedly rely on
the defense to avoid threatening circumstances. In stereotyped ways,
some clients rigidly engage regression rather than deal with immediate
conditions that elicit conflicted affect. In a counseling example, an early
adolescent client begins to bring her doll to school and act in immature
ways. The counselor learns that the girl's parents are constantly fighting,
as a result of bitter divorce proceedings. Through the employment of
regression, the client behaviorally retreats to a time in her childhood
when her parents' marriage was more secure and stable. The client's use
of regression averts the intolerable emotional impact of her parents'
separation, while providing a measure of support from familiar and
comforting experiences of an earlier developmental period. In some
instances in counseling, the possibility of establishing a purposeful
climate that permits a focus on topics of importance is restricted because
of a client's patterned use of regression. A young adult client, for
example, acts in fatuous ways by joking and laughing each time the
counselor attempts to introduce significant and pertinent issues.

Intensity. When regression is used excessively, individuals may encounter difficulties in social relationships. Inherently, the defense involves diminished self-restraint and intemperate actions, and people
frequently become dismayed or disgusted with a person who persistently
fails to assume more responsible behavior (Firestone, 1990). Consider,
for example, a situation involving Aaron, a preadolescent in counseling
with a school psychologist. Although Aaron has in the past demonstrated
a capacity for learning and appropriate behavior in the classroom, his
teacher ruefully reports that he "acts like a clown and simply doesn't do
his work." In meeting with the psychologist, Aaron attempts to play with

items carried in his pockets and avoids topics that focus on personal responsibility. It is also possible that individuals' habitual use of regression relates to their lifestyle. To continue with the cited example, Aaron appears to maintain core convictions that he is an inadequate person in a world that offers little support. Considered in this light, his employment of regression conceals his perceived inadequacies when Aaron feels threatened. Instead of attempting to work through conflicted affect, however, Aaron reverts to childish actions that divert attention away from his perceived lack of capabilities.

Reversibility. Qualitatively, regression involves a reversal to a lower level of development as a response to threat. Typically, persons resume their previous more adaptive mode of functioning after perceived dangers subside or become nonexistent. Some individuals, however, may continue to employ regression long after conditions that initially prompted the engagement of the defense have changed. Anna Freud (1965) observed that after traumatic stresses, anxieties, and illnesses, a person's employment of regression may take on a more permanent form. Consider the example of a client named Eric who experienced the trauma of witnessing his older brother fall to his death in a rock climbing accident. Almost immediately after the tragedy, Eric, who was 12 years old at the time, began acting out. Family members expected that after a time, his reckless actions would diminish. Two years after the accident, however, Eric continues to exhibit episodes of infantile functioning. It is also possible that individuals who have been exposed to extreme trauma may experience characteristic symptoms of post-traumatic stress disorder (American Psychiatric Association, 1994a), including a change in previous personality characteristics that now involve the engagement of regression.

Context. Negative experiences, such as poverty, illness, divorce, death of loved ones, and financial loss, can understandably challenge an individual's ability to sustain appropriate developmental levels of functioning. In other instances, various events with more positive connotations, including leaving home for the first time, getting married, starting a family, and achieving an important personal goal, may activate regression (Firestone, 1990). Clarifying social and cultural contexts of experiences in the lives of clients contributes to a counselor's understanding of diverse situational variables that influence the engagement of regression. In a counseling example, an adolescent client, living in a dangerous neighborhood, reverts to a pattern of infantile behavior representing a time in his life when as a young child he experienced a relative degree of personal safety and security. In a contrasting example, a young adulthood client receives a promotion to become a partner in a law firm and, significantly, is the first African American to receive this distinction. The promotion prompts a pattern of childish reactions by the client, who experiences difficulty in assimilating the enhanced degree of recognition for her assumed competency.

PROCESSING REGRESSION IN COUNSELING

Relationship Stage

The initial stage of counseling focuses on clarifying conflicted affect involving a client's use of regression. Prominent counseling techniques used in this period include reflection, assessment methods, and counselor self-disclosure.

Reflection. It is essential to the effective processing of regression that individuals first gain an awareness of their defensive stance. Reflection focuses on the clarification of client feelings and perceptions through the counselor's empathic and sensitive exchanges. In a counseling example, an adolescent, Daniel, alternates periods of refusing to talk with outbursts about inadequacies of the therapist. Although the counselor may feel irritated or dismayed in reaction to Daniel's oppositional behavior, expressing such emotional reactions at this point will likely be counterproductive. Instead, the counselor should attempt to reflect Daniel's feelings and consistently stay within his frame of reference. In a continuation of this counseling example, the counselor responds with a reflection of feeling, "You don't have much regard for me or for counseling, and you resent being pressured to meet with me." This response acknowledges Daniel's feelings of resentment and prompts an emotional release that may lead to a subsequent diminution of affect.

As the intensity of client feelings begins to subside, it may then be possible for the counselor to clarify a deeper understanding of their experiencing. To conclude the cited example, the counselor employs reflection of meaning with Daniel, "You resent being told what to do because there are a lot of pressures occurring in your life from which you would like to escape."

The counselor may infer client employment of regression through a range of immature and intemperate behavior in counseling. The following examples suggest specific possibilities related to the defense:

- A sixth-grade client has started bringing her favorite doll to school with her and is continually picked on by her classmates.
- Facing early retirement from a job that he really enjoys, a middle adulthood client has started to shirk his responsibilities at work and toward his family.
- A college freshman, who was at first conscientious and successful in his academic work, begins to drink quite heavily. He skips most of his classes and rarely submits assignments.
- After receiving a promotion at work, a client suddenly becomes unreliable and careless. Although she had unofficially been filling the position for several months, she has started to fall behind in her work and misses important assignments.
- Soon after enrolling in a comprehensive high school, a Native American student begins to act out and creates disciplinary problems. The client had previously attended schools on his tribal reservation and now takes a lengthy bus ride 20 miles from his home.

A counselor may use reflection as a response to a client's possible use of regression in each of these examples. In the next counseling example, a counselor employs reflection with a sixth-grade student who has recently been taking her doll to school and class.

Counselor:	I can tell that your doll means a lot to you.
Client:	She does. I really like her. The other kids make fun of me about her, but I don't care.
Counselor:	It must really mean a great deal to have her with you and not care what the other kids think about her.
Client:	Yeah (quietly).

Counselor:	What is it about her that makes her so special to you?
Client:	(pause) I got her from my dad when he was still living with me and mom.
Counselor:	She reminds you of a time when your whole family was together.
Client:	(starts to cry) Yeah. She makes me feel closer to my dad.

Assessment. The counselor should consider multiple perspectives in evaluating individuals' employment of regression. Behavioral observations, collateral sources, and projective material may collectively indicate immature levels of clients' functioning intrinsic to the defense mechanism. The following examples suggest the possible use of regression because client statements are inconsistent with other behavioral expressions and conditions:

1. *Statement:* It's not that important that I have my doll with me in school. I just like her, that's all.
   Nonverbal expression: The sixth-grade client holds on to her doll tightly.

2. *Statement:* It's time I started to think about myself since I have to retire. I'm doing things now that make me feel alive.
   Previous statement: My life is out of control.

3. *Statement:* I'm having a great time in college. My grades aren't good right now, but I'm happy here.
   Action: The client repeatedly skips classes and drinks heavily.

4. *Statement:* There's so much pressure involved in my new job. I just can't handle it.
   Objective condition: For 2 months prior to her promotion, the client had successfully been filling the position on an unofficial basis.

5. *Statement:* I can't stand the teachers in this school. All they do is get on my back.
   Omission: Each of the client's teachers has allowed him numerous opportunities to work on a more independent basis.

Collateral sources, such as anecdotal statements from a parent, spouse, or other family member, may provide significant data for assessing the occurrence of regression. To evaluate reversions in functioning, it is necessary for the counselor to appraise a client's prior level of development. Persons who are more intimately familiar with an individual's developmental history may be able to contribute pertinent observations. Consider, for example, an adolescent named Carl who manifests infantile actions on enrolling in a new school district. The counselor, through discussion with Carl's parents, hypothesizes that his immature conduct represents reversals in development consistent with the defense of regression. In other instances, more formal sources may be available to the counselor that suggest the operation of client regression. In the case of Carl, a psychological report indicates that he is prone to act in immature ways when faced with transitions or ambiguous situations.

Selected projective techniques provide another method for assessing client use of regression. Through the elicitation of early recollections, a counselor may clarify the relationship of individuals' employment of regression with their lifestyles. Consider the example of an early memory stated by Sylvia, a young adulthood client:

I was in the second grade, and the teacher divided the class into different reading groups. Each of the students was put into some type of bird group. When she put me with the yellow birds, I knew that it was the lowest group, but I felt it was probably where I belonged.

The counselor infers that Sylvia perceives herself as less capable in comparison with other people and that this self-evaluation is recognized by others. In accord with her core convictions, Sylvia began acting irresponsibly on the job almost immediately after a recent promotion at work and was therefore putting her position advancement in jeopardy. When she received a promotion, her psychological equilibrium was disturbed, and Sylvia's use of regression incurred a reversion to a developmental level that is possibly consistent with her perception of personal competencies.

Human figure drawings and sentence completion tasks are other projective techniques that may assist in clarifying client use of regression. Individuals may render productions of assigned drawings less mature than they are capable of by completing infantile human figures or using extensive scribbling (Levick, 1983). To assess developmental aspects of human figures that are critical in evaluating regression, the counselor may refer to especially dedicated volumes (Koppitz, 1968, 1984). The sentence completion tasks may also reflect individuals' developmental functioning and use of regression. For example, the counselor infers the use of regression when a 40-year-old client in good physical health completes the following sentence stems: "At home . . . I am able to hide from things." "My greatest worry . . . is having to be by myself." "I need . . . someone to take care of me." The same responses by a 7-year-old client, however, may simply reflect functioning within a relatively normal range of development.

Self-Disclosure. Recounting personal experiences involving regressive activity enables the counselor to demonstrate mutuality and linkage with clients' functioning. A counselor's self-disclosures may emphasize success or failure experiences among other dimensions. In the following example, a counselor discusses her personal behavior with a client who demonstrates regression after receiving a job promotion. The therapist states,

Not too long ago, I was elected as the president of a voluntary organization. I had doubts whether I could carry out the responsibilities of the position, and I thought about resigning. But then I told myself that because the members elected me to the office, they must believe that I could do the job. This made me feel better about things, and it all worked out OK.

It is also possible for a counselor to disclose past or present experiences with a client. Consider the example of a counselor who recounts a personal loss with an adolescent who has employed regression since observing the traumatic death of his brother.

When my mother died about 10 years ago, I had several dreams about being with her when I was a young boy. It felt so wonderful to be little again and be with my mom that I didn't want the dreams to end.

Similar or dissimilar experiences of the counselor may also be disclosed to clients in a supportive and timely way. In the following instance, a counselor observes a similarity of her past actions with a sixth-grade client who has been bringing a doll to school after her parents' divorce. The counselor says,

When I was a young girl, I didn't want my mother to leave my room when I went to bed. To help me through the bedtime hours, she gave me one of her rings and tied it on a string so that I could hold it until I fell asleep.

A therapist may also express self-involving statements relating to a client's use of regression in counseling. In a counseling session with a young adult who acts immaturely when significant and pertinent topics arise, the counselor states, "It seems that you joke around each time serious issues come up, and I find it difficult to communicate with you at these times."

Integration Stage

In the middle period of counseling, emphasis begins to focus on reconciling inconsistencies and conflicts inherent in regression as a defense mechanism. Clarifying a client's reversion to immature behavior occurs through the selected counseling techniques of confrontation, cognitive restructuring, reframing, and interpretation.

Confrontation. Inconsistencies between individuals' immature behavior and their developmentally appropriate level of functioning may be challenged through confrontation. In employing confrontation, the counselor attempts to clarify contradictions between client statements and nonverbal expressions, previous statements, actions, objective conditions, and omissions. The following examples illustrate clients' employment of regression and confrontations by a counselor:

1. *Statement—Nonverbal Expression*

    Client: It's not that important that I have my doll with me in school. I just like her, that's all.

    Counselor: You're saying that she doesn't mean that much to you, but I can see how tightly you're holding her.

2. *Statement—Previous Statement*

    Client: It's time I started to think about myself since I have to retire. I'm doing things now that make me feel alive.

    Counselor: Although you are now taking care of what you want to do, you said a few minutes ago that your life seems out of control.

3. *Statement—Action*

    Client: I'm having a great time in college. My grades aren't too good right now, but I'm happy here.

    Counselor: You say that you enjoy being here, but it looks as if you will be on academic probation next semester.

4. *Statement—Objective Condition*

    Client: There's so much pressure involved in my new job. I just can't handle it.

    Counselor: You do feel a lot of pressure at work, but you filled the position for several months on a provisional basis and were quite successful.

5. *Statement—Omission*

    Client: I can't stand the teachers in this school. All they do is get on my back.

    Counselor: It's important for you not to be told what to do, but you haven't mentioned anything about the independent assignments and projects that your teachers have offered you.

A client typically reacts to a counselor's use of confrontation with varying degrees of response from outright rejection to one of acceptance and integration. In the following counseling example, a client who had received a promotion to a position that she had been filling at work for several months responds to the counselor's confrontation by examining her behavior.

Client:	All the responsibility and pressure involved in my new job are just too much for me. I really want to succeed, but I just can't handle it.
Counselor:	The job means a lot to you, but right now it feels overwhelming.
Client:	Why make myself suffer? I know it's not for me.
Counselor:	You say that the position is not for you, but you have also told me that before you got the promotion, you basically performed the same work quite successfully.
Client:	I know, but somehow it isn't the same now in my mind since I officially became the director. I need to talk about this.

Cognitive Restructuring. Regression may be integral to an individual's lifestyle, and, by attempting to modify convictions at the core level, therapeutic change may occur at the intermediate level of defense functioning. Cognitive restructuring focuses on constructing alternative frames of reference to faulty or self-defeating perspectives that possibly relate to regression. In a counseling example, a high school student who demonstrates a pattern of insecure and timid behavior perceives himself as vulnerable and incapable of dealing with challenging circumstances. When faced with threatening situations that elicit anxiety, the client employs regression as a defense and withdraws by isolating himself from other people. Only by addressing the individual's ingrained perspectives that have prompted the withdrawal behavior is it likely that change will be effected in his use of regression.

In the following counseling example, a client, after receiving a promotion at work, began acting irresponsibly in a position in which she had been successful on an interim basis. The counselor attempts to alter the individual's core assumption that she is less than a worthy and deserving person.

Client:	My supervisor told me yesterday that I'm not following through on projects and I'm wasting time. I'm so sick of her.
Counselor:	You don't like hearing this, but since you received the promotion, there is a pattern to this type of criticism.

Client: (pause) I can't understand it. I did the same job well before I got the promotion. Now that I'm a regional director, something has changed.

Counselor: Could it be that there is something troublesome about your holding the title of this position?

Client: Well, I never expected to see myself in such a responsible position (pause). I don't feel as though I deserve it.

Counselor: Yet you were selected for the job over equally qualified candidates.

Client: I don't think about that much.

Counselor: Is it possible for you to believe that you are a deserving and capable person?

Client: I don't know. I'm having a difficult time seeing myself that way.

Counselor: I understand how it could seem unfamiliar to you, although in many ways you have already proved that this description is an accurate one.

Client: It's really something I need to work on. I need to realize that . . . .

Reframing. Enabling clients to gain new and alternative perspectives is also possible through the counseling technique of reframing. Reconceptualizing frames of references in constructive directions may stimulate change in clients' use of regression. Consider the example of an adolescent, Jessie, who has demonstrated a pattern of regression use since observing the accidental death of his brother several years ago. Jessie reports to the counselor that he experiences recurring frightening dreams but that he tries not to think about them because his brother seems to be in the dreams. After acknowledging Jessie's fearful feelings relating to the dreams, the counselor invites him to consider that the dreams may represent unresolved issues that are seeking expression. Through this reframe, the counselor attempts to change the meaning of Jessie's dreams from experiences to be avoided to those that possibly offer potentially therapeutic material. In another reframing example, a counselor suggests a semantic change in how a client perceives his behavior since his acceptance of an early retirement from a company at which he was employed for many years.

Client:	I guess I have been making kind of a fool of myself.
Counselor:	Well, the news that you had to take early retirement caught you by surprise.
Client:	Yeah, but then I started acting pretty juvenile after I got the news.
Counselor:	You call your actions juvenile, but maybe you could look at it in another way.
Client:	What do you mean?
Counselor:	Maybe you could view your recent behavior as part of a transition to a more mature level.
Client:	Actually, it has been a big transition for me, and maybe it is fair to see it that way.

Interpretation. Clarifying motivational considerations in a client's use of interpretation may be necessary to effect constructive change in the defense. Interpretation focuses on understanding causal relationships between an individual's current and past functioning. In a counseling example, a school counselor expresses an interpretation in relating an adolescent's immature actions to the traumatic period encompassing his observation of his brother's death.

Client:	I don't know. I just seem to get in trouble around here.
Counselor:	I'm wondering if there is more to this than you are telling me.
Client:	What do you mean?
Counselor:	Well, we talked some about the death of your brother and how you experienced a number of discipline problems after he died.
Client:	He had a horrible death, and I still miss him a lot.
Counselor:	He meant so much to you. What I'm saying is that since you left your tribal school, you also have had discipline problems here. Could it be that the change in schools has renewed feelings about your brother that are still unresolved or troubling to you?
Client:	Well, I do know that I've been having the same terrible dream that I had right after he fell off the cliff.

Accomplishment Stage

Expanding clients' control of their use of regression and developing more adaptive actions are primary goals of the final stage of counseling. Selected counseling strategies enable individuals to establish more purposeful and mature levels of functioning.

Catching Oneself. Even after making a commitment to restrain use of regression tendencies, some clients require support in regulating the defense. "Catching oneself" establishes a cuing device as a person is about to enact the use of regression, and the signaling procedure is a reminder to avoid engaging the defense. Consider, for instance, the middle school student who at this stage in counseling is attempting to break a pattern of immature and impulsive conduct in the classroom. As a means of interdiction, the individual wears a ring-sized elastic on his finger, and at the critical point that he feels compelled to misbehave, he snaps the elastic to alert himself to avert the action. In another example, a client who has demonstrated a pattern of regression after receiving a job promotion considers using a cuing response to restrict her engagement of the defense.

Client:	I realize now that I am capable of being successful at my job. But there are still times when I start to worry about failing.
Counselor:	You find it troublesome when these feelings come back, although you know that they don't make much sense.
Client:	Once I start thinking about falling flat on my face, I can't seem to stop dwelling on it.
Counselor:	Is it possible to stop those doubts when they start, just before you start to respond to them?
Client:	How can I do that?
Counselor:	Can you think of an object that makes you feel qualified and capable of being successful in your new position?
Client:	(pauses) I have a picture from the newspaper that went with a small article about my promotion. I remember how sure of myself I felt when the picture was taken. I knew then that I could do the job.
Counselor:	Perhaps you could carry the picture around with you. That way, when you start to question your abilities, you can take it out and recall how you felt so capable.

| Client: | It might give me a little boost of self-confidence to look at that picture. |

Acting As If. Individuals employing regression for extended periods may be unskilled in more mature modes of functioning. "Acting as if" enables clients to assume the role of a person who demonstrates more purposeful and age-appropriate qualities. As a counseling example, a client who used a pattern of regression immediately after he took an early retirement identifies characteristics of individuals who appear to have made successful adjustments to this life transition.

Client:	I know that I've been acting in irresponsible ways. The job meant so much to me, and now I have nothing to keep me going.
Counselor:	It is a big void to fill in your life. Are you able to identify persons who have made reasonable adjustments in their early retirement?
Client:	A lot of people have trouble adjusting, and I can think of only one or two persons who have done well.
Counselor:	What is it about these individuals that make them stand out?
Client:	Well, they seem to keep busy and stay involved with activities, on both a paid and a volunteer basis.
Counselor:	How might it help for you to use these individuals as models for a time?

Breaking It Down. Individuals employing regression typically experience difficulties with tempering and regulating their actions. "Breaking it down" focuses on establishing manageable plans that enable clients to accomplish age-appropriate goals. In a concluding counseling example, a client acknowledges an awareness of his avoidance behavior, but he continues to feel overwhelmed by academic requirements in his first year of college.

Client:	I can't believe the extent to which I was getting high to avoid my problems. I'm doing much better in looking at reality, but things still seem too much for me at times.
Counselor:	Too much for you?
Client:	I'm behind in two of my classes, and I know one is beyond hope.

Counselor:	I'm wondering if it may help for you to break down what you need to do, rather than think about it all at one time.
Client:	Well, I used to work with a schedule that listed day by day what I needed to do for each of my classes. I guess that I've gotten away from using it in the last few months.
Counselor:	Tell me about the schedule, and perhaps you could make it even more detailed and helpful until you get caught up with your assignments.

CONCLUSION

Regression involves a broad range of age-inappropriate behavior as individuals respond to emotional conflict and threat. A pattern of regression typically evokes interpersonal difficulties when other persons react negatively to persons' lack of assumption of responsibility manifest in the defense. Clients' use of regression includes a temporal quality as they revert to developmentally immature functioning. A three-stage conceptualization of the counseling process includes selected interventions for identifying and modifying regression.

10

REPRESSION

For if the darkness and corruption leave
A vestige of the thoughts that once I had,
Better by far you should forget and smile
Than that you should remember and be sad.

—Christina Rossetti, 1849/1970, p. 42

Personal violations and insults may be barred from consciousness for a period until individuals fortify themselves sufficiently to face painful events. A person's ability to block awareness of distressing experiences may prove to be adaptive, considering the emotional impact of particular circumstances. For example, a psychiatric nurse, when harshly and unfairly criticized by her supervisor in front of a group of colleagues, is able to continue through the day only by putting the ordeal out of her mind. Of an even more consequential nature, a young adult who has endured a series of sexual assaults as a child currently has only a dim recollection of the traumatic episodes. As a response to perceived threat, a person may employ repression as a defense mechanism by preventing the processing of intolerable thoughts and feelings. Although there may be beneficial outcomes from actively inhibiting the effect of emotionally tormenting experiences, this same reaction may also impair an individual's functioning. In a counseling example, an adolescent who, as a child, witnessed the shooting death of her older sister never mentions the incident even after several sessions with a counselor. Since observing the tragedy, the client's behavior has become guarded and emotionally constricted, and she experiences recurrent and terrifying dreams. Defining repression as a defense mechanism emphasizes excluding from awareness intolerable cognitions and affect.

THEORETICAL ASPECTS OF REPRESSION

Emergence of Repression

A fundamental aspect of Sigmund Freud's earliest formulations, his conceptualization of repression changed and evolved through many years (Brenner, 1957). After initially recognizing repression as one of a number of defenses through its effect of shutting out ideas from recollection, Freud (1896/1962a, 1894/1962b) began to equate the terms *repression* and *defense*. Freud (1900/1953a) observed the regular avoidance of distressing memories as a psychical process and clearly stated, *"The essence of repression lies simply in turning something away, and keeping it at a distance, from the consciousness"* (1915/1957b, p. 147). Years later, in a major theoretical revision, Freud (1926/1959) distinguished repression as a specific mechanism and reserved the term *defense* as a general designation similar to his earlier view presented late in the 19th century. Freud (1915/1957b) also recognized a primal repression in childhood involving a barring of awareness of threatening conflicts before they become conscious. Although Freud maintained that no fresh repressions emerge after childhood as old ones persist, he also referred to a second stage of repression, repression proper, in which individuals in their later years become aware of and relegate conflicted material out of consciousness. An essential quality that remained constant throughout Freud's theory development is that repression requires a persistent expenditure of psychic force by an individual to keep intolerable conflicts from conscious awareness and that repressed material may be revealed through dreams, jokes, and neurotic symptoms.

In identifying repression as a defense mechanism, Anna Freud (1936/1966) also recognized the construction of a mental barrier that limits ideas and affect from entering the conscious processing of a person. She further emphasized the significant consumption of energy required of an individual in maintaining this counterforce and its subsequent constrictive and inhibitory effect on the pursuit of vital activities. Further, a person employing the defense typically demonstrates an indifference to experiences that normally elicit interest and involvement among most people. Freud described instances of a child's lack of curiosity about sexuality as possibly indicative of a painful conflict that led to the young person's use of repression. In the same volume, she made reference to secondary repression as a central emphasis with adults in analysis by identifying material that was at one time conscious but had been barred from awareness. Only after a lengthy focus of addressing secondary repression, according to Freud, should therapeutic attention proceed to considerations of preverbal elements under primary repression that had never been considered.

Psychopathology and Repression

Age Adequateness. Depending on the relative age of persons, displays of interest and curiosity about particular topics are customarily expected, and their conspicuous absence may suggest the operation of repression (Freud, 1936/1966). Consider, for example, the 8-year-old child who demonstrates a lack of interest in the vicious fights that she has witnessed between her estranged parents. The client's behavior is also tense and constricted, in contrast to the more spontaneous and high-spirited qualities characteristic of childhood. In another counseling example, a 16-year-old client exhibits a minimal degree of animation and involvement in discussions relating to topics of sexuality and intimacy among her peers. Even after several meetings with the counselor, the client maintains a rigid posture and rarely expresses feelings, both behavioral manifestations that are uncharacteristic of adolescents. In another instance, a client approaching 50 years of age is emotionally unresponsive and repeatedly expresses an indifference and a lack of curiosity about her childhood. This reaction is unlike those of many adults who are intrigued by and find discussions of early life experiences therapeutically beneficial.

Balance. An individual may find relief from threat by employing a compelled pattern of repression. At the same time, persistently restricting the expression of conflicted material may limit psychic energy available for alternative activity. An active inhibitory counterforce may contrive to keep intolerable affect and cognitions from consciousness, but this expenditure of effort generally results in emotional fatigue and a constriction and rigidity in personality functioning (Sappenfield, 1965). In a counseling example, an early adulthood client who was severely abused as a child is anxious and guarded in counseling and complains of feeling chronically tired. Characteristic of persons who use repression for extended periods, the client experiences interpersonal difficulties, and other people often complain that she is constantly tense and withdrawn in social situations.

Intensity. When individuals employ other defense mechanisms, even at inordinate frequency levels, they do so in episodic reactions to perceived threat. Persons using rationalization, for example, express plausible statements to justify their objectionable behavior within a circumscribed and time-limited context. As threatening conditions diminish with the immediate employment of rationalization, individuals generally disengage the mechanism. In contrast to this dynamic, repression is constantly employed regarding sustained psychic energy expenditure. In effect, persons using repression are in a continuous state of guardedness and vigilance as a defensive posture. Further, with the operation of a counterforce, clients stave off intolerable conflicted affect from consciousness but, at the same time, preclude examination of issues inherent to the perpetuation of the defense. In a study completed with undergraduate students, Hansen and Hansen (1988) concluded that repression is fear motivated and that fear-tagged memories are particularly inaccessible within the repressive architecture.

Reversibility. Individuals can employ repression to exclude intolerable thoughts and feelings long after a perceived threat has diminished.

In a counseling example, a 40-year-old client named Althea experienced a pattern of abusive and fractious familial relationships as a child that resulted in intense feelings of shame. In response to the painful and degrading episodes, Althea assumed repression as a defense. Although she has not experienced insult from family members for many years, Althea continues to engage repression. Consequently, she demonstrates an emotional constriction and depletion of psychic energy, inherent with repression, that are now fully assimilated into her lifestyle. For Althea, and other clients like her, the therapeutic question arises whether it is advisable to disrupt a defense pattern that has been preserved into adulthood (Herman & Schatzow, 1987) and has provided a measure of psychological equilibrium and a buffer from unresolved conflict. At the same time, an exploration of painful developmental memories may afford clients an understanding of inexplicable and intolerable experiences that were beyond their capacity to endure and comprehend as a child or in earlier life stages (Sappenfield, 1965).

Context. Social and cultural forces relating to individuals' employment of repression are essential for the counselor to consider. Within an environmental context, persons may have experienced painful occasions that prompted the use of repression. By exploring past conditions, it becomes possible to clarify their current functioning. A difficulty occurs, however, with clients who use repression in that they typically resist discussion or have difficulty recalling past events or particular periods. It then becomes necessary for the counselor to evaluate collateral information or indirect sources that may suggest client experiences that are repressed. In a counseling example, a military veteran avoids discussing events relating to his combat experience during his tour of duty in Vietnam. The counselor, however, possesses a report indicating that the client participated in a high number of enemy assaults and likely witnessed numerous deaths and atrocities. In another counseling instance, a client's pattern of dreams may indirectly reveal the use of repression. Consider, for example, an interaction with Kim, an early adulthood client, who appears tense and withdrawn in initial sessions with a college counselor. Kim resists discussing her personal history prior to when she entered a private residential high school, and it is therefore difficult for the counselor to assess her developmental history. Attempting to gain increased client understanding, the counselor asks Kim if she dreams. In response, Kim haltingly describes a terrifying dream that she has experienced repeatedly since her childhood. The dream depicts Kim and her older sister being physically threatened at an early age by gang members in a part of the city that is widely known for extensive crime and violence. The dream suggests a relationship between Kim's percep- tions of her early experience in a hostile and threatening environment and her subsequent employment of repression.

PROCESSING REPRESSION IN COUNSELING

Relationship Stage

Individuals employing repression typically demonstrate behavior that is guarded, rigid, and tense. In response to clients' apprehension and hesitancy to become involved in the therapeutic process, the counseling techniques of reflection and assessment procedures offer supportive qual- ities. Self-disclosure of the counselor is another selected intervention that potentially promotes more open communication and rapport building.

Reflection. An essential purpose of individuals' use of repression is to avoid awareness of painful feelings and perceptions. The task of the counselor is to validate clients' hesitancy to engage in personal disclosure but, in time, to encourage them to express threatening material. Reflec- tion of feeling enables persons to begin to bring to the surface guilt, shame, anxiety, or other affect originally associated with a pattern of repression. In a counseling example, a late adolescent client exhibits constricted behavior and resists discussing developmental periods in his life. In response, a counselor uses reflection of feeling, "At this point, talking about your past makes you feel increasingly anxious." Sub- sequently, the counselor may use reflection of meaning to clarify the tacit communication of the client. The counselor continues, "When we approach discussion relating to earlier periods in your life, you find yourself becoming tense, and this warns you not to proceed further."

A client's employment of repression may be inferred through a variety of constricted and inhibited behaviors. The following examples suggest possible engagement of the defense:

- An early adulthood Asian American client is in counseling because of her inability to form close, personal relationships with others. She informs the counselor that she is doing well but appears tense and apprehensive and rarely offers information about her family or her childhood.
- A middle school student has been referred to the school counselor because he isolates himself from others. In counseling, the client is nonexpressive much of the time and assumes a rigid and immobile position in his chair.
- A client initiates counseling because she is repeatedly abused by her violence-prone husband. Although the client expresses no recollection of abuse in her family of origin, her mother informs the counselor that both she and her daughter were emotionally and physically abused by her husband.
- A Vietnam veteran is in counseling because he drinks excessively and has recently lost both his wife and his job. The client rarely refers to his military service although he experienced extenvesive combat duty.
- A 15-year-old African American client who demonstrates a minimal degree of emotion relates a recurrent dream that he has had for years. In the dream, he is running with a number of people on an open highway when a huge bird swoops down and carries away a person. As the sky darkens, other birds fly over his head. Just as one begins to attack, the client wakes up terrified.

In each of these cases, a counselor's use of reflection may clarify client perceptions and feelings. In the following counseling example, a middle school student rarely expresses emotion since the bitter divorce of his parents more than 3 years ago. The counselor uses reflection of feeling, but the client responds with only a minimal expression of affect.

Client:	Some people think that they need a best friend, but it's easier just not to bother with anyone.
Counselor:	You seem a little uncertain about this.
Client:	No, not really. I actually prefer to do things by myself.
Counselor:	You appear to feel a little sad when you say this.
Client:	I'm doing OK.

Assessment. Evaluating multiple perspectives allows the counselor to more accurately infer client use of repression. In combination, observations of client behavior, collateral sources, and projective techniques often provide sufficient data to discern a pattern of defense use. In the following counseling examples, client statements contradict other aspects of their behavior and suggest possible employment of repression.

1. *Statement:* I don't know why you keep asking me about my childhood. I already told you that it was fine.
   Nonverbal expression: The client becomes physically rigid and tense when issues relating to her early development are discussed.

2. *Statement:* I don't care if I'm alone quite a bit.
   Previous statement: Sometimes, I wish that I had somebody to do things with.

3. *Statement:* My marriage is pretty good; I'm happy enough. I really can't think of any major problems that we have.
   Action: Any discussion of intimacy in the client's marriage results in her becoming anxious and making obvious efforts to change the subject.

4. *Statement:* The war didn't really affect me all that much. I just did my time and came home.
   Objective condition: The client's tour of duty in Vietnam involved prolonged combat conditions, during which he witnessed numerous atrocities.

5. *Statement:* I can't figure out the dream because I can't see any of the people's faces.
   Omission: The client fails to inform the counselor that when he was 8 years old, he saw his older brother killed in a shooting outside his apartment building.

Employer and teacher reports are examples of collateral data that may enable the counselor to clarify client use of repression. Inconsistencies between clients' behavior and collateral information may suggest repression employment. In a counseling example, a tense and apprehensive young adulthood client resists discussing her childhood and dismisses her early years as largely uneventful. In contrast to this view, a social worker's report indicates that the client had been sexually abused by her mother's boyfriend. Considering the controversy surrounding the topic of false memory phenomena, careful corroboration of sexual abuse is an essential consideration in ascertaining the validity of repressed memories (Pope & Hudson, 1995; Reisner, 1996). The counselor should also be aware that bilingual clients speaking in their nondominant language may appear emotionally withdrawn and passive (Marcos, 1980). Linguistic demands of speaking in a less familiar language may produce slower speeds and pauses, and the counselor must account for this variable in evaluating client use of repression.

Selected projective techniques may also be of assistance in assessing a person's use of repression. Elicitation of early memories contributes to evaluating a client's lifestyle that may relate to repression use. Consider, for example, an emotionally constricted 60-year-old client who describes one of her early recollections:

> I was playing in the backyard of my house, and I was supposed to be minding my little sister. When my mother came into the yard, she asked me where my sister was, and I didn't know. She screamed at me, and I felt so scared and stupid.

The memory suggests that the client maintains core convictions of incompetency and shame, and these painful perceptions are excluded from consciousness through a repression barrier (Loughead, 1992).

Inferences about individuals' use of repression may also be construed through human figure drawings and sentence completion tasks. Contradictions between clients' overt behavior and hypotheses drawn from their drawings of a person may suggest the use of repression. A docile and submissive male client, for example, who draws a figure indicating evidence of aggression (such as exaggerated size, closed fists, and teeth emphasis) may be maintaining considerable tensions that are controlled by repression, suppression, or a combination of either counterforce

(Hammer, 1958). Inconsistencies between clients' demonstrated behavior and particular endings on sentence completion tasks may also suggest repression use. To continue with the example of the client who demonstrates passive and timid actions, his responses to the following sentence stems point to an inhibition of aggression and the employment of repression or suppression: "I feel . . . like punching people in the face sometimes." "I am afraid of . . . what I may do if I explode." "My greatest worry is . . . that I may hurt someone." In other instances, individuals' use of repression may be inferred by voids in responses and the omission of particular sentence stems that evoke conflict. Consider, for example, the case of a young adulthood client who was sexually abused by her mother's boyfriend when she was 11 years old. The client completes each of the 25 sentence stems with the following exceptions: "At home . . . " "My mother . . . " "I suffer . . . " "I hate . . ."

Self-Disclosure. A counselor's self-disclosure may relate to client use of repression and may clarify the function of the defense. Success or failure experiences of the counselor are among the various dimensions of self-disclosure that may also enhance the counseling relationship. In a counseling example, an adolescent has demonstrated rigid and emotionally inhibited behavior since witnessing the violent death of her younger sister. Although the client hesitatively describes a terrifying dream that appears to relate to the loss of her sister, she is reluctant to explore the dream further. In response, after acknowledging the client's feelings, the counselor relates how he used to avoid thinking about "bad" dreams but that he has learned, in recent years, that they are often helpful in understanding himself. A counselor may also disclose past or present experiences that are pertinent to a client's use of repression. For instance, a client who is suspected to have been sexually abused as a child mentions that she constantly feels tired and emotionally drained. The counselor hypothesizes that the individual's chronic fatigue may be a function of her sustained use of repression. Relating to the client's complaints, the counselor states that several years ago, she found herself depleted and lethargic much of the time. Only after several months did the counselor find relief from the fatigue after she began working through a personal conflict that she had attempted to put out of her mind.

Similar or dissimilar experiences are other dimensions of self-disclosure of the counselor that may be relevant to client employment of repression. Consider, for example, a client in counseling who fleetingly admits that he often feels tense and apprehensive. When the counselor attempts to explore in greater detail the source of the individual's tension, however, the client resists discussing the topic further. The counselor, in response, discusses a parallel experience in which he has attempted to block out thoughts that make him feel tense because he does not want to make matters worse by focusing on them. At the same time, the counselor relates that this tactic frequently results in his feeling even more anxious about the issues. A counselor may also express self-involving statements in reaction to a client's behavior in counseling. Take, for instance, an Asian American client who acts in a deferential and respectful way toward the counselor and avoids talking about his parents or any issue related to his family of origin. The counselor decides to acknowledge this pattern of omission by the client to determine whether he is respecting his family's privacy and reputation or possibly employing the defense of repression.

Integration Stage

Capitalizing on the trust and understanding established in the relationship stage, therapeutic focus in the middle period of counseling emphasizes the clarification of client contradictions and conflicts intrinsic to repression. Selected counseling techniques emphasized in this stage include confrontation, cognitive restructuring, reframing, and interpretation.

Confrontation. Contradictory client behavior relating to repression can be challenged through a counselor's employment of confrontation. Individuals' statements that are inconsistent with other aspects of their behavior, objective conditions, or significant omitted material are now recognized. The following counseling examples include ambiguous client statements and subsequent counselor confrontations.

1. *Statement—Nonverbal Expression*

Client: I don't know why you keep asking me about my childhood. I already told you that it was fine.

Counselor: You wish to emphasize that things were fine for you as a child, yet whenever this topic comes up, you appear to become tense.

2. *Statement—Previous Statement*

Client: I don't care if I'm alone quite a bit.

Counselor: You feel you do OK by yourself, but you said before that it would be nice to have someone to do things with.

3. *Statement—Action*

Client: My marriage is pretty good; I'm happy enough. I really can't think of any major problems that we have.

Counselor: You believe that your marriage relationship is pretty good, but you seem to avoid expressing feelings of affection toward your husband.

4. *Statement—Objective Condition*

Client: The war didn't really affect me all that much. I just did my time and came home.

Counselor: You say that the war did not have much of an impact on you, yet you tell me that you often have bad dreams about the atrocities you witnessed during combat.

5. *Statement—Omission*

Client: I can't figure out the dream because I can't see any of the faces of the people.

Counselor: Although you cannot see their faces, you seem worried about the people in the dream.

In a counseling example, a Vietnam veteran appears to employ repression relating to his combat experience, and the counselor uses a confrontation. In response, the client initially rejects the counselor's confrontation attempt.

Client: I already told you that I don't think about the war anymore. It's just part of my past. It has nothing to do with my life now.

Counselor:	You want to believe that your war experience is pretty much behind you, but whenever your duty in Vietnam is mentioned, you appear to become agitated.
Client:	So are you saying that I'm lying about everything here?
Counselor:	No. I'm describing the way you appear to react when we refer to your combat service.

Cognitive Restructuring. It is possible that the employment of repression relates to individuals' lifestyles and persists as an enduring personality pattern. To effect more enduring change in clients' use of repression, it may be necessary to address their core convictions integral to the defense. Cognitive restructuring focuses on modifying maladaptive client schemas in a more purposeful direction through the collaborative effort of the client and counselor. An individual, for example, holds core assumptions of feeling flawed and shamed, and her use of repression excludes the painful convictions. In this instance, unless the client's perception that she is not an adequate person is modified in a more constructive direction, it is unlikely that she will reduce the use of repression.

In the following example, a counselor begins to use cognitive restructuring with a 20-year-old client who experienced neglect and abuse as a child.

Client:	Well, there really isn't that much in my childhood that is important to talk about.
Counselor:	You feel fairly certain about this, but at the same time, you experience dreams from that period in which you are continually humiliated.
Client:	I need to forget the dreams to feel better about myself.
Counselor:	You do what you can to keep the shameful feelings in the dreams from affecting you.
Client:	This is hard for me to say, but I feel bad about myself just talking about this with you.
Counselor:	You are saying something that is difficult for you, but at the same time, this may be a breakthrough for you.
Client:	How can it be good if it feels so bad?
Counselor:	Perhaps you have been telling yourself for so long that you are less than adequate and that sharing this with another person makes it feel even worse.

Client: It hurts a lot inside (sobbing).

Counselor: Your pain is connecting with you more fully.

Client: I need to face this, though, but . . .

Counselor: You are now facing the deep hurt, and perhaps in time, you
               can begin to tell yourself that you are a worthy person.

Client: I really need to do both things.

Reframing. Modifying the self-defeating employment of repression
may also be possible by altering an individual's perspective of the
defense. Reframing emphasizes semantic change by constructing alternative meanings of a client's employment of repression. In a counseling
example, a middle school student hesitatively mentions to a counselor
that since his parents' divorce a few years ago, he seems to feel "uptight."
The counselor is aware that the client is possibly using repression to
block awareness of the brutal fights that his parents engaged in when he
was a child and acknowledges the individual's feelings of distress.
Subsequently, the counselor uses a reframe by stating that the client may
have needed to buffer himself and hold in his thoughts and feelings
relating to the divorce until he was older and more ready emotionally
to deal with it. In a related reframing example, a middle adulthood client
is resistant to exploring her past that involves early betrayals and
prolonged repression use.

Client: I stopped thinking about my past a long time ago. I just think
               that whatever is there should be left alone. I couldn't handle
               much earlier in my life.

Counselor: But you're not the same person that you were when you were
               younger.

Client: What do you mean?

Counselor: As a mature and independent adult, you are quite a different
               individual than you were as a vulnerable young person. You
               blocked out what you had to, but now you are more capable
               of dealing with threatening thoughts and feelings.

Interpretation. As another counseling technique that invites clients
to consider alternative perspectives, interpretation additionally focuses
on motivational and causal considerations. For some persons, it is
necessary to offer new explanations about their experience, including

the persistent use of repression (Myerson, 1977). Consider, for example, the instance of an adolescent who describes a recurrent dream and the counselor's interpretation response.

Client:	In my dream, I can't see people's faces, and it really scares me.
Counselor:	Although you can't see their faces, you are afraid that everyone is in danger.
Client:	Well, somehow I know that one of the persons is me, and a big bird is about to fly down and take me away.
Counselor:	This is frightening to you. I'm wondering if it could be possible that the dream brings back feelings that you are trying to hide even from yourself?
Client:	(pause) It's the same feeling that I had when I saw my brother shot and killed.
Counselor:	Perhaps you can begin to understand now how you have tried to block out your thoughts and feelings about this because you find them so terrible to think about.
Client:	I feel really scared now just talking about it, but maybe it's time that I begin to deal with it.

Accomplishment Stage

For some individuals, the constant use of repression results in an emotionally constricted range of functioning, and support is needed to establish alternative behavior patterns. In the final stage of counseling, selected action-oriented counseling strategies enable clients to achieve more adaptive and coherent behaviors.

Catching Oneself. In the integration stage, clients process conflicted material relating to repression that they have kept from awareness. As a consequence of this continuing effort, individuals tend to become emotionally more expressive. Some persons, however, find themselves uncomfortable in the change process and begin to assume previous constricted levels of functioning. Consequently, clients may benefit from employing "catching oneself" by engaging a cuing device at the moment that they are about to trigger inhibited features of the defense. In a counseling example, an early adulthood client named Kim, who, in earlier periods of counseling, addressed her early history of sexual abuse, relates that she is now affectively more open but also feels unsure of herself. In response, the counselor asks Kim if she could identify a small object that she owns that could provide a measure of comfort as she encounters new and unfamiliar experiences. After clarifying the counselor's request, Kim decides to wear a locket that had been given to her by her grandmother as an amulet. At the moment that she feels emotionally uncertain, Kim touches the neck locket and reminds herself that she is venturing into change but continues to possess a protective level of caring from a loving person in her past.

In another counseling example involving catching oneself, an adolescent expresses concerns about dealing with issues that he previously repressed.

Client:	I don't want to go back to the way things were. I know I now have to face what happened, but I still get scared and unsure of things.
Counselor:	You have worked through a lot of feelings about your parents' divorce, and this represents a big change for you.
Client:	I just wish I could be stronger in dealing with all this.
Counselor:	It sounds as if you could use a boost to stay on track and not go back to the way things were when you were keeping so much inside.
Client:	Yeah, my mom and I are a lot happier now that I've started talking to her about things. I don't want that to change.
Counselor:	That is important to you, and maybe there's a way to help keep this fresh in your mind. Would you happen to have a picture or something else that reminds you of how much better things are now for you?
Client:	Well, Mom and I went to a Red Sox baseball game last week and had a great time. I put the ticket stub on my desk at home, and when I look at it, I remember how much fun we had.
Counselor:	Maybe you could carry the ticket stub in your pocket. When you feel uncertain about things, take out the stub and remind yourself how far you have come.

Acting As If. Because of the prolonged employment of repression, some individuals are unpracticed or unfamiliar with more spontaneous expressions of behavior. Clients may need support in pursuing open and purposeful communication that may have been inhibited by extensive repression use. "Acting as if" enables individuals to act how they would like to behave in assumed and constructive roles and provides an alternative to the use of repression. In the following counseling example, a 35-year-old client has made therapeutic gains relating to her history of abuse, but she experiences difficulty in crystallizing a perception of herself as a capable and assertive person.

Client:	I know that I need to regain control of my life and find a way to deal with everything that happened. I'm just not sure if I'm strong enough.
Counselor:	So many new thoughts and feelings have come up that you question your ability to deal with them all.
Client:	Yes, part of the problem is that I've been a passive person for so long, I forgot how it used to be when I did stand up for myself.
Counselor:	It sounds as if you need some help in deciding how you would like to act—perhaps more assertively.
Client:	I'm open to just about anything now.
Counselor:	I'm wondering if there are any women you know who live the type of life you would like to live in the future?
Client:	There is the assistant director at the domestic violence center that I've been going to. Her husband used to beat her really bad but she's worked hard to turn her life around. I really respect her.
Counselor:	What is it about her behavior that you admire? If we can get an idea of how she acts, it may help you try to behave in some of the ways she does.

Breaking It Down. Although individuals may express an intent to control their use of repression, they sometimes become overwhelmed by the prospect of attempting to mitigate the mechanism. "Breaking it down" emphasizes making small and incremental changes in attempting to regulate repression and establish more adaptive actions. In a concluding counseling example, a Vietnam veteran who has made clear therapeutic gains in working through his violent war experiences begins to question his ability to manage change.

Client: When I start to think about everything—my memories from the war, losing my job, losing my wife—I just feel so overwhelmed. I want to find a way to get through all this, but I don't know where to start.

Counselor: There is so much to deal with all at one time. Perhaps it may help if you could decide which concern is the most important for you to work on first, and you could start there.

Client: I know that working through my combat background has been the most important topic for me. I think at this point, though, I need to find a job and deal with other things coming down.

Counselor: Would it make sense for you to focus on finding work for now, and then think about the next concern you wish to address? In this way, by pursuing one objective at a time, it may be less overwhelming.

CONCLUSION

Repression affords individuals a means to bar intolerable thoughts and feelings from awareness. Theoretically, persons construct a mental barrier that requires a constant expenditure of psychic energy. This counterforce results in emotionally constricted and depleted behavior that may be observed by a counselor. Clients typically resist exploring their past in counseling and appear to lack curiosity about topics that are of interest to most people. A three-stage conceptualization of the counseling process provides the counselor with a framework for using selected techniques and interventions in processing clients' employment of repression.

11

UNDOING

> "I have done that," says my memory.
> "I cannot have done that," says my pride,
> and remains inexorable. Eventually—memory yields.
>
> —Friedrich Nietzsche, 1886/1989, p. 80[1]

Pride is not the only emotion that prompts people to relinquish the memory of experiences that they wish to forget. Shame, regret, humiliation, and other painful feelings affect a person's desire to dismiss perceived transgressions. Depending on the contextual circumstances of the behavior that is attempted to be forgotten, the letting-go process may be purposeful or maladaptive. In a related direction, individuals may pursue a step beyond memory yield and take an action that seeks to negate or undo a prior act. Through an expiatory gesture, a person may retract a previous behavior. A woman, for instance, says to a friend, "I don't like the way John neglects his kids" and immediately nullifies the statement with "but in many ways, he is a good father." The second segment of the individual's assertion annuls the first part and possibly reduces embarrassment or anxiety that she experiences with her initial assertion. This dynamic has been conceptualized as the defense mechanism of undoing. In a counseling example, a client demonstrates a pattern of expressing caustic remarks followed by an immediate apology for his statements. Defining undoing as a defense mechanism emphasizes nullifying a perceived transgression through a reverse action.

THEORETICAL ASPECTS OF UNDOING

Emergence of Undoing

In a case study that introduced the operation of undoing, Freud (1909/1955e) details how a patient who became known as the "Rat Man" felt compelled to move a stone in the road in the event that his friend's horse carriage might be overturned by it. After a few minutes, the Rat Man, recognizing the absurdity of his behavior, decided to return the rock to its original position in the road. Freud further recognized the obsessive quality of undoing when it involves an expiation for a perceived transgression that negates its effect. An individual, for example, experiences hostility toward another person, which is immediately followed by a desire to make amends for having harbored hostile feelings. In a later work, Freud (1926/1959) specifically identified the function of undoing as a defense mechanism: "When anything has not happened in the desired way it is undone by being repeated in a different way" (p. 120).

In classifying undoing as a defense, Anna Freud (1936/1966) recognized that the mechanism involved two successive and paired steps involving an initial gesture and a reversal through a subsequent act. She also emphasized the role of undoing as a defense against anxiety in obsessional neurosis. A later publication (Sandler & Freud, 1985) clarified the function of undoing in obsessive-compulsive behavior. Freud conceptualized that just as a person can put a thing in its place and remove it again, this also can be mentally done in the mind to block out and undo an act.

Psychopathology and Undoing

Age Adequateness. As with other defense mechanisms, the relative age of an individual employing undoing is critical in determining its developmental appropriateness. The "magical" quality inherent in undoing that allows for the annulment of actions, as if they did not occur, may be more typical of childhood and may be expected to diminish as a person advances in age. A 6-year-old child, for example, repeatedly creates a mess in his room and immediately begins to clean it up. The young person, possibly fearing the loss of his parents' love and affection because of his misdeeds, attempts to reverse his initial actions. It may be difficult for a counselor to distinguish between this functioning characteristic of childlike behavior and the defense of undoing. In contrast, if an adolescent engages in a repetitive sequence of messing and cleaning, the likelihood of the employment of undoing becomes more viable. In another instance, a 45-year-old client who expresses demeaning comments toward others quickly retracts the statements and excuses himself for his improprieties. This pattern of behavior lacks an integrated quality that is more representative of a person in middle adulthood and therefore suggests the use of undoing.

Balance. Individuals may employ undoing in an entrenched pattern as a predominant means to fend off threat. In a two-step defensive sequence, after expressing or demonstrating an impulse, a person controls its threatening consequences through an expiatory action (White & Gilliland, 1975). Although reversing a behavior serves as a countermeasure to minimize its impact, the inherent conflict between opposing forces remains unaddressed. Consider the counseling example of a 30-year-old client who expresses a hostile comment about her father and immediately recants the statement. The client exclaims, "I really hate him, but I guess I shouldn't say that because he is a good person." The woman's ambivalence is evident in the retraction of the initial part of her statement, but her conflicted feelings persist with the sustained engagement of undoing.

Intensity. Some persons tend to employ undoing with excessive frequency as the defense assumes obsessive-compulsive qualities. An intense pattern of undoing may result in strained interpersonal relationships because of the ambivalent and capricious functioning manifest in the defense. In a counseling example, a client repeatedly evinces a sequence of expressing caustic comments and immediately retracting his statements. In response to the individual's mixed messages, his spouse and business associates typically react with confusion and dismay over what is perceived as false promises to change his behavior. Considering the intensity of clients' use of undoing, it may be possible that the defense use relates to their lifestyles. In the cited example, the client's inferred core convictions indicate that he perceives life as unpredictable and uncertain. Relatedly, the client's contradictory expressions evident in his employment of undoing possibly reflect his ambiguous perceptions of life.

Reversibility. A person may continue to employ undoing for extended periods, even after the threatening conditions that prompted the adoption of the defense have changed or become nonexistent. Rather than recognizing a diminution of threat, an individual may persist in engaging undoing to reverse situations. In a counseling example, a 25-year-old client who was raped in her mid-adolescence demonstrates obsessive-compulsive tendencies relating to personal hygiene and cleanliness. Although the sexual assault occurred years earlier, the client continues to use undoing as a defense that provides her with a semblance of control and symbolic renunciation of her traumatic experience. Instances of long-term use of undoing may also be assimilated into a client's lifestyle, including perceptions affected by trauma. In the example cited, the client's habitual cleaning pattern related to undoing suggests a core conviction in which she perceives herself as a defiled person.

Context. Social and cultural contexts can influence the adoption of undoing and provide an increased understanding of motivational forces relating to the defense. In a counseling example, an early adulthood client is physically abusive toward his spouse. Although he sincerely apologizes for his assaults after each incident, the client maintains his pattern of abuse. When explaining his developmental history, the client related that his father, who abused alcohol, frequently came home drunk and beat his mother. After his father sobered up, he was apologetic and attempted to make amends for his actions. The similarity is apparent between the pattern of behavior that the client witnessed in his family as a child and his current use of undoing. In another counseling instance, a late adulthood African American client named Marcus is frequently sarcastic toward other persons in his residential community. Immediately after each verbal outburst, Marcus attempts to retract his statements and says that he is sorry. In discussing his early life history, Marcus disclosed numerous instances of racial discrimination. Marcus's typical pattern in dealing with intolerance was to express his anger and resentment but then to recant his statements. Given the oppressive and threatening conditions surrounding his formative experiences, Marcus's partial protest became a functional compromise. Subsequently, it may be assumed, he expanded his use of undoing to other occasions that induced threat in his life.

PROCESSING UNDOING IN COUNSELING

Relationship Stage

Individuals employing undoing typically express conflicted feelings in the initial stage of counseling. Reflection, assessment methods, and self-disclosure of the counselor are counseling interventions that clarify clients' functioning and enhance the counseling alliance.

Reflection. Persons employing undoing maintain ambivalent feelings that require clarification in counseling. Reflection enables the counselor to respond to a client's ambivalence and confusion. In a counseling example, a client expresses anger and self-reproach when reflecting on those occasions when he physically abuses his wife. In response, the counselor uses the following reflection of feeling: "You, at the same time, feel angry toward your wife and shameful about abusing her." Understandably, the client may be unsettled by this clarification, and the counselor subsequently offers a reflection of meaning: "This is confusing to you because you seem to hold feelings that are opposed and contradictory."

Instances of a client's employment of undoing occur in counseling. The following examples illustrate various possibilities:

- Immediately after asking to borrow a pencil from a counselor, a preadolescent deliberately breaks the pencil and then profusely apologizes for her action.
- After losing his job because he arrived at work intoxicated, a client promises that he will never touch another drop of alcohol.
- A Hispanic American client who has been raped feels the need to take several showers a day and tends to be compulsive about cleaning.
- After being critical and intolerant of the shortcomings of others, a client demonstrates a pattern of apologizing for his actions a short time later.
- An 8-year-old student is bossy toward other children in his class and on the playground. When confronted by his teacher for his behavior, the client always says that he is sorry and will not act this way again.

In response to each of these examples, the counselor may employ reflection to promote client support and understanding. In the following counseling example, the counselor uses reflection with a rape victim.

Client:	I feel so dirty all the time. I just can't seem to get clean enough.
Counselor:	You feel as though you must constantly clean yourself and your surroundings, but somehow this still doesn't make you feel right.
Client:	Nothing seems to work. None of it seems to make much difference.
Counselor:	At the same time, you believe that you must do something to relieve the degraded feelings that you have.

Assessment. Although the ambivalent and tenuous quality of undoing may be readily recognizable by a counselor, additional data can confirm the employment of the defense. Client behavior, collateral sources, and projective material contribute to the evaluation of individuals' use of undoing. In the following counseling examples, inconsistencies between client statements and other behavioral manifestations suggest the use of undoing.

1. *Statement:* I'm really sorry for breaking your pencil.
   Nonverbal expression: Smiling.

2. *Statement:* I'm not going to lose this new job because of my drinking.
   Previous statement: I don't know whether I'll ever be able to stop drinking.

3. *Statement:* I think I'm doing better in some respects.
   Action: The client takes several showers a day and compulsively cleans her apartment.

4. *Statement:* Things usually go pretty well at work.
   Objective condition: Most people do not like to work with the client because she is frequently either faultfinding or apologizing for her actions.

5. *Statement:* I'm not going to bother the kids in my room anymore.
   Omission: An hour before meeting with the counselor, the student was sent to the principal by his teacher for teasing several classmates.

Collateral information from various sources, such as statements from family members or teachers, may corroborate a client's use of undoing. A classroom teacher, for example, reports that a student repeatedly teases other students but then appears contrite about his misbehavior. Despite numerous instances of a commitment to change, however, the individual persists with his infringement. In another example, a late adulthood client has alienated himself from old friends and relatives because of his capricious behavior. The client's sister states that he continually belittles others, and although he immediately asks for forgiveness, most people now avoid him.

Early recollections are among several selected projective techniques that may also clarify a person's use of undoing. Early memories may also suggest an integral relationship to a client's lifestyle. Consider, for example, the middle adulthood client who relates the following childhood memory: "I was in the kitchen with my mother, and I yelled at her that I hated her. My mother started crying, and I felt bad inside. I ran outside so that I could put it out of my mind." The essential aspect of the memory relates to the client's ambivalent feelings and his reluctance to express more intimate feelings. The recollection suggests that the client perceives himself as emotionally disconnected from others in expressing affection. Undoing as a defense wards off this conflicted core conviction.

Other projective techniques, including human figure drawings and sentence completion tasks, assist in understanding clients' use of undoing. When rendering a human figure drawing, persons employing undoing may scribble over lines and objects in an effort to drastically change or obliterate their graphic product (Levick, 1983). Clients' use of retractors when completing the human figures may also suggest the employment of undoing. Individuals, for instance, state, "This is such a waste of time, but I'll do my best." "I hate doing drawings, although that's not important." "I think this is stupid, but I guess I shouldn't say that." In completing sentence stems, a client engaging in undoing also tends to use retractions. To illustrate, consider the following responses to sentence stems: "I suffer . . . from frightening dreams, although they're really not too bad." "I hate school . . . but I guess it's necessary." "I regret . . . so many things, but there is so much that I have to be thankful for."

Self-Disclosure. Recounting experiences of success or failure are among the various dimensions of counselor self-disclosure that can enhance a client's awareness of undoing. In a counseling example, a middle adulthood client expresses conflicted feelings toward her elderly mother: "I really can't stand her, but she is my mother, and I love her." In response, the counselor relates how she experienced similar emotions toward her deceased father, and only by working through her ambivalent feelings was she able to find some relief. Past or present accounts of a counselor's use of undoing may also promote communication in counseling. Consider, for example, the early adulthood client who has demonstrated obsessive-compulsive cleaning tendencies since her rape several years earlier. In a supportive way, the counselor describes her experiences as an adolescent when her parents went through a divorce that was difficult and traumatic for her. For a lengthy period after their separation, the counselor kept her bedroom extremely clean, believing that somehow this would bring her parents together again.

It is also possible for a counselor to express similar or dissimilar experiences relating to a client's employment of undoing. For example, an adolescent who is ridiculed by other students demonstrates a pattern of undoing by retracting expressed statements. The client says, "Those kids really scare me, but I think some of them like me," and "I hate those kids, but I shouldn't say that." After acknowledging the client's conflicted feelings, the therapist describes a time in school when he was teased by other students and how he experienced mixed feelings toward them. Self-involving statements may also be expressed by a counselor relating to a client's employment of undoing. A counselor, for instance, recognizes a client's courage in his willingness to explore the conflicted feelings that he experiences as a result of peer ridicule.

Integration Stage

Building on the foundation of trust and understanding established in the relationship stage, counseling emphasis in the middle period of counseling begins to focus on clarifying contradictory dynamics that relate to undoing. Selected counseling techniques, including confrontation, cognitive restructuring, reframing, and interpretation, may be used to clarify a client's ambivalent behavior.

Confrontation. Perhaps more than with any other defense mechanism, an individual's contradictory and conflicted functioning becomes apparent with a patterned employment of undoing. Inconsistencies emerge between a client's statements and nonverbal expressions, previous statements, actions, objective conditions, and omissions. In the following examples, a counselor uses confrontation to challenge diverse clients.

1. *Statement—Nonverbal Expression*
   Client: I'm really sorry for breaking your pencil.
   Counselor: You say you are sorry, but you are smiling as you say this.

2. *Statement—Previous Statement*
   Client: I'm not going to lose this new job because of my drinking.

> **Counselor:**   You sound determined when you say this, but you just told me that you are not certain if you will ever be able to stop drinking.

3. Statement—Action

> **Client:**   I think I'm doing better in some respects.
>
> **Counselor:**   You want to believe that you are progressing, yet since the rape occurred, you take several showers a day and repeatedly clean your surroundings.

4. Statement—Objective Condition

> **Client:**   Things usually go pretty well at work.
>
> **Counselor:**   You feel that you are doing OK, but you recently told me that you have had a number of arguments with other employees.

5. Statement—Omission

> **Client:**   I'm not going to bother the kids in my room anymore.
>
> **Counselor:**   As determined as you seem to be about this, you teased some boys in your classroom this morning and were sent to the principal's office.

Clients respond with varying levels of acceptance of a counselor's use of confrontation. In the following example, a middle adulthood client begins to examine a confrontation by the counselor in regard to her ambivalent feelings toward her mother.

> **Client:**   Sometimes, I feel as though I can't stand her anymore, but I do love her.
>
> **Counselor:**   You are feeling angry at your mother, but at the same time, you have strong feelings of affection toward her.
>
> **Client:**   I'm really mixed up about it (pause). I'm embarrassed to say this, but I feel both hate and love toward her.

Cognitive Restructuring.   Individuals' patterned use of undoing may suggest an integral relationship of the defense to their lifestyles. To effect a more enduring change in client use of undoing as a defense, it may be necessary to address their core convictions. The counseling technique of cognitive restructuring focuses on transposing dysfunctional client schemas. Consider the example of the 50-year-old individual who attempts to reverse a sense of shame by compulsively cleaning himself. Unless the person's self-attribution of being less than sufficient is altered, it is unlikely that he will relinquish a defense pattern that wards off painful conflicted affect. In another counseling instance, a counselor uses cognitive restructuring with an early adulthood client.

Client:	I know that I'm always putting people down, and I feel bad after I do it, but I can't seem to stop.
Counselor:	You have an understanding about what seems to be a contradictory pattern, and you are able to admit that this creates problems for you.
Client:	I know, and it certainly does get me into a lot of bad situations.
Counselor:	It seems to me that first you are telling yourself that everyone else is wrong and that you are right, and then you immediately admit that you are wrong.
Client:	That's true. I guess I always see things and people as either all good or all bad. I always feel so sorry when I overreact and sound so critical.
Counselor:	It is perplexing to you. I'm wondering, though, if it is possible for you to look at this in another way?
Client:	What do you mean?
Counselor:	What if you begin to see the efforts of others in varying degrees of quality, rather than all or nothing? It seems as if you are really hard on people, then you regret what you say.
Client:	I think that this is beginning to make sense to me. If I weren't so absolute about things at the start, I wouldn't feel so let down when they don't always work out. That's when I become so critical toward people. I'm too harsh on them, and I realize that.

Reframing. Clients who employ undoing often hold self-defeating perspectives relating to the defense. Through reframing, it may be possible to transform the meaning of a person's behavior and construct alternative frames of reference. Consider, for example, the 17-year-old client who experiences shame over spontaneous sexual thoughts. The counselor believes that the client is overreacting and is unwarranted in regard to what may be normal adolescent sexual fantasies. Through a reframe, the counselor suggests the alternative perspective to the client that his fantasy activity is not unlike that of most individuals in his age range. In another reframing example, a 25-year-old client demonstrates repeated instances of alcohol abuse and immediate repentance for each episode.

Client:	I know now that I drink excessively and then feel very bad about my behavior.
Counselor:	There is some advantage of being aware of your pattern of abuse.
Client:	It helps to figure this out, but it still sounds like excuse making when I say that I'll change. Just the other day, my sister said to me, "You'll never make it, and it doesn't help when you say that you're sorry."
Counselor:	How did this make you feel?
Client:	I felt hurt and kind of angry at the same time.
Counselor:	I'm wondering if it would be possible for you to change how your sister's words affect you?
Client:	What are you saying?
Counselor:	Are you able to let her statement serve as a source of challenge rather than defeat? Her words, "You'll never make it," could help bolster you to change.
Client:	(pause) That begins to make sense to me. Her statement might be able to work as a motivator for me and . . .

Interpretation. To clarify the ambivalent quality of undoing, it may be necessary for some individuals to explore motivational and causal considerations relating to the defense. Interpretation focuses on clarifying relationships between clients' present and past functioning, including those lifestyle assumptions that are integral with undoing. A client, for instance, repeatedly expresses caustic comments that are immediately followed by retractors. Through an interpretation, a connection is made between the current purpose of undoing, which supports ambivalent positions, and uncertainties and lack of stability that the person experienced in his early development. In another counseling case with an early adulthood client who was raped, the counselor uses an interpretation.

Client:	I feel mixed up about things. Part of me wants to forget it ever happened, and another smaller part wants to talk about it.
Counselor:	It seems difficult for you to express your feelings about this terrible experience. Could it be that talking about your feelings is something less familiar to you?
Client:	(pause) Well, as a Hispanic American, my parents expected me to keep my feelings in. They didn't want the family to be associated with the cultural stereotype of overemotional Hispanics.

Accomplishment Stage

The final stage of counseling emphasizes the adaptive functioning of clients, including increased control of undoing. Selected action-oriented strategies can assist in facilitating purposeful client change.

Catching Oneself. Persons who have used undoing for extended periods may have difficulty modifying their use of the defense because of its habitual quality. "Catching oneself" enables clients to use cuing devices to avoid employing undoing. In a counseling example, a client demonstrates a pattern of drinking to excess and then expressing remorse for his behavior. Because the individual has become aware of his self-defeating actions, he is now determined to reverse this ritualistic sequence. In an effort to control his tendency to engage in undoing, the client intentionally elicits feelings of determination to break his habitual response whenever he considers having a drink by viewing a wallet-sized picture of his family. In another counseling instance, a 45-year-old client recognizes that she tends to persist in expressing caustic statements toward others and then immediately apologizing for her actions.

Client:	I still find myself falling back on old habits. I need to strike a balance between putting people down and then backing off.
Counselor:	Do you usually know when you are about to be overcritical toward other people?
Client:	Yes, I can feel it coming on.
Counselor:	What if at the critical point you find yourself getting ready to attack someone, you alert yourself to avoid acting?

Client:	But what could I possibly use to put the brakes on?
Counselor:	Would it be possible for you to use some tangible or symbolic item to remind yourself to act in a more balanced way?
Client:	(pause) Well, it just occurred to me that I own a silver ring with a yin-yang symbol on it, and I could touch the ring when I . . .

Acting As If. If individuals have gained increased understanding of their ambivalent functioning, it may be possible for them to act in more integrated and balanced ways. Persons employing undoing for prolonged periods, however, may be unpracticed in behavior that is less conflict laden. "Acting as if" enables clients to model their behavior after individuals who function more adaptively. Consider the following counseling example of an 8-year-old client who demonstrates a pattern of aggressive behavior followed by repentant actions.

Client:	I know that I bother other kids, and then I feel bad about what I do.
Counselor:	You understand what you do, but you still keep doing it.
Client:	Yeah, I guess I have always acted this way.
Counselor:	I have a thought. Can you tell me about some kids who act more in the middle? That is, tell me about someone who is not particularly bossy so that he doesn't always have to say that he is sorry for his actions.
Client:	I can think of a couple of kids who are really pretty friendly, and they never seem to bother anybody else.
Counselor:	Well, what if you acted like one of them for a short time and . . .

Breaking It Down. Modifying an established pattern of undoing can appear to be an imposing task for some individuals. "Breaking it down" enables clients to partialize changes in defense use through manageable segments. In a concluding counseling example, a late adulthood client struggles with attenuating a habitual practice of criticizing people and then apologizing for his actions.

| Client: | I know I'm doing a little better, but it is hard to stop something that I have done for years. |

Counselor:	It is difficult to change after such a long time. I'm wondering if it may make sense for you to try to take it one step at a time. What if you stop yourself from putting people down for maybe a day and see how things work out?
Client:	Maybe that would help because then I wouldn't have to worry about being perfect forever.

CONCLUSION

Undoing as a defense mechanism involves a conflict between opposing forces that becomes manifest in an individual's ambivalent functioning. In a two-step defensive sequence, a person attempts to annul or repudiate perceived transgressions. Undoing symbolically atones for intolerable behavior through obsessive-compulsive tendencies. Selected counseling techniques and strategies, through the three stages of the counseling process, emphasize adaptive client change related to undoing.

NOTE

1. Excerpt from *Beyond Good and Evil: Prelude to a Philosophy of the Future* (p. 80), by F. Nietzsche (W. Kaufman, Trans.), 1989, New York: Vintage Books. Original work published 1886. Copyright © 1989 by Random House, Inc. Reprinted with permission.

12

DEFENSE MECHANISMS IN THE
COUNSELING PROCESS IN GROUPS

I want by understanding myself, to understand others. I want to
be all that I am capable of becoming.

—Katherine Mansfield, 1927, p. 254

Defense mechanisms that impair an individual's ability to relate effectively on an interpersonal level frequently become apparent in social
exchanges in the group experience. A person's characteristic defense
pattern often emerges in the sometimes threatening social context of a
therapeutic group (Rutan & Stone, 1993). In a supportive and challenging group environment, the group leader and group members may
provide constructive feedback to participants employing maladaptive
defenses. Purposeful therapeutic interactions enable individuals in
groups to clarify their conflicted behavior and regulate defense use
(Clark, 1992, 1997).

Although groups may facilitate the processing of a person's defenses, they also are subject to producing counterproductive outcomes. Group members may prematurely confront or attack vulnerable group participants in a debilitating practice referred to as *stripping defenses*. Individuals may be coerced to disclose intimate information as their defenses break down, and emotional casualties resulting from such attacks have been chronicled (Yalom, 1995). At the same time, participants employing various patterns of defenses may also have a disruptive effect on a group and be perceived by other members as avoiding responsibility or distorting reality. Attempting to engender a safe and protective environment while promoting a climate of trust and open communication is a vital concern of the group leader in processing defenses in group.

PREPARATION FOR GROUP

A pregroup screening interview enables a counselor to assess individuals' defense functioning as a consideration in determining the composition of a group. Behavioral observations of potential group members, suggesting the presence of hostility, suspicion, and impulsivity, may relate to their use of defense mechanisms. Although persons tend to employ various mechanisms in individual sessions with a counselor, they may manifest the full extent and complement of their defenses only in the more threat-inducing environment of a group. Selected projective techniques, including human figure drawings, early recollections, and sentence completion tasks, provide another perspective for understanding individuals and the operation of their defense mechanisms (Clark, 1995d). Collateral information gathered from multiple perspectives including school and clinic records; observations of parents, spouses, and other individuals; and related sources may also contribute to evaluating candidates for group.

Some individuals may not be ready for a group, or their participation may produce a disruptive effect on therapeutic progress, and their membership in a group is contraindicated (Corey & Corey, 1997). A highly defensive person, for example, who is extremely suspicious of other people will likely find a group to be psychologically overwhelming. In another instance, individuals may be excessively threatening to other group members, and their inclusion becomes questionable. Consider, for example, what effect the participation of an acting-out adolescent who uses the defense of regression would have on a group of middle school students who are intimidated and ridiculed by their peers. Consideration of potential group members' defenses may also allow the group leader to plan for heterogeneity in groups. For example, a group composed of individuals who tend to use intense patterns of denial and rationalization may only reinforce each other's avoidant frames of reference.

STAGES OF DEFENSE
MECHANISM PROCESSING

Through the three stages of the counseling process in groups, individuals progress from an awareness of their defensive reactions to a position of more adaptive functioning. The initial, or relationship, period focuses on the development of trust and understanding among group participants. In the middle, or integration, stage, members tend to be less guarded as they examine conflicts and contradictions inherent in their employment of defense mechanisms. Group participants in the final, or accomplishment, period of group development are encouraged to control the use of their defenses and to establish more purposeful actions.

Relationship Stage

As individuals enter a group, they often employ defense mechanisms to reduce the threat evoked by interactions with others. Consequently, supportive counseling interventions that contribute to the development of a safe therapeutic group climate are appropriate and timely. Reflection, blocking, modification, universality, linking, and counselor self-disclosure are selected techniques emphasized in this initial stage.

Reflection. Acknowledging feelings and perceptions of group members who employ defense mechanisms is essential for reducing perceived threat. At the same time, other group participants emotionally react in both positive and negative ways to individuals using defenses, and it is also necessary for the group leader to recognize this interaction. In the following example, the counselor uses reflection of feeling with a group member who denies his need for medication after heart bypass surgery. The counselor states, "The idea of taking medication irritates you because you believe it is not necessary." Subsequently, another group participant addresses a comment to the individual employing denial, "I know what you're going through. I hate taking medication. It makes me feel old." In response, the counselor uses reflection of meaning, "It seems that you both feel determined to lead your lives in the manner that is most familiar to you." In time, group members frequently begin to model the group leader's use of reflection, and the understanding provided through this technique contributes to the development of cohesion in groups.

Blocking. Persons employing patterns of defenses may elicit resentful or hostile reactions from other group members for their failure to acknowledge manifest contradictions in their behavior. Group participants using defenses are susceptible to verbal attacks by other members who perceive them as distorting conditions or refusing to face reality. As with other counterproductive behavior, such as gossiping, breaking confidences, and invasion of privacy, the counselor must intervene through the technique of blocking to prevent group members from continuing in a destructive direction against individuals who employ defense mechanisms (Corey & Corey, 1997). In the following exchange among young adults, a group member engages reaction formation in response to another participant who discloses intimate feelings. The counselor intervenes by blocking the verbal threat against the member using the defense in a way that respects the integrity of the perpetrator.

Alice: Sometimes, I have sexual fantasies about having an affair with a man who happens to be married.

Mary: I find what you just said repulsive. I have never in my life even entertained such lewd thoughts.

Alice: I feel like punching you in the face for that remark. You sound like some kind of saint or something.

Counselor: Alice, you have strong feelings about what Mary just said to you, but I cannot allow you to threaten her because our group will never be a safe place for anyone if that type of talk is permitted.

Modification. It is imperative that the counselor intervene to prevent the continuation of behavior that places undue pressure on group members. In other instances, however, an intermediate condition exists in which the statements of a group participant evince counterproductive qualities but also contain potentially constructive elements. A group leader may recognize that an individual's feedback relating to another member's defense includes therapeutically useful content but, as initially expressed, is unacceptable in group. Feedback from group members as to how they observe a participant's defense mechanism use is essential, and a balance is needed between barring outright assaults on a person's defense functioning and encouraging constructive member observations. Through the use of modification, it is possible for the group leader to request group members to revise their feedback statements in a more sensitive way, without eliminating the essential quality of the message (Clark, 1995b). In an adolescent group, for example, Carla says to another participant, Len, who employs the defense of regression, "You act like such a fool in class. You have the ability if only you would use it." The counselor, after empathizing with Len, requests Carla to modify her statement: "You want Len to hear what you are saying, but the way you express it is hard to accept. Can you say what you mean so that Len is able to hear you?" Almost invariably, when the communication of group members is motivated primarily by constructive intent, they will alter their feedback to individuals employing defenses in more purposeful directions. To conclude the cited example, Carla states to Len, "What I mean is that you could do really well in class if you would pay attention more often."

Universality. The contradictory behavioral quality intrinsic to defense mechanism use frequently results in interpersonal difficulties for individuals. Problems in maintaining social relationships may leave persons who employ various defenses feeling isolated from and different from other people. It is often a relief in a group when such individuals are able to gain a new perspective about their feelings of isolation and uniqueness by recognizing that they are not alone and that others share similar life experiences and perspectives (Yalom, 1995). Clarifying the universality of a participant's defense posture occurs by acknowledging related behavioral patterns among other group members. In a group example, a member repeatedly offers justifications in support of her avoidance of assuming responsibility. The counselor attempts to promote universality by saying,

> Lisa, you suggest to us a number of reasons why you are not able to follow through on various commitments and responsibilities. I don't think that you are alone in doing this. Does anyone else in the group react this way when you have to account for your behavior?

Expressed in an inviting tone by the group leader, this statement enables other group participants to reflect on the occurrence of rationalization in their lives while providing awareness and support to an individual member. This approach, used early in the initial stage of the counseling process in groups, may advance a sense of experiencing common ground among members, but as individuals progress in their development through the group experience, they may begin to distance themselves from members who continue to demonstrate intense patterns of defense.

Linking. The group leader can also promote member awareness and relatedness by pointing out the existence of corresponding defenses between two or more group participants. Linking or associating defense use also reduces threat for individuals because they perceive a sense of mutuality with another member or members (Posthuma, 1996). In the following group example, the counselor responds by linking the experiences of two participants using the defense of repression.

Curtis:	I just can't remember that much about growing up, and I really don't want to talk about it.
Counselor:	This period seems vague to you, and at this point, you do not wish to discuss your childhood years. Andrea, I have noticed that you feel the same way Curtis does about preferring not to talk at this time about your experiences as a child.

Self-Disclosure. A group leader's disclosure of personal experiences relating to defense mechanism employment may be potentially useful in clarifying the operation of defenses in a group. Recounting various dimensions of defense use by the counselor may promote understanding of defense reactions of group members and serve as a model for the group. In a group example, the defense mechanism of undoing becomes evident through a participant's frequent use of retractions after expressing harsh or inappropriate comments. The member states, "My boss at work is incompetent, but she has a lot of responsibilities to worry about." In response, after acknowledging the individual's mixed feelings toward his supervisor, the counselor says, "Sometimes, I find myself saying things that I feel strongly about and almost immediately stating something that is quite the opposite." Statements of this type may also stimulate other group participants to become aware of this behavioral pattern in their lives. The group leader may also employ self-involving statements in reaction to the defense engagement of a group member or members. For example, in a statement directed to the group as a whole, the counselor relates, "Each person in our group, including myself, reacts to threat at some level."

Integration Stage

The support and understanding developed in the initial stage of the counseling process in groups generally lessen the affective intensity of member defenses. Individuals who initially found the group to be threatening and destabilizing now may experience a level of trust that allows for the examination of contradictions and conflicts intrinsic to their defense use. Member feedback in the middle period of counseling typically becomes more supportive, yet challenging, and the group leader's use of protective interventions becomes less frequent. Prominent treatment techniques in this stage include confrontation, cognitive restructuring, reframing, and interpretation.

Confrontation. As a form of feedback, confrontation provides a means for individuals to become aware of behavioral incongruities manifest in their defense use (Posthuma, 1996). The group leader or more advanced group participants may demonstrate how to effectively confront in a descriptive and nonjudgmental style (Corey & Corey, 1997). Other group members gain an increased understanding of their defense functioning when inconsistencies between group members' statements and other manifestations of their behavior are challenged. In a group, for example, George repeatedly states that he has not been able to find a job for various reasons. Each time that one of the other group participants suggests a possible solution to this problem, George provides a somewhat plausible response. In reaction to George's defense, the other group members become irritated at what they perceive is his constant excuse making. Subsequently, Eleanor says, "George, each time that one of us suggests a reasonable possibility for you to consider about finding work, you respond with a reason why you choose not to follow up on the idea." In this instance, Eleanor's confrontation is effectively stated, and the group leader has only to wait for George's reaction.

Cognitive Restructuring. Core convictions that relate to defense use may also be inferred when individuals express statements that are contradictory and conflicted. The group experience offers a means for participants to become aware of and to evaluate their lifestyle convictions through the multiple perspectives of group members. Group participants may suggest alternative ways for individuals to develop constructive and purposeful core assumptions. In a group example, Bob repeatedly expresses suspicion and distrust toward other people, including the group members. In response, the counselor initiates cognitive restructuring by suggesting that Bob also has a choice of viewing others as neutral or even benign. Other group members then express their perceptions as to how they generally view other people. After a lengthy discussion, Bob acknowledges that he is somewhat receptive to reconsidering his assumptions. The group leader points out that Bob frequently employs negative self-statements relating to his perceptions of others, and Bob agrees to try using counterstatements as alternative responses that will allow for more tolerant views. In subsequent sessions, Bob continues, with the support of the group, to examine his core convictions and to report on his employment of counterstatements.

Reframing. Within groups, reframing offers another means for members to contribute to therapeutically expanding the perceptions of individuals, including their maladaptive use of defenses. Reframing is a type of interpretation that provides new meanings to rigid and constricted perspectives through the interaction and collaboration of group members (Clark, 1998b; LaFountain, Garner, & Eliason, 1996). Diverse social and cultural backgrounds of individuals in groups potentially enrich the perceptions of other members in constructive directions (Merta, 1995). The group leader or other group participants may offer a reframe, suggested as a plausible consideration and in an inviting tone. In an adolescent group, for example, Samantha exhibits a pattern of immature behavior that is indicative of regression use. In a group session, Samantha acknowledges that she likes the feeling of being carefree and independent but that this has also gotten her into a lot of trouble. In response, Joan, who was recently released from a correctional facility, suggests that in actuality Samantha's behavior may be less free because she doesn't get the privileges and choices that usually come with acting responsibly. This observation, stated in a caring way by a respected peer, introduces Samantha to a new frame of reference, and in group she begins to reflect on its implications.

Interpretation. For many group participants, clarifying contradictory functioning and developing more adaptive perspectives enable them to act in more constructive ways. Other individuals, however, may need to gain a motivational level of understanding before they are able to progress to more purposeful actions. In groups, the effective use of interpretation enables persons to relate the meaning of their current behavior, including defense mechanism use, to developmental experiences (Clark, 1994b, 1998). Expressed at a time when members appear to be emotionally receptive to processing an interpretation, the exchange should be discussed in a supportive way to allow for thoughtful examination in group. It is possible that premature or inappropriate interpretations may be stated by group participants, requiring the group leader to block or modify antitherapeutic exchanges. Individuals' prevailing defense employment may also relate to their lifestyles, and interpretation clarifies this relationship. A group participant, for instance, speaks about her pattern of isolating her feelings and acting in an emotionally detached way.

Ann:	I feel terrified in saying this, but I have a real difficulty in expressing my feelings about almost anything on an intimate level.
Ed:	I give you a lot of credit for telling us what you just said.
Sarah:	I'm wondering if it is possible that the reason you find it difficult to express personal feelings is something that you learned early in your life?
Ann:	In my family, it wasn't even permitted to raise your voice.
Sarah:	This is what I'm talking about.
Ed:	Ann, can you talk more about what it was like for you growing up in your family?

Accomplishment Stage

Consolidating insights and perspectives gained during the counseling process in groups occurs in the final stage of counseling. With an increased understanding of the dynamics of their defenses and with the encouragement of other group members, individuals may focus on adaptive actions. The group serves as a vehicle for change as participants strive to control their engagement of defense mechanisms and develop more purposeful functioning. Group members in collaboration with the group leader may pursue various action strategies during this period, and the following examples illustrate specific possibilities. Ideas for cuing devices for use by individuals to moderate their defense use may be made by group members in conjunction with "catching oneself." The group may also provide support to participants as they attempt to model alternative behavior to defense use by "acting as if." By recognizing the incremental steps that persons make in behavioral change, including regulating the employment of defenses, group members may become directly involved through "breaking it down." In yet another instance, individuals who have made gains in controlling their frequency of regression use may share with the group written notations of responsible actions that they accomplished during the week.

In the final stage of counseling, group members work through termination issues and frequently reflect on their experiences in counseling, including the recognition of therapeutic gains made by individuals. Regarding defense mechanisms, participants often provide feedback relating to changes in a person's actions: "You are letting your feelings out more now" (isolation). "You are much easier to be with now. I used to feel that you would be trying to find fault with me for no real reason" (projection). "You don't make as many excuses for your behavior as you used to" (rationalization). "When you first came to group, you acted as if you were superior to us. I don't get this feeling from you now" (reaction formation).

CONCLUSION

The counseling process in groups frequently involves intense social interactions among group members and tends to elicit threat and the use of defense mechanisms by individuals. The group experience has the potential to provide support and challenge to participants who use a pattern of defenses, but it also may be counterproductive and produce emotional casualties. The group leader has a crucial role in establishing a safe and trust-inducing climate and in employing a range of interventions that stimulate collaborative efforts among group members. A three-stage model of group development provides a conceptual framework in the identification and modification of group member defense mechanisms.

13

DEFENSE MECHANISMS IN THE COUNSELING PROCESS: A CASE STUDY

The urgent telephone call came in from Ellen, a residence director of a dormitory in the state university where I am employed as a college counselor. Ellen wanted to provide me with information about Gary, a student with whom I was scheduled to meet in the afternoon. She described Gary's relationship with other students in his dormitory as strained and tense. According to Ellen, Gary had an excuse for everything he did, and he continually accused other people of starting trouble. Although Gary was not required to see me, Ellen had strongly urged him to do so, and he reluctantly agreed. Ellen also informed me that Gary received several below-average grades at midterm as a freshman, and unless he improved his work, he would be placed on academic probation at the end of the semester. After talking with Ellen, I realized that I had already heard about Gary from his English composition instructor. Gary had insisted on meeting with the professor several times because he felt singled out in class and wished to voice his complaint that the course assignments seemed irrelevant. With this brief background, I felt at least minimally prepared to meet with 18-year-old Gary for our initial counseling session.

STAGES OF DEFENSE
MECHANISM PROCESSING

Relationship Stage

Almost immediately after I greeted Gary, he said, "Why are you staring at me? Do you have a problem?" Somehow, I was caught off guard by Gary's statement, perhaps because it did not fit my expectations of how we would begin our session. In my response to Gary, I reflected his feelings that he seemed uncomfortable in the way that I looked at him. For most clients with whom I work, reflection of feelings enables them to feel understood, and this is essential in fostering a counseling relationship. Perhaps Gary did experience some degree of understanding on my part, but this did not prevent him from questioning the value and purpose of counseling and my potential effectiveness.

Gary: How do you think that this is going to help? What good can you possibly do?

AC: You have your doubts that meeting with me is going to make any difference.

Gary: Most of what you people do is listen to other people so you can dig up dirt about their lives.

AC: I guess you question not only my usefulness but the whole idea of counseling as a service.

Gary: You say service. I'm not just going to come in here and spill my guts to you. You're like all the rest of them who just want to get something on me.

AC: You feel distrustful because you've learned that you can be hurt by getting close to people.

In my last comment to Gary, I used reflection of meaning to abstract the essence of his implied communication. In a curious way, Gary seemed to respond to this intervention as he paused and shifted in his chair. His distrust and suspicion seemed to subside slightly, but then he started to defiantly justify his actions.

> **Gary:** I don't have to explain myself to anybody. I know that the resident director called you. Ellen has problems. She is one of the worst administrators on this campus. Students in her dorm act like animals, and she doesn't know what to do.
>
> **AC:** Given your doubts about her administrative skills, you are questioning whether she can accurately appraise your behavior.
>
> **Gary:** Yes, that's it. If anything, I'm one of the few people who stand up to those idiots, and I get in trouble for doing it.

At this point, I did not challenge the validity of Gary's assertions, because in doing so I possibly could entrench his defensive posture even further. The remainder of our first meeting continued with Gary essentially complaining that he is right and others are wrong. Begrudgingly, Gary agreed to return the following week, and on his way out the door, said over his shoulder, "My coming here shows Ellen and the rest of the people in the dorm how bad they really are."

After Gary left my office and I had a few minutes to myself, I realized how drained I felt. Although I also experienced some relief that the session had progressed fairly well largely because of my use of reflection, I was troubled that Gary believed our interactions seemed to affirm that Ellen was "bad." My attempt was to convey an understanding of Gary, not necessarily to acknowledge agreement with his views. I did feel somewhat better about this, however, when I considered that through the counseling process, possible distortions in Gary's beliefs should eventually be clarified. I was also struck by how certain Gary felt about himself and how absolute he was about his assertions. He seemed to leave no room for self-doubt, and I was concerned about how I could begin to suggest alternative views. A corroborating piece of information about Gary that I had not used was that of the English instructor's perception of him. My thought was that it seemed premature and possibly threatening to introduce this in our first meeting. I did know that I wanted Gary to complete several projective techniques in our next session because I needed more information about the dynamics of his functioning, including what was becoming apparent in his use of defense mechanisms.

During the next week, I heard from Ellen that a stink bomb had been set off outside Gary's room, and the entire floor had to be cleared for several hours. Gary began the session by accusing students in his dorm of trying to ruin his life and saying how the bomb represented just one more example of their attacks on him. As Gary expressed hostility toward the students and toward Ellen, I began to think that perhaps there was an objective reality and some grounds for his suspiciousness. I needed, however, to go beyond Gary's expressed views and assess his subjective functioning through selected projective techniques. After I introduced the instruments, Gary immediately voiced his objections and distrust.

> **Gary:** Why do we have to do this? What are you trying to find out?
>
> **AC:** You are suspect about how I will use the information. Well, it will help me understand you better, and this may help in our meetings.
>
> **Gary:** I think that this will be used against me somehow, and you know it.

After a discussion of confidentiality issues and safeguards to protect assessment materials, Gary tentatively agreed to draw a human figure. Like many other resistant clients with whom I have worked, once Gary started the drawing, he became absorbed in the intrinsically interesting nature of the medium. Gary's figure was revealing in the inferences that it generated. He drew a small person of less than 3 inches. The diminutive size of the drawing suggests a reduced self-concept. This hypothesis contradicts Gary's manifest behavior; he appears certain about himself. Gary also drew dark piercing eyes and used shading and heavy lines in completing the figure. Representations of this type indicate the possibility of suspicion and aggression, both characteristics that appear evident in Gary's interactions.

After Gary completed the drawing, I elicited Gary's early recollections: "Think back to a long time ago, when you were little, and try to recall one of your earliest memories, one of the first things you can remember." Gary responded with interest, and he subsequently related the following three memories:

1. I was standing on a beach at the ocean with my aunt and uncle, who were making fun of me because I was cold. I felt really cold but also upset because they didn't help me.
2. I had just received an immunization shot in my arm, and a neighborhood kid was sitting on my chest punching my arm, and it really hurt.
3. I was out playing with my brother, and I realized that I had lost all the money that I was carrying that I had saved up. I was so angry at myself for losing the money.

Thematically, Gary's early recollections suggest that he maintains core convictions of ineptness and insignificance in a hurtful and punishing world.

Gary also completed the sentence completion tasks after a brief emotional exchange about the purpose and security of the information derived from this instrument. The data from Gary's completion of the sentence stems provided illuminating material, particularly as it related to his defensive functioning. Although I had hypothesized earlier about salient defense mechanisms that Gary might be employing on the basis of behavioral observations and collateral information, his responses to the sentence completion tasks pointed to some specific tendencies. Projection was indicated when Gary wrote, "What bothers me . . . is when people talk about me for no reason." "I suffer . . . because the other students are out to get me." I was able to infer the use of rationalization by Gary on the basis of his responses to the following sentence stems: "I regret . . . that I can't succeed in college because of the students in my dorm." "I failed . . . because of my poor professors." "Whenever I have to study . . . I can't because this college makes it impossible." Immediately after finishing the sentence completion tasks, Gary said that he had to leave but that he felt better about "getting some things off his chest."

Several of Gary's responses on the sentence completion tasks related to his developmental history. As an example, Gary completed the sentence stem, "My father . . . never really bothered with me." My plan was to discuss and clarify particular responses that Gary made on his sentence completion in our third counseling session, but this possibility had to be deferred. Gary entered the counseling office and slammed the door. In an angry tone, he recounted an incident that occurred a few days earlier in his dorm. Gary stated that as he walked by the student lounge, he heard several students talking about him, and he decided to confront them. Gary admonished the individuals for gossiping behind his back and then ran to his room. For the remainder of the session, discussion focused on this incident and how, from Gary's perspective, people constantly try to "do me in."

Our fourth counseling session was in marked contrast to our previous meeting. Gary was somewhat subdued as he discussed a paper assigned by his English instructor. Gary was required to write an essay about a rock that the professor had brought to class. Like other assignments in this class, Gary felt that it was "a waste of time." In response to Gary, I decided to discuss an assignment that I had in college that I also found of questionable value. Only after I completed the work, however, did I realize how much I had learned. My disclosure seemed only to annoy Gary, and he then began to criticize my efforts. "I'm not finding my time with you that worthwhile, and I don't think I want to come here anymore." My internal response to Gary's statement was, "Good, you can take your obnoxious behavior and go bother someone else." Instead of acting on this reaction, with restraint, I decided to use a self-involving statement: "Perhaps you haven't felt that our meetings are helpful, but you are expressing yourself and sorting out things, and this takes courage on your part." Was I stretching the truth here or using a sound strategy? At any rate, Gary then asked me about the experience that I had in college, which he had refused to hear about only a few minutes earlier.

The remainder of our meeting progressed with somewhat more open communication as Gary again focused on how he is always right and others are wrong. Our next counseling session continued with a similar theme but with a lessened degree of emotional intensity. This change and a clearer understanding of Gary's behavior, including his employment of projection and rationalization, suggested to me that we were entering the middle period of counseling.

Integration Stage

During our initial counseling sessions, I attempted to provide support and understanding by acknowledging Gary's feelings and perceptions.

Although we had met only five times, I felt that we had established a reasonable level of communication and that I now needed to challenge Gary's frames of reference to further effect therapeutic change. It was my intention to begin to confront Gary when he demonstrated inconsistent or contradictory behavior. Only minutes into our sixth session, the opportunity arose:

Gary: Nobody around here really cares if I flunk out of college.

AC: This leaves you feeling pretty unimportant.

Gary: Sure, but you would think that somebody would care what happens to me.

AC: You feel strongly about this, but you also said a few minutes ago that your English professor was willing to meet with you to work on your compositions outside class.

Gary: Oh yeah, but who has the time? I'm just too busy.

In this instance, Gary was rejecting my confrontation by using rationalization to support his position. I considered it important, however, for me to question his contradictory behavior, and I continued this effort throughout the middle stage of counseling.

At this point, I wanted to particularly focus on inconsistencies relating to Gary's use of projection and rationalization. He responded in various ways to my confrontations, from rejection and dismissal to a considered examination of my observations. In the seventh counseling session, Gary for the first time began to evaluate contradictions inherent in his defensive functioning.

Gary: I walked by the lounge yesterday where I had the big blowup a few weeks ago when the students were talking about me.

AC: You still feel some pain from that experience.

Gary: Well, it isn't over. I couldn't hear what they were saying, but I could guess that it was about me.

AC: How could you tell?

Gary: Well, they stopped talking when I walked in the room.

AC: You are saying that you are sure they were talking about you, but at the same time, you couldn't really hear what they were saying.

Gary: I know what you are getting at, but I could see it in their eyes.

AC: Somehow, when you say this, you don't really seem convinced.

> Gary: (pause) I feel a little uncomfortable admitting this, but I guess it is possible that they weren't talking about me. I'm so used to certain things happening that I probably expect to find them.

As Gary became somewhat more open to examining his contradictory behavior through confrontation, the question emerged: What is he specifically defending against? I made the assumption that Gary's defense functioning protects himself from an awareness of painful lifestyle perceptions. To effect change at the intermediate defense level, Gary's core-level cognitions needed to be addressed. Earlier in the counseling process, I hypothesized that Gary perceives himself as inept and inconsequential in a hurtful and punishing world. My plan was to collaborate with Gary in an attempt to modify these schemas in a more constructive and purposeful direction. When Gary alluded to his core assumptions, the timing seemed right to initiate cognitive restructuring:

> Gary: I'm so sick of people getting on my case. Nobody seems to give me a break.
>
> AC: I'm wondering if somehow this could be changed, and all of a sudden you had everybody on your side. How would your life be different?
>
> Gary: It won't happen, so why even bother talking about it?
>
> AC: Say that it did. What would it be like for you?
>
> Gary: Well, it would be great. Everything would be just right.
>
> AC: Would it? What about how you feel about yourself?
>
> Gary: I think you know (pause). I don't feel that good about myself.
>
> AC: That's not easy to admit or even to think about. I'm wondering, though, that if you felt better about yourself, then how you think other people look at you may not make that much difference.
>
> Gary: (pause) That kind of makes sense. But how do I get to feel better about myself?

Using Gary's question as a starting point, we discussed how he tends to express negative statements repeatedly about himself and toward others. Gary recognized this trend, and we explored a pattern of behavior that extended back as long as he could remember. We then went on to identify a few thoughts that he could employ as counters on occasions when he used self-defeating cognitions. Gary occasionally stated that he didn't seem to make any difference to anyone, and he decided instead to use the self-reference "I matter." We both agreed that this effort was a beginning for Gary to revise his self-perception and see himself as a person of significance and worth. In our next counseling session, Gary's perception of other people was similarly addressed through cognitive restructuring. He acknowledged that his view of others was that they treated him badly. Although Gary recognized that this assumption was possibly not true to the degree that he thought, he felt comfortable concluding that perhaps people seemed to treat him largely as a result of how he treated them.

The possibility of Gary's effecting constructive change by modifying his assumptions toward himself and toward others was beginning to take hold through cognitive restructuring. At the same time, however, Gary experienced disequilibrium as he reassessed his core convictions. In the following interaction in the ninth counseling session, I used a reframe in attempting to transform the meaning of Gary's perspective on personal control.

Gary: I feel kind of mixed up by what we have been talking about in the last few weeks.

AC: It is unsettling for you to evaluate some of your deeper feelings about life.

Gary: I guess what is really bothering me is that I felt better about things when I was able to blame other people for making me feel bad about myself. It has been this way for a long time, you know. I don't feel that I have much control now.

AC: In important ways, you feel more comfortable in your old ways of looking at things. Taking more responsibility for your behavior is not easy. I'm not sure, though, what you mean when you say that you now don't have much control?

Gary: I feel as if I have more control over my life when I can blame other people for causing problems for me.

AC: I see now how you connect feeling mixed up and not having as much control. I'm wondering, though, if it is possible for you to look at this in another way?

Gary: What are you saying?

AC: You just said that when you blame people for making your life difficult, you believe that you are more in control. Could it actually be that you are relinquishing control? It may be easier for you to find fault with others, but this does not put you in a position to make active and purposeful decisions to direct your life.

Gary: I know what you are saying. I spend so much time looking to blame other people that this really doesn't amount to much in improving my situation.

As Gary more fully acknowledged the dynamics relating to his defensive functioning, he began to question why he felt so negative about himself and toward other persons. In our 10th meeting, Gary reflected on his developmental experiences and provided a referent to associate with his use of defenses. Although my interpretation only began to clarify motivational and causal considerations, it did provide a perspective that made sense to Gary.

Gary: I know that I still don't feel that good about myself, although I've been practicing positive counterthoughts.

AC: It is difficult to change beliefs that you have held for many years.

Gary: As we have talked about, I can't remember when I felt good about myself or toward other people.

AC: For a long time, you have felt less significant and less capable.

Gary: You know me pretty well. I have tried to think back and understand why I don't feel better about things. My family seemed OK. Somehow, though, I have never believed that I am important or that I matter much.

AC: I'm wondering if it is possible that the way you believe that people are against you and how you make excuses for your behavior relate to this sense of feeling insignificant.

Gary: Possibly, I hate having this worthless feeling, and I can blame other people and situations for causing problems.

In the following counseling session, Gary and I collaborated on another interpretation that clarified past-present associations relating to his lifestyle.

Gary: I told you last time that I felt OK growing up in my family. I have been thinking about it, though, and I can recall feeling unimportant.

AC: Does there seem to be any pattern to your recollections?

Gary: Possibly, but it seems more like impressions or a sense of being passed over. Somehow, I can't remember being cared for, but this can't be.

AC: You don't want to overstate the situation.

Gary: It is more as if I felt less cared for, but then I can't recall asking for help or affection either. I just don't want to set up an excuse of why I act as I do today.

AC: Could it be that you don't feel that good about yourself or others because in growing up you felt less important, but you also did not act on your dissatisfaction with this situation?

Gary: That is very close to it. I don't think that the family circumstances were great, but I really didn't do much to seek out care or affection, and I seemed to put people off. In a lot of ways, I behave in the same way today.

Accomplishment Stage

As Gary clarified various contradictions and conflicts in the integration stage of counseling, he also enhanced his potential for acting more purposefully. In our concluding three sessions, we focused on action strategies that enabled Gary to more effectively control his defense use and to establish more adaptive functioning. Early in this final period of counseling, Gary expressed uncertainties about his ability to sustain therapeutic gains that he had made, and I suggested that he use a cued reminder through "catching oneself."

Gary: I don't want to go back to blaming everyone for my problems, but there are some days that I can feel myself slipping back into my old ways.

AC: It may be that you do revert occasionally to old patterns, but now you are aware of this.

Gary: Yes, and I'm not looking for perfection, but I'd like to do better.

AC: What if you use an approach that alerts you when you are about to be accusatory or make excuses, and you catch yourself and stop the behavior?

Gary: What am I supposed to do, ring a bell?

AC: That might be a little hard to do. I'm wondering, though, is there something you could use to remind yourself as a warning device just before you get defensive?

Gary: I could carry a mirror around and look at my face to keep me honest.

AC: Actually, if you use a small mirror, that may work.

Gary: I guess that I could carry a little mirror in my shirt pocket and touch it as a reminder.

Gary seemed to respond to using "catching oneself" because he used the strategy effectively during the week between counseling sessions. Although he was able to limit his defense use, Gary felt uncomfortable and uncertain in expressing more direct and honest communication.

Gary: I just don't feel at all familiar with this new role of being more honest with my feelings. I'm not even sure how to act this way.

AC: Would it be helpful if you had in your mind a concept of an individual who acts the way that you would like to act?

Gary: You mean a person whose behavior I could copy?

AC: Not necessarily to copy but to serve as a guide or as a model. Can you think of someone who is fairly honest and direct with his or her feelings but is not offensive?

Gary: This may surprise you, but a person whom I respect who has these qualities is the residence director, Ellen.

AC: I remember that Ellen suggested that you come to see me a number of weeks ago.

Gary: Well, I like how she deals with people, and what I could try out is her way of . . .

OUTCOME

As Gary and I addressed termination issues in our final sessions together, he reflected on the gains that he made through the counseling process. Gary wondered how anyone used to put up with him because he continually made excuses for his behavior and acted as if everyone was against him. Yet although we had met for 14 counseling sessions, Gary was concerned that he still found himself unable to trust other people more readily. He also expressed uncertainty about our not meeting on a weekly basis, but he felt it was time to be more independent. He agreed to use the strategy "breaking it down" and approach the weeks ahead a day at a time and focus on purposeful actions. I reminded Gary about how suspicious he was of me when we first met and how this changed during our time together. As a way of acknowledging that he could still call on his defenses, Gary humorously used a final rationalization, "At that point, it was a choice between meeting with you and taking a bus ride home."

REFERENCES

Abend, S. M., & Porder, M. S. (1986). Identification in the neuroses. *International Journal of Psycho-Analysis, 67,* 201-208.

Adler, A. (1936). Compulsion neurosis. *International Journal of Individual Psychology, 2,* 3-22.

Adler, A. (1958). *What life should mean to you* (A. Porter, Ed.). New York: G. P. Putnam. (Original work published 1931)

à Kempis, T. (1964). *Of the imitation of Christ; four books.* Boston: E. P. Dutton. (Original work published 1441)

Allport, G. W. (1961). *Pattern and growth in personality.* New York: Holt, Rinehart & Winston.

American Psychiatric Association. (1994a). *Diagnostic and statistical manual of mental disorders* (4th ed.). Washington, DC: Author.

American Psychiatric Association. (1994b). *A psychiatric glossary* (7th ed.). Washington, DC: Author.

Anastasi, A., & Urbina, S. (1997). *Psychological testing* (7th ed.). New York: Macmillan.

Arlow, J. A., & Brenner, C. (1964). The concept of regression and structural theory. In J. A. Arlow & C. Brenner (Eds.), *Psychoanalytic concepts and structural theory* (pp. 56-83). New York: International Universities Press.

Audi, R. (1988). Self-deception, rationalization, and reasons for acting. In B. P. McLaughlin & A. O. Rorty (Eds.), *Perspectives on self-deception* (pp. 92-120). Berkeley: University of California Press.

Axelson, J. A. (1993). *Counseling and development in a multicultural society* (2nd ed.). Pacific Grove, CA: Brooks/Cole.

237

Beck, A. T., & Weishaar, M. (1995). Cognitive therapy. In R. J. Corsini & D. Wedding (Eds.), *Current psychotherapies* (5th ed., pp. 229-261). Itasca, IL: F. E. Peacock.

Bellak, L., & Abrams, D. M. (1997). *The T.A.T., C.A.T., and S.A.T. in clinical use* (6th ed.). Needham Heights, MA: Allyn & Bacon.

Bibring, G. L., Dwyer, T. F., Huntington, D. S., & Valenstein, A. F. (1961). A study of the psychological processes in pregnancy and of the earliest mother-child relationship. *Psychoanalytic Study of the Child, 16,* 9-72.

Bieri, J., Lobeck, R., & Galinsky, M. D. (1959). A comparison of direct, indirect, and fantasy measures of identification. *Journal of Abnormal and Social Psychology, 58,* 253-258.

Bishop, D. R. (1991). Clinical aspects of denial in chemical dependency. *Individual Psychology: The Journal of Adlerian Theory, Research and Practice, 47,* 199-209.

Blos, P. (1979). *The adolescent passage: Developmental issues.* New York: International Universities Press.

Blum, H. P. (1987). The role of identification in the resolution of trauma: The Anna Freud memorial lecture. *Psychoanalytic Quarterly, 56,* 609-627.

Blum, H. P. (Ed.). (1985). *Defense and resistance: Historical perspectives and current concepts.* New York: International Universities Press.

Bond, M. (1995). The development and properties of the Defense Style Questionnaire. In H. R. Conte & R. Plutchik (Eds.), *Ego defenses: Theory and measurement* (pp. 202-220). New York: John Wiley.

Bond, M., Gardner, S. T., Christian, J., & Sigal, J. J. (1983). Empirical study of self-rated defense styles. *Archives of General Psychiatry, 40,* 333-338.

Bradshaw, J. (1988). *Healing the shame that binds you.* Deerfield Beach, FL: Health Communications.

Brems, C. (1990). Defense mechanisms in clients and non-clients as mediated by gender and sex-role. *Journal of Clinical Psychology, 46,* 669-674.

Brenner, C. (1957). The nature and development of the concept of repression in Freud's writings. *Psychoanalytic Study of the Child, 12,* 19-46.

Brezin, M. A. (1980). Intrapsychic isolation in the elderly. *Journal of Geriatric Psychiatry, 13,* 5-18.

Breznitz, S. (1983). The seven kinds of denial. In S. Breznitz (Ed.), *The denial of stress* (pp. 257-280). New York: International Universities Press.

Brown, L. M., & Gilligan, C. (1992). *Meeting at the crossroads: Women's psychology and girls' development.* Cambridge, MA: Harvard University Press.

Browning, E. B. (1974). *The poetical works of Elizabeth Barrett Browning* (R. M. Adams, Ed.). Boston: Houghton Mifflin. (Original work published 1844)

Bruhn, A. R. (1984). Use of early memories as a projective technique. In P. McReynolds & G. J. Chelune (Eds.), *Advances in psychological assessment* (Vol. 6, pp. 109-150). San Francisco: Jossey-Bass.

Carlyle, T. (1993). *On heroes, hero-worship, and the heroic in history.* Berkeley: University of California Press. (Original work published 1841)

Chandler, L. A., & Johnson, V. J. (1991). *Using projective techniques with children: A guide to clinical assessment.* Springfield, IL: Charles C Thomas.

Chang, V., & James, M. (1987). Anxiety and projection as related to games and scripts. *Transactional Analysis Journal, 17,* 178-184.

Clark, A. J. (1991). The identification and modification of defense mechanisms in counseling. *Journal of Counseling & Development, 69,* 231-236.

Clark, A. J. (1992). Defense mechanisms in group counseling. *The Journal for Specialists in Group Work, 17,* 151-160.

Clark, A. J. (1993). Interpretation in group counseling: Theoretical and operational issues. *The Journal for Specialists in Group Work, 18,* 174-181.

Clark, A. J. (1994a). Early recollections: A personality assessment tool for elementary school counselors. *Elementary School Guidance & Counseling, 29,* 92-101.

Clark, A. J. (1994b). Working with dreams in group counseling: Advantages and challenges. *Journal of Counseling & Development, 73,* 141-144.

Clark, A. J. (1995a). An examination of the technique of interpretation in counseling. *Journal of Counseling & Development, 73,* 483-490.

Clark, A. J. (1995b). Modification: A leader skill in group work. *The Journal for Specialists in Group Work, 20,* 14-17.

Clark, A. J. (1995c). Projective identification in counselling: Theoretical and therapeutic considerations. *Canadian Journal of Counselling, 29,* 37-49.

Clark, A. J. (1995d). Projective techniques in the counseling process. *Journal of Counseling & Development, 73,* 245-251.

Clark, A. J. (1995e). Rationalization and the role of the school counselor. *The School Counselor, 42,* 283-291.

Clark, A. J. (1995f). Techniques in the counseling process with adolescents. In K. V. Chandras (Ed.), *Handbook on counseling adolescents, adults and older persons* (pp. 13-22). Alexandria, VA: American Counseling Association.

Clark, A. J. (1997). Projective identification as a defense mechanism in group counseling and therapy. *The Journal for Specialists in Group Work, 22,* 85-96.

Clark, A. J. (1998a). The defense never rests. In L. B. Golden (Ed.), *Case studies in child and adolescent counseling* (2nd ed., pp. 28-40). New York: Merrill.

Clark, A. J. (1998b). Reframing: A therapeutic technique in group counseling. *The Journal for Specialists in Group Work, 28,* 80-87.

Clarkson, P. (1989). *Gestalt counselling in action.* London: Sage.

Conte, H. R., & Apter, A. (1995). The life style index: A self-report measure of ego defenses. In H. R. Conte & R. Plutchik (Eds.), *Ego defenses: Theory and measurement* (pp. 179-201). New York: John Wiley.

Conte, H. R., & Plutchik, R. (Eds.). (1995). *Ego defenses: Theory and measurement.* New York: John Wiley.

Corey, M. S., & Corey, G. (1997). *Groups: Process and practice* (5th ed.). Pacific Grove, CA: Brooks/Cole.

Cormier, S., & Cormier, B. (1998). *Interviewing strategies for helpers: Fundamental skills and cognitive behavioral interventions* (4th ed.). Pacific Grove, CA: Brooks/Cole.

Cramer, P. (1991). *The development of defense mechanisms: Theory, research, and assessment.* New York: Springer-Verlag.

Cramer, P., & Carter, T. (1978). The relationship between sexual identification and the use of defense mechanisms. *Journal of Personality Assessment, 42,* 63-73.

Cummings, J. A. (1986). Projective drawings. In H. M. Knoff (Ed.), *The assessment of child and adolescent personality* (pp. 199-244). New York: Guilford.

Dinkmeyer, D. C., Dinkmeyer, D. C., Jr., & Sperry, L. (1987). *Adlerian counseling and psychotherapy* (2nd ed.). New York: Macmillan.

Dorpat, T. L. (1985). *Denial and defense in the therapeutic situation.* New York: Jason Aronson.

Dorpat, T. L. (1987). A new look at denial and defense. *Annual of Psychoanalysis, 15,* 23-47.

Eissler, K. R. (1959). On isolation. *Psychoanalytic Study of the Child, 14,* 29-60.

Ellis, A. (1995). Rational emotive behavior therapy. In R. J. Corsini & D. Wedding (Eds.), *Current psychotherapies* (5th ed., pp. 162-196). Itasca, IL: F. E. Peacock.

English, H. B., & English, A. C. (1958). *A comprehensive dictionary of psychological and psychoanalytical terms.* New York: McKay.

Evans, R. G. (1982). Defense mechanisms in females as a function of sex-role orientation. *Journal of Clinical Psychology, 38,* 816-817.

Firestone, R. W. (1990). The bipolar causality of regression. *American Journal of Psychoanalysis, 50,* 121-135.

Freud, A. (1963). Regression as a principle in mental development. *Bulletin of the Menninger Clinic, 27,* 122-139.

Freud, A. (1965). *Normality and pathology in childhood: Assessments of development.* New York: International Universities Press.

Freud, A. (1966). *The ego and the mechanisms of defense* (Rev. ed.). New York: International Universities Press. (Original work published 1936)

Freud, S. (1953a). The interpretation of dreams. In J. Strachey (Ed. and Trans.), *The standard edition of the complete psychological works of Sigmund Freud* (Vols. 4 & 5). London: Hogarth. (Original work published 1900)

Freud, S. (1953b). Three essays on the theory of sexuality. In J. Strachey (Ed. and Trans.), *The standard edition of the complete psychological works of Sigmund Freud* (Vol. 7, pp. 135-243). London: Hogarth. (Original work published 1905)

Freud, S. (1955a). Analysis of a phobia in a five-year old boy. In J. Strachey (Ed. and Trans.), *The standard edition of the complete psychological works of Sigmund Freud* (Vol. 10, pp. 5-149). London: Hogarth. (Original work published 1909)

Freud, S. (1955b). Beyond the pleasure principle. In J. Strachey (Ed. and Trans.), *The standard edition of the complete psychological works of Sigmund Freud* (Vol. 18, pp. 7-64). London: Hogarth. (Original work published 1920)

Freud, S. (1955c). The claims of psycho-analysis to scientific interest. In J. Strachey (Ed. and Trans.), *The standard edition of the complete psychological works of Sigmund Freud* (Vol. 13, pp. 165-190). London: Hogarth. (Original work published 1913)

Freud, S. (1955d). Group psychology and the analysis of the ego. In J. Strachey (Ed. and Trans.), *The standard edition of the complete psychological works of Sigmund Freud* (Vol. 18, pp. 69-143). London: Hogarth (Original work published 1921)

Freud, S. (1955e). Notes upon a case of obsessional neurosis. In J. Strachey (Ed. and Trans.), *The standard edition of the complete psychological works of Sigmund Freud* (Vol. 10, pp. 155-249). London: Hogarth. (Original work published 1909)

Freud, S. (1957a). Instincts and their vicissitudes. In J. Strachey (Ed. and Trans.), *The standard edition of the complete psychological works of Sigmund Freud* (Vol. 14, pp. 117-140). London: Hogarth. (Original work published 1915)

Freud, S. (1957b). Repression. In J. Strachey (Ed. and Trans.), *The standard edition of the complete psychological works of Sigmund Freud* (Vol. 14, pp. 146-158). London: Hogarth. (Original work published 1915)

Freud, S. (1958). Psycho-analytic notes on an autobiographical account of a case of paranoia (dementia paranoides). In J. Strachey (Ed. and Trans.), *The standard edition of the complete psychological works of Sigmund Freud* (Vol. 12, pp. 9-82). London: Hogarth. (Original work published 1911)

Freud, S. (1959). Inhibitions, symptoms and anxiety. In J. Strachey (Ed. and Trans.), *The standard edition of the complete psychological works of Sigmund Freud* (Vol. 20, pp. 87-172). London: Hogarth. (Original work published 1926)

Freud, S. (1960). Jokes and their relation to the unconscious. In J. Strachey (Ed. and Trans.), *The standard edition of the complete psychological works of Sigmund Freud* (Vol. 8). London: Hogarth. (Original work published 1905)

Freud, S. (1961a). Dr. Ernest Jones (on his 50th birthday). In J. Strachey (Ed. and Trans.), *The standard edition of the complete psychological works of Sigmund Freud* (Vol. 21, pp. 249-250). London: Hogarth. (Original work published 1929)

Freud, S. (1961b). The ego and the id. In J. Strachey (Ed. and Trans.), *The standard edition of the complete psychological works of Sigmund Freud* (Vol. 19, pp. 13-59). London: Hogarth. (Original work published 1923)

Freud, S. (1962a). Further remarks on the neuro-psychoses of defence. In J. Strachey (Ed. and Trans.), *The standard edition of the complete psychological works of Sigmund Freud* (Vol. 3, pp. 162-185). London: Hogarth. (Original work published 1896)

Freud, S. (1962b). The neuro-psychoses of defence. In J. Strachey (Ed. and Trans.), *The standard edition of the complete psychological works of Sigmund Freud* (Vol. 3, pp. 45-61). London: Hogarth. (Original work published 1894)

George, R. L., & Cristiani, T. S. (1995). *Counseling: Theory and practice* (4th ed.). Englewood Cliffs, NJ: Prentice Hall.

Gergen, K. J. (1985). The social constructionist movement in modern psychology. *American Psychologist, 40,* 266-275.

Gibbon, E. (1932). *The decline and fall of the Roman empire.* New York: Modern Library. (Original work published 1788)

Gilliland, B. E., & James, R. K. (1998). *Theories and strategies in counseling and psychotherapy* (4th ed.). Boston: Allyn & Bacon.

Gladding, S. T. (1996). *Counseling: A comprehensive profession* (3rd ed.). New York: Merrill.

Goldstein, W. N. (1991). Clarification of projective identification. *American Journal of Psychiatry, 148,* 153-161.

Gray, P. (1994). *The ego and analysis of defense.* Northvale, NJ: Jason Aronson.

Grieger, I., & Ponterotto, J. G. (1995). A framework for assessment in multicultural counseling. In J. G. Ponterotto, J. M. Casas, L. A. Suzuki, & C. M. Alexander (Eds.), *Handbook of multicultural counseling* (pp. 357-374). Thousand Oaks, CA: Sage.

Guterman, J. T. (1994). A social constructivist position for mental health counseling. *Journal of Mental Health Counseling, 16,* 226-244.

Haan, N. (1977). *Coping and defending: Processes of self-environment organization.* New York: Academic Press.

Hammer, E. F. (Ed.). (1958). *The clinical application of projective drawings.* Springfield, IL: Charles C Thomas.

Handler, L. (1996). The clinical use of figure drawings. In C. S. Newmark (Ed.), *Major psychological assessment instruments* (2nd ed., pp. 206-293). Boston: Allyn & Bacon.

Hansen, J. C., Rossberg, R. H., & Cramer, S. H. (1994). *Counseling: Theory and process* (5th ed.). Boston: Allyn & Bacon.

Hansen, R. D., & Hansen, C. H. (1988). Repression of emotionally tagged memories: The architecture of less complex emotions. *Journal of Personality and Social Psychology, 55,* 811-818.

Hart, D. H. (1986). The sentence completion techniques. In H. M. Knoff (Ed.), *The assessment of child and adolescent personality* (pp. 245-272). New York: Guilford.

Hartman, H. (1958). *Ego psychology and the problem of adaptation.* New York: International Universities Press. (Original work published 1939)

Harway, M., & Hansen, M. (1993). Therapist perceptions of family violence. In M. Hansen & M. Harway (Eds.), *Battering and family therapy: A feminist perspective* (pp. 42-53). Newbury Park, CA: Sage.

Heath, D. (1958). Projective tests as measures of defensive activity. *Journal of Projective Techniques, 22,* 284-292.

Hentschel, V., Ehlers, W., & Peter, R. (1993). The measurement of defense mechanisms by self-report questionnaires. In V. Hentschel, G. J. W. Smith, W. Ehlers, & J. G. Draguns (Eds.), *The concept of defense mechanisms in contemporary psychology: Theoretical, research, and clinical perspectives* (pp. 53-86). New York: Springer-Verlag.

Herman, J. L., & Schatzow, E. (1987). Recovery and verification of memories of childhood sexual trauma. *Psychoanalytic Psychology, 4,* 1-14.

Hoffman, L. (1990). Constructing realities: An art of lenses. *Family Process, 29,* 1-12.

Ihilevich, D., & Gleser, G. C. (1995). The Defense Mechanisms Inventory: Its development and clinical applications. In H. R. Conte & R. Plutchik (Eds.), *Ego defenses: Theory and measurement* (pp. 221-246). New York: John Wiley.

Ivey, A. E. (1994). *Intentional interviewing and counseling: Facilitating client development in a multicultural society* (3rd ed.). Pacific Grove, CA: Brooks/Cole.

Ivey, A. E., Ivey, M. B., & Simek-Morgan, L. (1997). *Counseling and psychotherapy: A multicultural perspective* (4th ed.). Needham Heights, MA: Allyn & Bacon.

Jackson, S. W. (1969). The history of Freud's concepts of regression. *Journal of the American Psychoanalytic Association, 17,* 743-784.

Jacobson, A. M., Beardslee, W., Gelfand, E., Hauser, S. T., Noam, G. G., & Powers, S. I. (1992). An approach to evaluating adolescent ego defense mechanisms using clinical interviews. In G. E. Vaillant (Ed.), *Ego mechanisms of defense: A guide for clinicians and researchers* (pp. 181-194). Washington, DC: American Psychiatric Press.

Jarrell, R. (1965). *The lost world.* New York: Macmillan.

Johnson, N. L., & Gold, S. N. (1995). The Defense Mechanism Profile: A sentence completion test. In H. R. Conte & R. Plutchik (Eds.), *Ego defenses: Theory and measurement* (pp. 247-262). New York: John Wiley.

Jones, E. (1908). Rationalisation in every-day life. *Journal of Abnormal Psychology, 3,* 161-169.

Juni, S. (1981). Theoretical foundations of reaction formation as a defense mechanism. *Genetic Psychology Monographs, 104,* 107-135.

Kelly, G. A. (1955). *A theory of personality: The psychology of personal constructs.* New York: Norton.

Killingmo, B. (1990). Beyond semantics: A clinical and theoretical study of isolation. *International Journal of Psycho-Analysis, 71,* 113-125.

Koff, R. H. (1961). A definition of identification: A review of the literature. *International Journal of Psycho-Analysis, 42,* 362-370.

Koppitz, E. (1968). *Psychological evaluation of children's human figure drawings.* New York: Grune & Stratton.

Koppitz, E. (1984). *Psychological evaluation of human figure drawings by middle school pupils.* New York: Grune & Stratton.

Kris, E. (1952). *Psychoanalytic explorations in art.* New York: International Universities Press.

Kübler-Ross, E. (1969). *On death and dying.* New York: Macmillan.

LaFountain, R. M., Garner, N. E., & Eliason, G. T. (1996). Solution-focused counseling groups: A key for school counselors. *The School Counselor, 43,* 256-267.

Laughlin, H. P. (1979). *The ego and its defenses* (2nd ed.). New York: Jason Aronson.

Levant, R. F. (1995). Toward the reconstruction of masculinity. In R. F. Levant & W. S. Pollack (Eds.), *A new psychology of men.* New York: Basic Books.

Levick, M. F. (1983). *They could not talk and so they drew: Children's styles of coping and thinking.* Springfield, IL: Charles C Thomas.

Levit, D. B. (1991). Gender differences in ego defenses in adolescence: Sex roles as one way to understand the differences. *Journal of Personality and Social Psychology, 61,* 992-999.

Levy, L. H. (1963). *Psychological interpretation.* New York: Holt, Rinehart & Winston.

Liotti, G. (1987). Structural cognitive therapy. In W. Dryden & W. L. Golden (Eds.), *Cognitive behavioural approaches to psychotherapy* (pp. 92-128). London: Hemisphere.

Loughead, T. A. (1992). Freudian repression revisited: The power and pain of shame. *International Journal for the Advancement of Counseling, 15,* 127-136.

MacGregor, J. R. (1991). Identification with the victim. *Psychoanalytic Quarterly, 60,* 53-68.

Machover, K. (1949). *Personality projection in the drawing of the human figure.* Springfield, IL: Charles C Thomas.

Magid, B. (1986). The meaning of projection in self psychology. *Journal of the American Academy of Self Psychology, 14,* 473-483.

Mahl, G. F. (1969). *Psychological conflict and defense.* New York: Harcourt Brace Jovanovich.

Mansfield, K. (1927). *The Journal of Katherine Mansfield* (J. M. Murry, Ed.). New York: Knopf.

Marcos, L. (1980). Bilinguals in psychotherapy. In M. A. Simpson (Ed.), *Psycholinguistics in clinical practice: Languages of illness and healing* (pp. 91-109). New York: Irvington.

Martin, J. (1994). *The construction and understanding of psychotherapeutic change: Conversations, memories, and theories.* New York: Teachers College Press.

Maxmen, J. S., & Ward, N. G. (1995). *Essential psychopathology and its treatment* (2nd ed.). New York: Norton.

Meichenbaum, D. (1977). *Cognitive-behavior modification: An integrative approach.* New York: Plenum.

Merta, R. J. (1995). Group work: Multicultural perspectives. In J. G. Ponterotto, J. M. Casas, L. A. Suzuki, & C. M. Alexander (Eds.), *Handbook of multicultural counseling* (pp. 567-585). Thousand Oaks, CA: Sage.

Miller, D. R., & Swanson, G. E. (1960). *Inner conflict and defense.* New York: Henry Holt.

Miller, J. B. (1986). *Toward a new psychology of women* (2nd ed.). Boston: Beacon.

Murray, E. J., & Berkun, M. M. (1955). Displacement as a function of conflict. *Journal of Abnormal and Social Psychology, 51,* 47-56.

Murstein, B. I., & Pryer, R. S. (1959). The concept of projection: A review. *Psychological Bulletin, 56,* 353-374.

Myerson, P. G. (1977). Therapeutic dilemmas relevant to the lifting of repression. *International Journal of Psycho-Analysis, 58,* 453-462.

Nietzsche, F. (1989). *Beyond good and evil: Prelude to a philosophy of the future* (W. Kaufman, Trans.). New York: Vintage. (Original work published 1886)

Ogden, T. H. (1982). *Projective identification and psychotherapeutic technique.* New York: Jason Aronson.

Oster, G. D., & Gould, P. (1987). *Using drawings in assessment and therapy: A guide for mental health professionals.* New York: Brunner/Mazel.

Pascal, B. (1966). *Pensées* (A. J. Krailsheimer, Trans.). Baltimore: Penguin. (Original work published 1662)

Patterson, L. E., & Welfel, E. R. (1994). *The counseling process* (4th ed.). Pacific Grove, CA: Brooks/Cole.

Pedersen, P., & Carey, J. C. (1994). *Multicultural counseling in schools: A practical handbook.* Boston: Allyn & Bacon.

Perry, J. C., & Kardos, M. E. (1995). A review of the Defense Mechanism Rating Scales. In H. R. Conte & R. Plutchik (Eds.), *Ego defenses: Theory and measurement* (pp. 283-299). New York: John Wiley.

Peterson, C., Maier, S. F., & Seligman, M. E. P. (1993). *Learned helplessness: A theory for the age of personal control.* New York: Oxford University Press.

Pleck, J. H. (1995). The gender role strain paradigm: An update. In R. F. Levant & W. S. Pollack (Eds.), *A new psychology of men.* New York: Basic Books.

Plutchik, R. (1995). A theory of ego defenses. In H. R. Conte & R. Plutchik (Eds.), *Ego defenses: Theory and measurement* (pp. 13-37). New York: John Wiley.

Ponterotto, J. G., Casas, J. M., Suzuki, L. A., & Alexander, C. M. (Eds.). (1995). *Handbook of multicultural counseling.* Thousand Oaks, CA: Sage.

Pope, H. G., Jr., & Hudson, J. I. (1995). Can memories of childhood sexual abuse be repressed? *Psychological Medicine, 25,* 121-126.

Posthuma, B. W. (1996). *Small groups in counseling and therapy: Process and leadership* (2nd ed.). Boston: Allyn & Bacon.

Raskin, N. J., & Rogers, C. R. (1995). Person-centered therapy. In R. J. Corsini & D. Wedding (Eds.), *Current psychotherapies* (5th ed., pp. 128-161). Itasca, IL: F. E. Peacock.

Reisner, A. D. (1996). Repressed memories: True and false. *Psychological Record, 46,* 563-579.

Ritzler, B. (1995). The Rorschach: Defense or adaptation. In H. R. Conte & R. Plutchik (Eds.), *Ego defenses: Theory and measurement* (pp. 263-282). New York: John Wiley.

Rossetti, C. (1970). *Selected poems of Christina Rossetti* (M. Zaturenska, Ed.). New York: Macmillan. (Original work published 1849)

Rousseau, J. J. (1911). *Émile* (B. Foxley, Trans.). New York: E. P. Dutton. (Original work published 1764)

Rutan, J. S., & Stone, W. N. (1993). *Psychodynamic group psychotherapy* (2nd ed.). New York: Guilford.

Rycroft, C. (1995). *A critical dictionary of psychoanalysis* (2nd ed.). London: Penguin.

Safyer, A. W., & Hauser, S. T. (1995). A developmental view of defenses: Empirical approaches. In H. R. Conte & R. Plutchik (Eds.), *Ego defenses: Theory and measurement* (pp. 120-138). New York: John Wiley.

Sampson, H., Weiss, J., Mlodnosky, L., & Hause, E. (1972). Defense analysis and the emergence of warded-off mental contents. *Archives of General Psychiatry, 26,* 524-531.

Sandler, J., & Freud, A. (1985). *The analysis of defense: The ego and the mechanisms of defense revisited.* New York: International Universities Press.

Sanford, N. (1955). The dynamics of identification. *Psychological Review, 62,* 106-118.

Sappenfield, B. R. (1965). Repression and the dynamics of conflict. *Journal of Consulting Psychology, 29,* 266-270.

Sarnoff, I. (1960). Reaction formation and cynicism. *Journal of Personality, 28,* 129-143.

Schafer, R. (1954). *Psychoanalytic interpretation in Rorschach testing.* New York: Grune & Stratton.

Schafer, R. (1958). Regression in the service of the ego: The relevance of a psychoanalytic concept for personality assessment. In G. Lindzey (Ed.), *The assessment of human motives* (pp. 119-148). New York: Rinehart.

Schafer, R. (1967). *Projective testing and psychoanalysis.* New York: International Universities Press.

Schlesinger, H. J. (1994). The role of the intellect in the process of defense. *Bulletin of the Menninger Clinic, 58,* 15-36.

Seltzer, L. F. (1986). *Paradoxical strategies in psychotherapy: A comprehensive overview and guidebook.* New York: John Wiley.

Semrad, E. V., Grinspoon, L., & Feinberg, S. E. (1973). Development of an Ego Profile Scale. *Archives of General Psychiatry, 28,* 70-77.

Shakespeare, W. (1917). *Romeo and Juliet* (W. H. Durham, Ed.). New Haven, CT: Yale University Press. (Original work published 1595)

Shakespeare, W. (1990). *King John* (L. A. Beaurline, Ed.). New York: Cambridge University Press. (Original work published 1623)

Sharf, R. S. (1996). *Theories of psychotherapy and counseling: Concepts and cases.* Pacific Grove, CA: Brooks/Cole.

Shedler, J., Mayman, M., & Manis, M. (1993). The illusion of mental health. *American Psychologist, 48,* 1117-1131.

Sherwood, G. C. (1981). Self-serving bias in person perception: A reexamination of projection as a mechanism of defense. *Psychological Bulletin, 90,* 445-459.

Sjöbäck, H. (1973). *The psychoanalytic theory of defensive processes*. New York: John Wiley.

Sperling, S. J. (1958). On denial and the essential nature of defense. *International Journal of Psychoanalysis, 39*, 25-38.

Suppes, P., & Warren, H. (1975). On the generation and classification of defense mechanisms. *International Journal of Psychoanalysis, 56*, 405-414.

Swanson, G. E. (1988). *Ego defenses and the legitimization of behavior.* New York: Cambridge University Press.

Tennyson, A. (1898). *The poetic and dramatic works of Alfred, Lord Tennyson.* Boston: Houghton Mifflin.

Vaillant, G. E. (1977). *Adaptation to life.* Boston: Little, Brown.

Vaillant, G. E. (1992). *Ego mechanisms of defense: A guide for clinicians and researchers.* Washington, DC: American Psychiatric Press.

Vaillant, G. E. (1997). *Changing character: Short-term anxiety-regulating psychotherapy for restructuring defenses, affects, and attachment.* New York: Basic Books.

Vickers, R. R., & Hervig, L. K. (1981). Comparison of three psychological defense mechanism questionnaires. *Journal of Personality Assessment, 45*, 630-638.

Watkins, C. E., Jr. (1990). The effects of counselor self-disclosure: A research review. *The Counseling Psychologist, 18*, 477-500.

Weinstock, A. R. (1967). Family environment and the development of defense and coping mechanisms. *Journal of Personality and Social Psychology, 5*, 67-75.

White, R. B., & Gilliland, R. M. (1975). *Elements of psychopathology: The mechanisms of defense.* New York: Harcourt Brace Jovanovich.

Yalom, I. D. (1995). *The theory and practice of group psychotherapy* (4th ed.). New York: Basic Books.

INDEX

ABOUT THE AUTHOR

Arthur J. Clark is Associate Professor and Coordinator of the Counseling and Development Program at St. Lawrence University in Canton, New York. He received his Ed.D. in counseling from Oklahoma State University in 1974 and has held positions as a school counselor, director of guidance, and school psychologist. His professional experience also includes counseling in a substance abuse treatment center and maintaining a private practice as a licensed psychologist. He has been an editorial board member of *Elementary School Guidance and Counseling* and the *Journal for Specialists in Group Work* and holds memberships in the American Counseling Association and the American Psychological Association. His publications in counseling and psychology journals focus on issues critical to practitioners in the helping professions. He currently resides in Canton, New York, with his wife, Marybeth, and their daughters, Heather, Tara, and Kayla.